Solutions to Cases in Management Accounting and Business Finance

Second Edition

Solutions to Cases in Management Accounting and Business Finance

Second Edition

Edited by Noel Hyndman and Donal McKillop

Published by
Chartered Accountants Ireland
Chartered Accountants House
47–49 Pearse Street
Dublin 2
www.charteredaccountants.ie

©The Institute of Chartered Accountants in Ireland, 2009

Copyright in this publication is owned by the Institute of Chartered Accountants in Ireland. All rights reserved. No part of this text may be reproduced or transmitted or communicated to the public in any form or by any means, including photocopying, Internet or e-mail dissemination, without the written permission of the Institute of Chartered Accountants in Ireland. Such written permission must also be obtained before any part of this document is stored in a retrieval system of any nature.

This publication is designed to provide accurate and authoritative information in regard to the subject matter covered. It is provided on the understanding that the Institute of Chartered Accountants in Ireland is not engaged in rendering professional services. The Institute of Chartered Accountants in Ireland disclaims all liability for any reliance placed on the information contained within this publication and recommends that if professional advice or other expert assistance is required, the services of a competent professional should be sought.

ISBN: 978-1-908199-03-4

First published 2006
Second edition 2009
Reprinted with corrections 2012

Typeset by: Datapage
Printed by the MPG Books Group

Contents

Section A: Solutions to Cases in Management Accounting

No.	Case name	Main topics	Author(s)	Page
1.	Beara Bay Cheese	CVP analysis; decision making; activity-based costing	Margaret Healy, University College Cork	3
2.	Terra Inc.	CVP analysis; decision making; balanced scorecard; kaizen costing	Tony O'Dea and Tony Brabazon, University College Dublin	11
4.	EasyONline	CVP analysis; sensitivity analysis; optimal pricing strategies	Tony Brabazon and Tony O'Dea, University College Dublin	17
6.	Castlegrove Enterprises	Absorption and variable costing income statements; decision making	Tom Kennedy, University of Limerick	21
8.	Chicken Pieces	Non-financial performance measures; cost allocation; CVP analysis; decision making	Peter Clarke, University College Dublin	39
10.	Newtown Manufacturing Limited	Activity-based costing; decision making	Tom Kennedy, University of Limerick	45
11.	Lennon Department Stores Limited	Budgeting; decision making; risk and uncertainty	Bernard Pierce and Barbara Flood, Dublin City University	57
12.	Autoparts SA	Divisional performance; compensation schemes	Tony Brabazon and Tony O'Dea, University College Dublin	77
13.	IXL Limited	Return on investment; capital investment decisions; decision making	Joan Ballantine, University of Ulster	81

Section B: Solutions to Cases in Business Finance

No.	Case name	Main topics	Author(s)	Page
18.	The Corner Café	Sources of finance; cash and profit budgets; working capital management	Jill Lyttle, Queen's University Belfast	93
19.	Calvin plc	Investment appraisal; capital structure; dividend policy	Peter Green, University of Ulster at Jordanstown	101
21.	Sun Shine Limited	Investment appraisal; foreign exchange risk	John Cotter, University College Dublin	109
22.	Blackwater Hotel Group plc	Investment appraisal; cost of capital; sensitivity analysis	Peter Green, University of Ulster at Jordanstown	119
23.	Tannam plc	Investment appraisal; cost of capital; financing decisions; diversification	Louis Murray, University College Dublin	131
24.	Salmon Spray	Investment appraisal; cost of capital; accounting profit and DCF; sensitivity analysis	Ray Donnelly, University College Cork	145
25.	Waterlife plc	Cost of capital; capital structure; financing decisions	Evarist Stoja, University of Bristol	157
29.	Good Eating Company plc	Valuation of pension funds; CAPM; defined contribution and defined benefit pension schemes	John Cotter, University College Dublin	171
30.	Personal Financial Planning: Tom Smith	Personal financial plans; personal financial objectives; net worth and net income; risk and return	Anne Marie Ward, University of Ulster	179

Section C: Solutions to Integrated Cases in Management Accounting/Business Finance

No.	Case name	Main topics	Author(s)	Page
32.	Toffer Group plc	Absorption and marginal costing; budgeting; company valuation; dividend policy	Ciaran Connolly and Martin Kelly, Queen's University Belfast	203

33.	Glenview House Hotel	Decision making; leasing	Margaret Healy and John Doran, University College Cork	213
34.	Delaney's Bakehouse Breads	Decision making; activity-based costing; investment appraisal; working capital management	John Doran and Margaret Healy, University College Cork	221
36.	Malvern Limited	Budgeting; investment appraisal; working capital management	Ciaran Connolly and Martin Kelly, Queen's University Belfast	229
38.	Drumview Limited	Variance analysis; budgeting; foreign exchange risk; cost of capital	Ciaran Connolly and Martin Kelly, Queen's University Belfast	239
42.	Plastic Products	Investment appraisal and cost of capital; company valuation; JIT and optimal pricing policy; activity-based costing	Michelle Carr and Derry Cotter, University College Cork	251
	Index			267

Preface

Solutions to Cases in Management Accounting and Business Finance
(Second Edition)

To aid independent student learning this book contains a substantial selection of solutions to the material included in *Cases in Management Accounting and Business Finance* (Second Edition); the solutions to the remainder of the cases are available to lecturers on adoption of the book (to facilitate use in a classroom situation). As appropriate, these solutions contain, among other things, computations for quantitative requirements, discussions of qualitative factors and recommended courses of action. Many are presented in report or memorandum form, as demanded by the author(s) in the case requirements. As they use the material, lecturers may develop alternative approaches for some of the cases. If this is so, they are invited to submit such ideas to the editors by e-mail (n.hyndman@qub.ac.uk or dg.mckillop@qub.ac.uk) so that they may be considered in any future edition. The solutions are numbered as per the case book, with the solutions to the management accounting cases being presented first (Section A), followed by the solutions to the cases in business finance (Section B) and then by the integrated management accounting/business finance cases (Section C).

Section A

Solutions to Cases in Management Accounting

Case 1
Solution to Beara Bay Cheese
Margaret Healy, University College Cork

**REPORT ON ISSUES FACING
BEARA BAY CHEESE**

Prepared by: Andrew Healy
Healy O'Rourke Consulting

For: Jana Williams and Thom Williams
Beara Bay Cheese

Date: x/x/xxx

1. Terms of Reference

This report reviews the sales and marketing strategy of Beara Bay Cheese and considers the adequacy or otherwise of the existing management accounting system in informing such decisions. Following preliminary discussions as of xx/xx/xxxx, I now present the report requested. Costing and breakeven calculations generated for Beara Bay Cheese are presented and reviewed. The relevance and limitations of cost-volume-profit analysis to business decisions at Beara Bay Cheese is explained and the proposed implementation of an activity-based costing system is considered. The viability of expanding turnover via the outsourcing of sales activity to Thom is also considered, both from Thom's perspective and in light of its impact on the existing business. All calculations included in this report are based on figures supplied by Beara Bay Cheese and have not been independently verified.

2. Recommendations

(a) The benefits of installing an extensive activity-based costing system for monitoring product costs are unlikely to justify the costs involved, particularly given that Beara Bay Cheese does not employ a full-time accounting professional.

(b) Reliance on a single unit level overhead allocation base in the current costing system does not reflect the underlying economics of the sales process at Beara Bay Cheese. Careful consideration should be given to the periodic use of an ABC model for ad hoc studies, providing Beara Bay Cheese with greater insights into the factors driving the consumption of organisational resources.

(c) Weighted average contribution rather than simply average contribution should be used in determining breakeven product volumes.

(d) Thom's proposal offers a return greater than that currently available from all existing customer segments. It should therefore be taken up by Beara Bay Cheese.

3. Concerns Regarding the Existing Management Accounting System

Concerns regarding the existing management accounting system at Beara Bay Cheese are reflected in the perceived usefulness or otherwise of the resulting accounting information, in particular that regarding breakeven analysis and that regarding overhead allocation. Each of these aspects of the accounting information system is discussed in greater detail in the following paragraphs.

(a) Breakeven Analysis

Breakeven or CVP analysis is a way of systematically evaluating the relationship between changes in activity and changes in sales revenues, expenses and net profits. This information is vital to the management of Beara Bay Cheese as it allows identification of the critical levels of sales such that no losses will occur in the short term. Extending the analysis to the longer term is complex and questionable, in that the relevant ranges assumed in the short term may no longer apply. Extending production at Beara Bay Cheese, for example, requires increments in fixed costs, e.g. additional sales-persons salary; acquisition of additional capacity once the current excess capacity is used up. In the longer term, volume will not be the only factor that impacts on total costs, total revenues and profits.

In situations involving more than one product, breakeven calculations should be based on the weighted average unit contribution. The initial analysis did not differentiate between the contribution available from 1 kg of CaiseBui cheese and 1 kg of BearaBeag cheese, even though the latter offers a significantly higher level of contribution per unit. Recalculating the contribution per kilogram of cheese for each of the products individually recognises the differing levels of contribution of each product and allows the use of cost-volume-profit analysis to provide insights into the breakeven level of sales mix. Revised breakeven results for Beara Bay Cheese based on the business plan estimates provided for the current year (detailed analysis shown in Appendix 1) are as follows.

	CaiseBui	BearaBeag
Contribution per kg	€8.12	€10.48
Breakeven sales volume	2,948 kgs	4,128 kgs

CVP analysis also has a number of other limitations.

(i) All variables other than volume are assumed to remain constant, i.e. volume is the only factor assumed to affect fixed costs. However, as will be shown in the results of the ABC analysis presented later in this report, some of the causal factors for fixed costs are related to non-unit level activities. If there are significant changes in the levels of these activities, then the outcomes of the CVP analysis will be incorrect.

(ii) CVP analysis assumes that the levels of sales for each product will be in accordance with the sales mix as anticipated in the business plan. However, if this initial assumption does not hold true (as the information supplied indicates is the case at Beara Bay Cheese), then the analysis must be viewed with caution.

(iii) Total costs and total revenue are assumed to be linear functions of output. CVP analysis assumes unit costs and selling price are constant, i.e. that the behaviour of sales and costs will remain constant despite increases or decreases in the level of sales.

(iv) Profits are calculated on a variable costing basis. It is assumed that the fixed costs incurred during the period are charged as an expense for that period only.

(v) Complexity-related fixed costs are assumed to not change.

(b) Overhead Allocation Process

At Beara Bay Cheese overheads represent a substantial proportion of the total costs. When these overheads are traced back to their underlying causal factors, it can be seen that they are not primarily driven by volume, but are related instead to the complexity of the sales process and the unequal consumption of overhead resources by each customer grouping. Simply allocating overheads on a 'per kilogram of cheese' sold basis does not reflect the differing selling activities and consequent costs involved in selling each kilogram. Reviewing the costs per customer using activity-based costing principles yields the following information (see Appendix 2 for detailed calculations):

	Midleton Market	Bantry Market	Catering Trade
Sales Revenues	€59,330	€21,470	€153,100
Contribution	€24,124	€10,066	€63,891
(as % of Revenues)	41%	47%	42%
Net Profit	€6,991	€3,614	€12,626
(as % of Revenues)	12%	17%	8%

Activity-based costing systems consider the activities undertaken in the production and sale of products to be the causal factor explaining overhead costs. Rather than simply allocate overheads to costs using a unit-level driver (e.g. kilogram of cheese), activity-based costing systems instead seek to trace those costs to the underlying activities causing the costs to increment. ABC uses measures of activity rather than volume to trace indirect costs to the cost objects, thus recognising that:

- costs may be related to batches of a product rather than units of that product, as is the instance of the €8,635 of overheads incurred for 'transactions' – related activity;
- costs may be related to one product or customer only, as is the case in relation to the €3,756 cost of rush orders to the catering trade.

ABC systems therefore use cause-and-effect allocation bases, unlike the existing absorption costing system at Beara Bay Cheese, which relied on an arbitrary unit-level allocation – 'kilogram of cheese'.

(c) Implementing an ABC System

The current costing system at Beara Bay Cheese does not provide adequate information for distinguishing the most profitable customer segments available to the company – key information in relation to the decision scenario currently facing the organisation. Inaccuracies resulting from the inability of the absorption costing system to capture sufficiently the consumption of overhead resources by product or customer groupings distort reported costs.

Simple cost systems such as that in present use at Beara Bay Cheese are inexpensive to operate, making extensive use of arbitrary cost allocations, but in turn providing lower levels of accuracy in circumstances such as that pertaining to Beara Bay Cheese. At Beara Bay Cheese, overheads are a large percentage of total costs (51% of actual costs in the current year). These overhead costs are not primarily driven by volume or some other unit-level driver, but are instead related to a variety of other transaction drivers, as was indicated in both the information supplied by Beara Bay Cheese and that underpinning the customer cost and profitability calculations provided in Appendix 2 of this report.

Sophisticated costing systems such as ABC rely on cause-and-effect allocation mechanisms. They are more expensive to operate given the amount of information required to identify and operationalise such drivers, however this investment is often more than redeemed in terms of the higher levels of accuracy provided and low cost of errors. When considered *vis-à-vis* each other, products/customers do not consume organisational resources in similar proportions. More sophisticated cost information than that currently available is required, therefore, to capture this diversity and to assign overhead costs to products more accurately.

4. Feasibility of the Proposal to Expand Sales

The proposal currently on offer to Beara Bay Cheese from Thom is reviewed in this section of the report. This review is conducted in respect of two perspectives: that of Thom (see (i) below) and that of Beara Bay Cheese (discussed in (ii) below).

(i) For Thom's proposal to reach its target profit level of €2,500, the maximum he should pay for the cheese is €13.23 per kilogram (see Appendix 3). In order to simply breakeven (assuming a purchase price of €13.23 per kilogram), Thom will need to sell 767 kg of cheese. However this purchase price is below that at which Jana is prepared to accept the offer.

(ii) Appendix 4 details the profits available to Beara Bay Cheese (based on the information provided) for each of the cheese purchase prices proposed. At €14 per kilogram, the proposal generates an expected return of 42% or €7,112. At the lower price of €13.23 per kilogram, the proposal offers an expected return of 39% or €6,188.

Rather than focus solely on the financial consequences of the proposal as outlined above, there are a number of other issues that also have a bearing on the proposal.

(i) Lack of product availability seems to be the biggest factor preventing expansion of existing sales. Beara Bay Cheese products are popular in the market place, with demand exceeding supply. The agency proposal, even if it is only availed of in the shorter term, may allow Jana extra time to concentrate on expanding cheese production.

(ii) The return available from sales to Thom is far in excess of that available to Beara Bay Cheese via sales to existing customers. Jana may have strategic marketing reasons for continuing to serve the Midleton and Bantry farmers markets, but should also consider out-sourcing this activity to Thom.

(iii) The €10,000 charge for marketing consultancy services is adversely impacting on the profitability of the catering trade customer segment. The charge is unlikely to be incurred in the future however.

(iv) Beara Bay Cheese should consider the introduction of a charge for rush orders. Given existing demand and supply conditions in the market place, this more is unlikely to impact adversely upon sales. Greater insights into the pattern of rush orders would also help determine if such orders occur randomly or are largely related to one or a few trade customers. Information regarding the catering trade customer segment currently groups all such customers as one homogeneous entity.

Appendix 1: Breakeven Analysis, Based on Business Plan

	CaiseBui	BearaBeag
Net Profit	€12,600	€34,160
Contribution	€40,600	€73,360
Overheads:	**€28,000**	**€39,200**
At €5.60 per kg – the number of kgs of cheese sold:	5,000	7,000
% of sales mix	42%	58%
Contribution per kg	€40,600 / 5,000	€73,360 / 7,000
	= €8.12	= €10.48

Weighted Average Contribution:
(42% × €8.12) + (58% × €10.48) = €9.50

Breakeven point:
€67,200 / €9.50 ≈ 7,076 kgs of cheese

Of this breakeven volume:
CaiseBui   42% ≈ 2,948 kgs
BearaBeag   58% ≈ 4,128 kgs

Appendix 2: Analysis of Customer Profitability Using Activity-based Costing Principles

(Based on actual figures as supplied by Beara Bay Cheese)

	Midleton Market	Bantry Market	Catering Trade
Sales (w1):			
- CaiseBui	25,330	4,470	59,600
- BearaBeag	34,000	17,000	93,500
	59,330	21,470	153,100
Direct Costs (w1):			
- Materials	13,270	4,930	34,400
- Labour	13,111	4,449	33,470
Production Overheads (w2)	8,825	2,025	21,339
Contribution	**24,124**	**10,066**	**63,891**
Market-related overheads:			
- Packaging (w3)	1,850	650	4,750
- Travel mileage (w4)	3,120	416	22,753
- Advertising	633	633	10,000
- Product promotions (w5)	1,605	648	-
- Rush orders	-	-	3,756
- Administration:			
• Market registration fee	250	100	-
• Bookkeeper's salary (w6)	3,805	1,377	9,818
• Transactions (w7)	5,869	2,578	188
	17,133	6,452	51,265
Net Profit	**€6,991**	**€3,614**	**€12,626**
(as % of Revenues)	12%	17%	8%

w1	CaiseBui	BearaBeag
Total sales – kgs of cheese	6,000	8,500
Actual sales revenue per kg	€14.90	€17.00
Actual materials cost per kg	€3.10	€4.00
Actual labour cost per kg	€3.83	€3.30

w2: Production overheads	CaiseBui	BearaBeag
Total sales – kgs of cheese	6,000	8,500
Months in maturation per kg	6 months	1 month
-> total 'maturation-months'	36,000	8,500

Cost per 'maturation-month': [32190 / (36000 + 8500)] = €0.72

	CaiseBui	BearaBeag
Production overhead per kg	€4.34	€0.72

w3: Packaging (€7,511)	CaiseBui	BearaBeag
Total sales – kgs of cheese	6,000	8,500
In 2 kg boxes -> no. of boxes	3,000	4,250

Total boxes: 3000 + 4250 + 216 (stock) = 7511
-> cost of packaging per 2kg of cheese = €1.00

w4: Mileage (€26,289)	Midleton	Bantry	Catering
At €0.40 per mile, 52 weeks p.a.	3,120	416	Remainder = 22,753

w5: Promotions (€2,253)	CaiseBui	BearaBeag
Cost of promotions	25% = 563	75% = 1690
Sales to Farmers markets (kg)	2,000 kg	3,000 kg
Promotion cost per kg	€0.28	€0.56

w6: Salary (€15,000)	Midleton	Bantry	Catering
Turnover	59,330	21,470	15,3100
Percentage of total turnover	25.4%	9.2%	65.4%
Allocation of salary	3,805	1,377	9,818

w7: Transactions (€8,635)	Midleton	Bantry	Catering
No. of transactions	[3700 / 0.25] = 14,800	[1300 / 0.20] = 6,500	[9500 / 20] = 475

Cost per transaction: 8635 / (14800 + 6500 + 475) = €0.396

	Midleton	Bantry	Catering
Transaction costs	5,869	2,578	188

Appendix 3: Analysis of Thom's Proposal

(Based on actual figures as supplied by Beara Bay Cheese)

Costs of Thom's proposal	€'s
Registration Fee	300
Levy – insurance	100
Mileage (130 × 0.40 × 52)	2,704
Display stand & scales	520
Packaging costs	800
	€4,424

Anticipated sales revenue:
1,200 kgs × €19 per kg: €22,800

Calculation of contribution per unit:
1,200 units = (4424 + 2500) / contribution per unit
Contribution per unit = (4424 + 2500) / 1200 units
= €5.77

Sales price €19.00 − Contribution €5.77 = Cost €13.23

Breakeven:
Fixed costs / contribution per unit = 4424 / 5.77
= 767 kgs
OR €14,568

Appendix 4: Net Profits from the Agency Proposal

(Based on actual figures as supplied by Beara Bay Cheese)

	At €14.00 per kg of cheese	At €13.23 per kg of cheese
Sales:	16,800	15,876
Direct Costs:		
- Materials	4,800	4,800
- Labour	3,960	3,960
Production Overheads	868	868
Contribution	**7,172**	**6,248**
Market-related overheads:		
- Packaging	60	60
Net Profit	**€7,112**	**€6,188**
(as % of Revenues)	(42%)	(39%)

Case 2
Solution to Terra Inc.
Tony O'Dea and Tony Brabazon, University College Dublin

1. Moninicol Generic

(a)

Fixed Costs	$
Marketing	250,000
Manufacturing	
Heating	Nil
Blending	250,000
Reducing	200,000
Quality	25,000
	725,000

Note: the manufacturing costs are split into fixed and variable elements using the high-low method.

Variable Overhead Cost per Batch	$
Marketing (5% revenue)	1,750
Quality	750
Manufacturing	
Heating	7,500
Blending	5,000
Reducing	1,000
	16,000

Note: sales revenue per batch is $1000 \times (\$50\text{-}30\%) = \$35,000$.

Contribution margin is $\$35,000 - \$16,000 - \$8,500$ (materials + labour) $= \$10,500$.

(i) Therefore, the BEP is $725,000 / $10,500 = 69.04 batches or 69,048 units.

(ii) The target volume is $1,725,000 / $10,500 = 164.29 batches or 164,286 units.

(b) The expected sales volume is 20% of the current market. The current selling price per batch is $50,000, therefore the current sales volume is $50m / $50k = 1,000 cases.

20% of this gives 200 cases. The BEP and target volume) is substantially below this.

(c)

(i) If there is no competition, the selling price for the generic will remain at $50-30% = $35.

Assuming that Terra does indeed sell 200 batches (captures a 20% market share), the annual surplus generated once annual fixed (and variable) costs are covered is as follows:

	$
Sales Revenue ($35,000 × 200 batches)	7,000,000
Variable costs - Materials + labour ($8,500 × 200)	1,700,000
- Overheads ($16,000 × 200)	3,200,000
Contribution margin	2,100,000
Less Fixed Costs	725,000
Surplus	1,375,000
The up-front costs are:	
Marketing	500,000
Development	2,000,000
	2,500,000

Therefore the expected breakeven time is $2.5 million / $1.375 million = 1.82 years.

(ii) If competition does emerge, the selling price and therefore the contribution margin earned will reduce in years 2 and 3 (and thereafter).

The surplus generated in year 1 (over annual fixed costs) was calculated above as $1.375 million.

In year 2 this surplus will be: ($30,000 - $16,000 - $8,500) × 200 batches - $725,000 (fixed costs) = $0.375 million.

In year 3 the surplus will be: ($28,000 - $16,000 - $8,500) × 200 batches - $725,000 (fixed costs) = -$25,000 (a loss)

Therefore the firm will never breakeven on the project, and the financial position will deteriorate from year 2 onwards.

Year	Surplus/(deficit)	Cumulative surplus
1	$1.375m	$1.375m
2	$0.375m	$1.750m
3	($25)k	$1.725m

(d) Fixed costs and variable costs have already been calculated in part **(a)**.

Cost Increases	$
Fixed costs ($725,000 +10%)	797,500
Variable cost per batch (($16,000 + $8,500) + 10%)	26,950

Selling Price (per batch) = $35,000 – 5% = $33,250

Sales volume = 1,000 (market volume) × 25% = 250 batches

	$
Sales revenue ($33,250 × 250)	8,312,500
Variable costs ($26,950 × 250)	(6,737,500)
Contribution margin	1,575,000
Fixed Costs	(797,500)
Profit	777,500

Note: in answering this part of the question, you could assume that the variable selling cost also increased by 10% (to 5.5% of sales revenues).

2. Active Ingredients Division

To get 1,000 'good' kg of output, 1,250 kg of gross output is required (1000/0.80). Therefore 2,500 kg of inputs are required.

Relevant Cost Statement		$
Material A	(625 kg × $50)	31,250
Material B	(1250 kg × $70)	87,500
Material C	(625 kg × $10)	6,250
Labour	(125 hours × $125)	15,625
	(100 hours /0.8=125)	
Overheads	(125 hours × ($500 × 25%))	15,625
Inspection cost		2,500
		158,750

3. Diagnostic Tests Division

(a)

	2XX0		2XX2	
	(€000)	% Sales	(€000)	% Sales
Sales	€25,000	100	€30,000	100
Costs				
Prevention				
Quality training	-		500	
Supplier evaluations	-	-	230	
	-		730	2.4%

continued

Appraisal

Inspection costs (finished units)	400		300	
Incoming inspection	—		400	
	400	1.6%	700	2.3%
Internal failure				
Re-work	2,000		1,000	
Scrap	600		200	
	2,600	10.4%	1,200	4.0%
External failure				
Warranty costs	3,000		750	
Sales returns	1,000		435	
Customer complaints	500		325	
	4,500	18.0%	1,510	5.0%
Total quality costs	€7,500	30.0%	€4,140	13.7%

Additional information for 2XX1.

Sales ($000) $26,000;

Re-work costs ($000) $1,500 (5.7% of sales).
This compares with re-work costs/sales percentages of 8% in 2XX0 and 3.3% in 2XX2.

Evaluation of the Success of Quality Driven Turnaround Strategy:

The following points can be made comparing 2XX2 with 2XX0:

- sales revenues have increased by 20%;
- cost of quality as a percentage of sales has declined from 30% to 13.7%;
- failure costs have declined from 28.4% of revenues to 9% of revenues (a very significant improvement);
- re-work costs have declined by 50%, scrap by 66%, warranty costs by 75%, sales returns by 56% and customer complaints costs by 35%;
- the spending of $730,000 in 2XX2 on prevention costs appears to have had a significant positive impact on internal and external failure costs;
- internal failure costs have declined over the two years by 54%, while external failure costs have declined by 66%;
- from a loss of $1 million in 2XX0, Malvern has made a profit of $2.2 million in 2XX2.

(b) Additional Information Which Could be Useful:

- cost of quality figures for the year 2XX1.
- targets for each cost category for 2XX1 and 2XX2;

- non-financial information, such as the number of sales returns, customer complaints, warranty claims, etc.

(c) Kaizen standard 2XX1: 6% of $26 million = $1,560,000. Actual re-work costs were $1,500,000 (5.7% of sales). Therefore, the standard was met. Kaizen is the Japanese term for making improvements to a process through small incremental amounts, rather than through large innovations. Kaizen costing focuses on the production processes and cost reductions are derived primarily through the increased efficiency of the production process. The aim of kaizen costing is to reduce the cost of components and products by a pre-specified amount. Kaizen costing relies heavily on employee empowerment. They are assumed to have superior knowledge about how to improve processes because they are closest to the manufacturing processes and customers, and are likely to have greater insights into how costs can be reduced.

(d) The balanced scorecard provides a means for directed continuous improvement. It also links performance measures to the strategy itself and thus articulates and communicates the strategy to employees, increasing the chances of obtaining an alignment of employees' goals with organisational goals.

(e)

Balanced Scorecard Perspectives	Performance Measures
Financial	
- Increase profitability	ROI
- Increase new customers and markets	% of revenue from new sources
- Reduce unit cost	Unit cost
Customer	
- Increase customer acquisition	New customers
- Increase market share	Market share %
- Increase customer satisfaction	Survey ratings
- Increase product quality	Returns
Internal process	
- Improve process quality	Quality costs; percentage of defective units
- Increase quality of purchased components	Percentage of defective units
Learning and growth	
- Increase employee capabilities	Training hours
- Increase motivation and alignment	Suggestions implemented per employee

Case 4
Solution to EasyONline
Tony Brabazon and Tony O'Dea, University College Dublin

Question 1
Monthly Sales

		Manchester (€)	London (€)
9.00 am – 6.00 pm (12,000×1×€1)	12,000	(80,000 × 1 × €1)	80,000
6.00 pm – 9.00 am (28,000×2×€1)	56,000	(100,000 × 2 × €1)	200,000
	68,000		280,000
Computer Usage = 60%			
=> 'Other Sales' = 40%	45,333		186,667
Total Sales	113,333		466,667

Question 2
Number of half-hour blocks to breakeven

	Manchester
Fixed Costs:	
Staff	10,000
Lease	20,000
Connection	15,000
General	5,000
	50,000

Next, work out the contribution margin per half-hour block of time:

Selling price per half-hour block of computer time	€1.00
Add: 'other sales' per half-hour (€1 / 60% × 40%)	0.66
Total sales	€1.66

Variable costs per half-hour block:	€
Staff	0.167
Computer rental (0.1 × €1)	0.10
Other: Admin (0.05 × €1.67)	0.083
Other: Costs of 'other revenue' (30% × €0.66)	0.198
	0.548

Therefore, contribution margin per half-hour is: €1.66 – €0.548 = €1.112, and the breakeven point is:

50,000 / 1.112 = 44,964 half-hour blocks per month.

(**Note:** assume that all the costs of 'other sales' are variable => the contribution margin on these sales is also 30%.)

Question 3

Current Levels	Manchester (€)	London (€)
Sales	113,333	466,667
Less Variable Costs:		
Staff (10% of revenue)	11,333	46,667
P.C. leasing (10% of computer rev.)	6,800	28,000
Administration (5% all)	5,667	23,334
Costs of 'other revenue' (30% of 'other rev.')	13,600	56,000
Total Contribution Margin	75,933	312,666
Less Fixed Costs:		
Staff (1/12)	10,000	10,000
Lease (1/12)	20,000	300,000
Connection	15,000	35,000
Administration	5,000	5,000
Profit (Loss)	**25,933**	**(37,334)**

Sales + 10%	Manchester (€)	London (€)
Sales	124,666	513,334
Less Variable Costs:		
Staff (10% of revenue)	12,467	51,333
P.C. leasing (10% of computer rev.)	7,480	30,800
Administration (5% all)	6,233	25,667
Costs of 'other revenue' (30% of 'other rev.')	14,960	61,600
Total Contribution Margin	83,526	343,934
Less Fixed Costs:		
Staff (1/12)	10,000	10,000
Lease (1/12)	20,000	300,000
Connection	15,000	35,000
Administration	5,000	5,000
Profit (Loss)	**33,526**	**(6,066)**

Question 4

- Why might the chain's profitability have slipped?
- Set-up costs of new cafés may have impacted on profitability (marketing costs, slow ramp-up of customer demand, staff training, etc.).
- Mix of cafés may have veered towards smaller cafés, in which it is harder to recover fixed costs.
- There may be a change in usage patterns, even though total number of customers has not declined (staying online for less time).
- 'Other revenues' may have declined.

Question 5

Pricing strategy is a critical decision in any organisation as it impacts directly on sales volume, cash-flows and profitability. While the current pricing strategy (flat rate pricing) is easy to implement and is easy for customers to understand, it fails to consider that different customers will place differing value on the product (internet access), and that the same customer will place differing value on the product at different times of the day.

Ideally, the optimal pricing strategy is to charge each customer the full value they receive from consuming the product (perfect price discrimination), but this is rarely possible as firms do not have complete information on their customers. A variant on this idea which is commonly seen in high fixed cost industries, such as power generation or indeed running an internet café, is to offer lower rates during off-peak. This can help reduce peak demand and therefore reduce the level of (expensive) capacity that the firm needs to invest in. Variants on offering off-peak rates would be to offer additional services off-peak (for example, free coffee or reduced-cost printing).

Case 6
Solution to Castlegrove Enterprises
Tom Kennedy, University of Limerick

Pedagogical Objectives

The case is intended to make students aware of the difficulty in determining the most appropriate costing systems to use in organisations and the application of those systems in different situations. The case content has the potential to cover all three elements of management accounting, namely full costing, differential costing and responsibility accounting.

Required

To prepare a draft set of guidelines and briefing notes on how McGuire might structure her presentation to the Castlegrove senior management team. Your response should deal with the overall concerns expressed by Maloney and the specific issues arising from the new product decision.

REPORT FROM THE MANAGEMENT CONSULTANT TO MARY MCGUIRE, CASTLEGROVE ACCOUNTING MANAGER

Presentation Objective

The overall aim of your presentation should be to convince the Castlegrove senior management team of the potential contribution that the management accounting function can make to strategic development and its operational implementation. It should facilitate an inclusive discussion on how to address the substantive issues raised by Maloney and, specifically, in regard to the projected performance of the 'Pulse' project. The presentation should be pitched at a level suitable for a non-accounting audience. It should result in an understanding of the context and the language that accountants use to communicate economic information on a regular basis.

Presentation Structure

In order to achieve your objective, I suggest that you use the following structure or an appropriate variation. I also attach some background notes in the Appendix that your colleagues might find useful.

(i)   Overview of the management accounting framework.
(ii) Overview of the different costing system choices facing organisations, with particular reference to Castlegrove's situation.
(iii) Presentation of a revised variable costing income statement for 2XX6 and 2XX7.
(iv) Presentation of an absorption costing income statement for 2XX6 and 2XX7.
(v)   Explanation of the difference between the operating income statements.
(vi) Key issues to be addressed by the Castlegrove senior management team in reviewing the projected performance of the 'Pulse' new product line.

I advise you to prepare your presentation slides from the attached supporting material and edit, as appropriate, to suit your specific audience, style and the time available. I have prepared the supporting material, based on our discussions and the information you gave me. I, also, reviewed the Castlegrove audit file. Based on your experience to date, I emphasise that your task is not likely to be achieved at a once-off event. I see it as part of a long-term and ongoing educational process.

Executive Summary

Castlegrove should continue to use its job costing system to determine the cost of its products. It should present its operating income statements under both absorption and variable costing formats. Absorption costing is required in order to satisfy statutory and regulatory requirements. Variable costing is a fundamental component of the managerial decision-making process and you should exploit the capability you have acquired in classifying costs between fixed and variable. Consequently, the reliability and relevance characteristics of good accounting information are delivered and this underpins the integrity of non-routine decision making at Castlegrove. This should mitigate against dysfunction behaviour and motivate all management to seek the more efficient use of resources and agree optimal performance levels.

The application of variable costing can also help to highlight the phenomenon of 'unintended consequences' through inventory building caused by absorption costing. The 'Pulse' project provides some evidence of how this could happen and this aspect of the project needs to be addressed, as a matter of urgency. Specifically, the appropriate balance between the production and sales volumes projected for 'Pulse' needs to be reviewed in order to protect its viability and the overall Castlegrove business performance. Revised operating income statements should then be prepared and updated regularly to reflect performance.

Castlegrove should continue to use the normal costing valuation method in order to incorporate some element of pre-determination. The choice of the practical capacity denominator is appropriate for its financial reporting, product costing and pricing requirements. Some thought should be given to replacing volume with transaction-based drivers in order to better identify the underlying causes of its overhead. The above scenario at Castlegrove is consistent with the notion that there are 'different systems for different purposes'.

Finally, in addition to operating both cost classification systems to varying degrees, Castlegrove could develop its own balanced scorecard set of performance measures in order to reduce the emphasis on financial measures. This would widen the scope of performance evaluation and, if properly implemented, could encourage behaviour that is consistent with the organisation's strategy.

Supporting Material

(i) Overview of the Management Accounting Framework

Definition

There are many different definitions of management accounting. As a compromise, one could adopt the normative definition put forward by Wilson and Chua (1993): "managerial accounting encompasses techniques and processes that are intended to provide financial and non-financial information to people within the organisation to make better decisions and, thereby, achieve organisational control and enhance effectiveness."

Relationship with Financial Accounting

- Optional versus mandatory.
- Internal focus largely versus external.
- Future versus the past.
- Disaggregated versus aggregated.
- Subjective versus objective.

Primary Functions of Management Accounting

- Inventory valuation/profit determination (full costing – scorekeeping).
- Decision-making (differential costing – problem-solving).
- Operational control and performance measurement (responsibility accounting – attention directing).

Scope of Management Accounting

Management accounting is important in its ramifications and social impact and is not just a collection of techniques. It can range from social/behavioural to closed/prescriptive/rational. The challenge today is "how to put the management back into management accounting" (Otley, 2001, *British Accounting Review*, 33, 243–261).

Changing Role of Management Accountant

- From functional to holistic.
- From what to why and how.
- From inward-looking to outward-looking.
- From backward-looking to forward-looking.
- From accountant to information manager.
- From country based to global.
- From slave to technology to master of technology.
- From closed department overhead role to integrated specialist.

(ii) Overview of the Different Costing System Choices Facing Organisations, with Particular Reference to Castlegrove's Situation

Objective of a costing system: to record, classify, trace and assign costs for inventory valuation/profit determination, decision-making and performance measurement purposes.

There are three substantive questions that organisations need to address before deciding on the appropriate costing system(s) to use:

(a) what costing system to use in order to assign costs to products or services?
(b) what cost classifications to make?
(c) what valuation method to adopt?

(a) What Costing System to Use?

Job costing and process costing are the *principal systems* that determine the cost of products or services through the *assignment of costs to the cost object* (product or service). In practice, hybrid systems can be used for different parts of the operation. The choice of system should reflect the underlying operations of the business, provide information that is useful for financial reporting and decision making and be subject to a cost/benefit test.

Specific to Castlegrove

Castlegrove currently uses a job costing system because of the product-oriented layout of its plant and the relative uniqueness of its individual product lines and customers. Some consideration could be given to using activity-based costing, as the cost profile of the plant has changed in recent years due to automation. However, like any commodity, its installation should be subject to a cost/benefit test. This is unlikely to be positive at this time.

Process costing is not appropriate because Castlegrove does not mass-produce homogeneous products. I understand some consideration has been given to changing the plant layout to a more functional model, due to the overlap in the material specifications for some of the products and in order to maximise machine utilisation. This may result in the introduction of a process costing system to that part of the plant in the future.

(b) What Cost Classifications to Make?

Variable costing, absorption costing and throughput costing systems primarily describe the *cost classifications* or *types of cost* included in inventory. These classifications are *direct material, direct labour, variable or fixed overhead*. The absorption costing format includes all four cost classification elements, variable costing includes direct material, direct labour and variable overhead and throughput costing only includes direct material. These systems or formats can all be used with job, process or hybrid costing systems. The manner in which an organisation can operate these systems is quite flexible. Surveys of company practice show that up to 30% of companies use them as stand-alone, with many others extracting the relevant variable cost data from their absorption costing system.

Specific to Castlegrove

Castlegrove currently uses an absorption costing system to value its inventory. This 'full costing' approach is in compliance with regulatory accounting standards and is the current basis used by Castlegrove for performance measurement, both internally and externally. This means that the fixed manufacturing overhead element of product cost associated with 'Pulse' is recorded on Castlegrove's balance sheet as an asset and only expensed when the product is sold.

Castlegrove currently uses a variable costing presentation format to inform its decision-making process. It extracts the relevant information from the absorption costing system, as it does not have the resources or the need to operate two stand-alone systems. This is the appropriate basis to use in assessing the likely impact of non-routine decisions, such as whether it should manufacture 'Pulse'. This format means that the fixed manufacturing overhead element of product cost associated with 'Pulse' is expensed in the period in which it is incurred and is not recorded on Castlegrove's balance sheet as an asset. This decision-relevant approach seeks to identify the quantitative differential costs and revenues associated with a decision. It does not reflect the qualitative factors, which should always be considered before the final decision is made.

(c) What Valuation Method to Adopt?

Actual costing, normal costing and standard costing describe the *valuation method* that can be used by the job or process costing systems. This reflects the time frame and the degree of sophistication used to prepare the income statements. An actual costing system records costs historically. Normal costing involves some element of pre-determination by incorporating a budgeted indirect or manufacturing overhead rate. Standard costing incorporates 'carefully' set standards for all inputs and facilitates comparison with the outputs. All three systems can be used in conjunction with the absorption costing, variable costing or throughput costing cost-classification processes.

Specific to Castlegrove

Castlegrove currently uses a normal costing system. This allows it to accumulate its product costs by recording the direct manufacturing (material & labour) costs by product line and adding the appropriate level of indirect costs using a pre-determined overhead rate by product line. It operates this in conjunction with a budgeting system that is organised by responsibility centre. This process involves estimating the overhead for the year, allocating it and re-allocating it to the production cost centres and classifying it into fixed and variable. It then selects the appropriate absorption base and the activity level in order to compute the pre-determined overhead rate by product line.

Castlegrove currently uses allocation bases such as floor area, book value of equipment, number of employees and the value of material in order to allocate overhead that it cannot trace directly to its cost centres. It then uses an agreed formula to re-allocate the approximate benefit received by the production departments resulting from the administration and engineering support departments. I understand this formula has been the subject of intense debate at the annual budget meetings and is likely to continue to be a contentious issue.

Castlegrove currently uses volume (number of units) as the absorption base, primarily because of its size and the nature of its product lines. As it grows and develops new products, it could consider alternatives such as machine hours, labour hours and percentage of material costs. As its product variety and level of automation increase, it may need to look at a more sophisticated way of determining the underlying 'drivers' of its overhead by using activity-based costing.

Castlegrove currently uses the practical capacity denominator level, as it is required for financial- and tax-reporting purposes. This recognises the fact that capacity usually takes time to build up and that some reasonable level of excess is sustainable in the early stages of any product life-cycle. This denominator level identifies the cost of idle/excess capacity and, in effect, treats it as a planning variance. It is important that the performance evaluation process takes that into account and holds management accountable for the operational aspect over which they have control. In practice, this is impossible to achieve because of the natural interdependencies that exist in most organisations. A working compromise that could be discussed is "to hold managers accountable for the performance areas that you want them to pay attention to" (Merchant, 1998), even if they have less than full control.

By using the practical capacity denominator level, management should be able to make a better-informed and more sustainable long-term pricing decision. This is particularly important in a new and/or highly competitive market, where a company should not seek to recover too large a burden of fixed manufacturing overhead at the outset or recover the cost of its idle capacity too quickly. If it attempts to do this, by using the master-budget level denominator, it may fall well short of achieving its immediate sales targets. This can lead to the company becoming more un-competitive, losing more market share and being effectively in a sales volume 'downward spiral'.

(iii) Revised Variable Costing Income Statement for 2XX6 and 2XX7

The revised variable costing statements, in Appendix 1 provide useful information for managerial decision-making. They supplement the information presented to the board in October 2XX5 and show that 'Pulse' is generating a very acceptable level of 'contribution' at €22 per unit. They confirm that the expected profit-volume ratio is well in excess of the company target of 20%, at 26% (€22/€85). They also confirm the breakeven level of sales at approximately 4,109 units (€90,400/€22) and the very acceptable anticipated margin of safety of 25% (1,391/5,500) in 2XX6 and 37% (2,391/6,500) in 2XX7. Based on this information, the board was right to approve the 'Pulse' project. It is projected to contribute €30,600 and €52,600 to operating income in 2XX6 and 2XX7, respectively. This should act as a stimulus to the commercialisation of the other new product ideas under investigation.

(iv) Absorption Costing Income Statement for 2XX6 and 2XX7

As Castlegrove must prepare an absorption costing income statement for financial and tax reporting, the anticipated performance of 'Pulse' is presented, using that method, in Appendix 2. This shows that the projected operating income for 2XX6 and 2XX7 is €39,600 and €64,600, respectively. Appendix 2 shows the 'full' cost for 'Pulse' and that it is well capable of paying its 'fair share' of overhead. This positive outcome is evidenced by the projected gross margin of 22% and the increase in operating income from 8% in 2XX6 to 12% in 2XX7.

However, caution needs to be exercised in interpreting the operating income increase from 2XX6 to 2XX7. This increase has the potential to give a misleading impression, as it is partly driven by the choice of capacity denominator and inventory valuation methodology. This aspect is addressed under the next heading.

(v) Explanation of the Difference Between the Operating Income Statements

In identifying the difference between the operating income statements, it is useful to summarise them (a) by year and (b) by format.

(a) Difference by Year

As the variable costing statements reflect the impact of sales only, this results in the 1,000 additional sales units in 2XX7 adding €22,000 to the operating income, as shown in Appendix 3. This means that Castlegrove's operating income for 2XX7 gets the 'full contribution' effect of the additional 1,000 sales units, as it is projected to be operating well above the breakeven point that year.

As the absorption costing statements reflect the impact of both sales and production volumes, this results in the additional 1,000 sales units in 2XX7, combined with the comparative stock increase of 500 units (sales + 1,000/production + 1,500), adding €25,000 to the bottom line, as shown in Appendix 3. This means that the

Castlegrove operating income statement in 2XX7 is getting the benefit of deferring an additional €3,000 of fixed manufacturing overhead allocated to the 500 'Pulse' units at €6 per unit.

(b) Difference by Format

As the variable costing statements treat fixed manufacturing overhead as a period cost, the €60,000 budgeted fixed manufacturing overhead is written off in both years. In contrast, the absorption costing statements treat fixed manufacturing overhead as part of product cost and assign the amount associated with the units still in inventory. This means that the €9,000 (1,500 units × €6) assigned to inventory in 2XX6 and the €12,000 (2,000 × €6) assigned to inventory in 2XX7 account for the difference between the projected operating income statement under the different formats. In effect, €51,000 (€33,000 + €18,000) of the fixed manufacturing overhead will be expensed in 2XX6 and €48,000 (€39,000 + €9,000) in 2XX7 under absorption costing versus €60,000 under variable costing in both years.

(vi) Key Issues to be Addressed by Senior Management in Reviewing the Projected Performance of the 'Pulse' Product Line

The projected positive results, prepared by you for the first two years of the project, confirm its strong viability. This is also the case if one extrapolates the data for another three years, as I have done in the attached Appendices 5, 6 and 7. Based on your cost data and incorporating the stated assumptions about production and sales volume, the 'Pulse' project is projected to increase operating income significantly each year, under both formats.

However, the projected operating income statements mask a potential significant problem in regard to the appropriate balance that is sustainable between production and sales volume, particularly with the launch of a new product. A small variation that is well managed and part of an integrated sales and production strategy is to be expected and is sustainable. However, Appendix 4 presents a situation that is worrying at this early stage.

Appendix 4 shows a continuous and significant stock build-up that peaks at the end of 2XX8. As a result, Castlegrove would need to be able to finance a stock valuation that rises to approximately €300,000. This is a significant figure for Castlegrove, based on its previous history, and I suggest it needs to be reviewed as a matter of urgency. The following profile may be a useful way to generate some serious discussion, so that agreement can be reached now on the appropriate action, rather than later in crisis mode.

> Year-end stock level 2XX6: 1,500 units or about 12 weeks 2XX7 anticipated sales.
> Year-end stock level 2XX7: 3,500 units or about 24 weeks 2XX8 anticipated sales.
> Year-end stock level 2XX8: 4,525 units or about 27 weeks 2XX9 anticipated sales.
> Year-end stock level 2XX9: 4,429 units or about 23 weeks 2X10 anticipated sales.

The above profile is completely at variance with the sales strategy articulated by Jones and reflects the need to ensure that the individual goals of the sales and production managers are synchronised in the best interests of Castlegrove. The problem could be further exacerbated by Holmes's personal anxiety to increase plant capacity utilisation further in the short-term. As the projected income statements do not properly reflect this underlying trend, there is a real danger that a significant write-off of unsaleable stock may have to take place at a later date or plant capacity for 'Pulse' may have to be retired for a prolonged period, with obvious consequences.

Alternatively, this situation could lead to undue pressure being placed on Jones to deliver more sales, even if it means pushing distributors and wholesalers beyond comfortable stocking levels. This manifestation of serious dysfunctional behaviour needs to be tackled by the managing director and the board, if necessary, in order to protect the underlying viability of 'Pulse' and Castlegrove's business, in general. The following questions would be a good basis from which to start the discussion.

- What strategy is Castlegrove pursuing in regard to 'Pulse'? Is it one of cost leadership, product differentiation or some combination of both?
- Can sales volume be boosted by pursuing a more aggressive pricing and/or marketing strategy?
- What is the logic in building up such high levels of inventory when the vast majority of sales are anticipated to be made to order?
- Should production be matched more closely with sales projections, even if it means 'retiring' some of the skilled operatives and running the plant at a lower capacity level? What are the cost implications of these alternatives?
- Can some of the plant capacity be used for some other productive internal purposes or outsourced?
- Is there any potential for productivity and expenditure improvements?
- Is this the time to incorporate a carrying charge for inventory in order to reflect its financing cost?

The outcome of this review process should be reflected in a revision of the projected revised operating income statements. These should then become the basis of the performance evaluation process and be subject to revision in the usual way.

Brief Summary of the Merits of Variable and Absorption Costing Systems

Absorption Costing

- Consistent with financial and tax-reporting requirements.
- Does not understate the importance of fixed costs.
- Fixed costs are assigned to the product rather than to the passage of time.
- Avoids fictitious losses being reported for businesses with a high degree of seasonality.
- Theoretically superior to variable costing, because of the application of the revenue production concept.

Variable Costing

- Provides more useful information for decision making and has a more user-friendly format.
- Removes from profit the effect of stock changes.
- If used as a basis for performance reward system, can help to prevent the unnecessary build-up of inventory or 'cherry-picking' products with high fixed manufacturing overhead absorption rates.
- Avoids fixed costs being capitalised in unsaleable stocks.

Different capacity options available and their possible application

Possible Capacity Levels	Possible Applications (Not Definitive)
Theoretical	Academic
Normal	Product Costing/Capacity Management and Pricing
Practical	Financial Statements/Regulatory Requirements
	Product Costing/Capacity Management and Pricing
Master-Budget	Performance Evaluation

Appendix 1: Projected Operating Income Statement for 'Pulse'

Revised Variable (Relevance) Costing Statement

Period: 12 months ended

	Dec. 2XX6 Unit €	Dec. 2XX6 Gross €	Dec. 2XX7 Unit €	Dec. 2XX7 Gross €
Revenue	85	467,500	85	552,500
Variable Costs				
Variable Manufacturing				
Direct Material	5	27,500	5	32,500
Direct Labour	25	137,500	25	162,500
Variable Manufacturing overhead	30	165,000	30	195,000
Variable Cost of Goods Sold	60	330,000	60	390,000
Variable Non-Manufacturing overhead	3	16,500	3	19,500
Total Variable Costs	63	346,500	63	409,500
Contribution Margin	22	121,000	22	143,000
Fixed Costs				
Fixed Manufacturing overhead		60,000		60,000
Fixed Non-Manufacturing overhead		30,400		30,400
Total Fixed Costs		90,400		90,400
Operating Income		30,600		52,600
Note				
Sales (units)		5,500		6,500
Production (units)		7,000		8,500
Breakeven level of sales (units)		4,109		4,109
Profit-volume ratio		26%		26%
Margin of safety		25%		37%

Appendix 2: Projected Operating Income Statement for 'Pulse'

Absorption Costing Statement

Period: 12 months ended

	Dec. 2XX6 Unit €	Dec. 2XX6 Gross €	%	Dec. 2XX7 Unit €	Dec. 2XX7 Gross €	%
Revenue	85	467,500		85	552,500	
Cost of Goods Sold						
Variable Manufacturing						
Direct Material	5	27,500		5	32,500	
Direct Labour	25	137,500		25	162,500	
Variable Manufacturing overhead	30	165,000		30	195,000	
Fixed Manufacturing overhead absorbed	6	33,000		6	39,000	
Cost of Goods Sold	66	363,000		66	429,000	
Gross Margin	19	104,500	22	19	123,500	22
Production Volume Variance	3.27	18,000	*	1.38	9,000	*
Adjusted Gross Margin	15.73	86,500	19	17.62	114,500	21

Appendix 2 (continued)

Operating Costs

Variable Non-Manufacturing overhead	3.00	16,500		3.00	19,500	
Fixed Non-Manufacturing overhead	5.53	30,400		4.68	30,400	
Total Operating Costs	**8.53**	**46,900**		**7.68**	**49,900**	
Operating Income	**7.20**	**39,600**	8	**9.94**	**64,600**	12

Note 1

Stock Input/Output Matrix (units)	2XX6	2XX7	Difference
Opening	0	1,500	1,500
Production	7,000	8,500	1,500
Less Sales	5,500	6,500	1,000
Closing	1,500	3,500	2,000
Stock Movement	**1,500**	**2,000**	**500**

Note 2

Production-Volume Variance	2XX6	2XX7
Practical Capacity Denominator Level (units)	10,000	10,000
Actual Production (units)	7,000	8,500
Under/Over Recovery (units)	3,000	1,500
Fixed Manufacturing Overhead Rate per Unit €	6.0*	6.0*
Production-Volume Variance €	18,000	9,000

*€60,000/10,000 units

Appendix 3: Difference in Operating Income between the Two Statements

Operating Income	Dec. 2XX6	Dec. 2XX7	Difference
Variable (Relevance) Costing	30,600	52,600	−22,000*4
Absorption Costing	39,600	64,600	−25,000*3
Difference	-9,000*1	-12,000*2	

*1 1,500 (Stock Increase) Units at €6 fixed mnfg o/head p.u.
*2 2,000 (Stock Increase) Units at €6 fixed mnfg.o/head p.u.
*3 1,000 (More Sales) Units at €19 (gross margin) p.u. + PVV €9k - Var NMF o/head 1,000 Units at €3 p.u.
*4 1,000 (More Sales) Units at €22 contribution p.u.

Fixed Manufacturing overhead Reconciliation	€ Dec. 2XX6	€ Dec. 2XX7
Fixed Manufacturing overhead absorbed	33,000	39,000
Add Production-Volume Variance	18,000	9,000
Add Profit Difference (Absorption v Variable)	9,000	12,000
= Budgeted Fixed Manufacturing Overhead	60,000	60,000

Appendix 4: Projected Stock Input/Output Matrix (units)

Details	2XX6	2XX7	2XX8	2XX9	2X10	Summary
Opening	0	1,500	3,500	4,525	4,429	0
Production	7,000	8,500	8,500	8,500	8,500	41,000
Less Sales	5,500	6,500	7,475	8,596	9,885	37,956
Closing	1,500	3,500	4,525	4,429	3,044	3,044
Stock Movement	1,500	2,000	1,025	-96	-1,385	3,044
Stock Valuation (p.u.)	€66	€66	€66	€66	€66	
Stock Valuation (gross)	€99,000	€231,000	€298,650	€292,314	€200,904	

Appendix 5: Absorption Costing Statement

Period: 12 months ended	Dec 2XX6 Unit €	Dec 2XX6 Gross €	Dec 2XX6 %	Dec. 2XX7 Unit €	Dec. 2XX7 Gross €	Dec. 2XX7 %	Dec. 2XX8 Unit €	Dec. 2XX8 Gross €	Dec. 2XX8 %	Dec. 2XX9 Unit €	Dec. 2XX9 Gross €	Dec. 2XX9 %	Dec. 2X10 Unit €	Dec. 2X10 Gross €	Dec. 2X10 %
Revenue	85	467,500		85	552,500		85	635,375		85	730,660		85	840,225	
Cost of Goods Sold															
Variable Manufacturing															
Direct Material	5	27,500		5	32,500		5	37,375		5	42,980		5	49,425	
Direct Labour	25	137,500		25	162,500		25	186,875		25	214,900		25	247,125	
Variable Manufacturing overhead	30	165,000		30	195,000		30	224,250		30	257,880		30	296,550	
Fixed Manufacturing overhead absorbed	6	33,000		6	39,000		6	44,850		6	51,576		6	59,310	
Cost of Goods Sold	66	363,000		66	429,000		66	493,350		66	567,336		66	652,410	
Gross Margin	19	104,500	22	19	123,500	22	19	142,025	22	19	163,324	22	19	187,815	22
Production Volume Variance	3.27	18,000	*	1.38	9,000	*	1.20	9,000	*	1.05	9,000	*	0.91	9,000	*
Adjusted Gross Margin	15.73	86,500	19	17.62	114,500	21	17.80	133,025	21	17.95	154,324	21	18.09	178,815	21
Operating Costs															
Variable Non-Manufacturing overhead	3	16,500		3	19,500		3	22,425		3	25,788		3	29,655	
Fixed Non-Manufacturing overhead	5.53	30,400		4.68	30,400		4.07	30,400		3.54	30,400		3.08	30,400	
Total Operating Costs	8.53	46,900		7.68	49,900		7.07	52,825		6.54	56,188		6.08	60,055	
Operating Income	7.20	39,600	8	9.94	64,600	12	10.73	80,200	13	11.41	98,136	13	12.01	118,760	14

Note 1

Stock Input/Output Matrix (units)

	2XX6	2XX7	2XX8	2XX9	2X10
Opening	0	1,500	3,500	4,525	4,429
Production	7,000	8,500	8,500	8,500	8,500
Less Sales	5,500	6,500	7,475	8,596	9,885
Closing	1,500	3,500	4,525	4,429	3,044
Stock Movement	1,500	2,000	1,025	−96	−1,385
Stock Valuation €	99,000	231,000	298,650	292,314	200,904

Note 2

Production-Volume Variance Calculation

	2XX6	2XX7	2XX8	2XX9	2X10
Practical Capacity Denominator Level (units)	10,000	10,000	10,000	10,000	10,000
Actual Production (units)	7,000	8,500	8,500	8,500	8,500
Under/Over Recovery (units)	3,000	1,500	1,500	1,500	1,500
Fixed Manufacturing Overhead Rate per unit €	6	6	6	6	6
Production-Volume Variance €	18,000	9,000	9,000	9,000	9,000

*€60,000/10,000 units

Appendix 6: Revised Variable (Relevance) Costing Statement

Period: 12 months ended	Dec. 2XX6		Dec. 2XX7		Dec. 2XX8		Dec. 2XX9		Dec. 2X10	
	Unit €	Gross €	Unit €	Gross €	Unit €	Gross €	Unit €	Gross €	Unit €	Gross €
Revenue	85	467,500	85	552,500	85	635,375	85	730,660	85	840,225
Variable Costs										
Variable Manufacturing										
Direct Material	5	27,500	5	32,500	5	37,375	5	42,980	5	49,425
Direct Labour	25	137,500	25	162,500	25	186,875	25	214,900	25	247,125
Variable Manufacturing overhead	30	165,000	30	195,000	30	224,250	30	257,880	30	296,550
Variable Cost of Goods Sold	60	330,000	60	390,000	60	448,500	60	515,760	60	593,100
Variable Non-Manufacturing overhead	3	16,500	3	19,500	3	22,425	3	25,788	3	29,655
Total Variable Costs	63	346,500	63	409,500	63	470,925	63	541,548	63	622,755
Contribution Margin	22	121,000	22	143,000	22	164,450	22	189,112	22	217,470
Fixed Costs										
Fixed manufacturing overhead		60,000		60,000		60,000		60,000		60,000
Fixed non-manufacturing overhead		30,400		30,400		30,400		30,400		30,400
Total Fixed Costs		90,400		90,400		90,400		90,400		90,400
Operating Income		30,600		52,600		74,050		98,712		127,070

Note

Period: 12 months ended	Dec. 2XX6	Dec. 2XX7	Dec. 2XX8	Dec. 2XX9	Dec. 2X10
Sales (units)	5,500	6,500	7,475	8,596	9,885
Production (units)	7,000	8,500	8,500	8,500	8,500
Breakeven level of Sales (units)	4,109	4,109	4,109	4,109	4,109
Profit-volume ratio	26%	26%	26%	26%	26%
Margin of safety	25%	37%	45%	52%	58%

Appendix 7: Difference in Operating Income Between the Two Statements

Operating Income	Dec. 2XX6 €	Dec. 2XX7 €	Dec. 2XX8 €	Dec. 2XX9 €	Dec. 2X10 €
Variable (Relevance) Costing	30,600	52,600	74,050	98,712	127,070
Absorption Costing	39,600	64,600	80,200	98,136	118,760
Difference	–9,000	–12,000	–6,150	576	8,310
Stock Difference	1,500	2,000	1,025	–96	–1,385
Fixed Manufacturing overhead p.u €6					

Fixed Manufacturing Overhead Reconciliation	Dec. 2XX6 €	Dec. 2XX7 €	Dec. 2XX8 €	Dec. 2XX9 €	Dec. 2X10 €
Fixed Manufacturing overhead absorbed	33,000	39,000	44,850	51,576	59,310
Add Production-Volume Variance	18,000	9,000	9,000	9,000	9,000
Add Profit Difference (Absorption v Variable)	9,000	12,000	6,150	–576	–8,310
= Budgeted Fixed Manufacturing Overhead	60,000	60,000	60,000	60,000	60,000

Case 8
Solution to Chicken Pieces
Peter Clarke, University College Dublin

MEMORANDUM

To: Ray Fullam
From: A. Student
Re: Major issues faced by the company
Date: As per postmark

Further to our recent meeting, I have undertaken a preliminary assessment of the major issues currently facing the company and report my main findings below. Please appreciate that I had a limited amount of time and information available to prepare this memo for you, so that my recommendations and conclusions are, necessarily, tentative. However, I hope that they highlight some important aspects that need your attention. I have structured my memo to coincide with some of the questions that you raised with me.

1. Critical Issues and Performance Measures

There are several critical success factors that are relevant to your business, but these should be considered in the context of overall company goals and strategy. It appears to me that your company can pursue either of two strategic options, namely cost leadership or product differentiation. The former consists of being, above all else, cost competitive. The second requires the company to excel in product quality and/or customer service. It is usual to 'drive' strategy throughout the firm by the identification of appropriate critical success factors. A critical success factor represents a key area in which performance must excel if the company is to be successful and will usually include reference to product quality, customer service and cost competitiveness. In turn, it is usual to highlight these areas to employees and management staff by way of related performance measures. Based on my quick assessment of your operations, it appears that critical success factors and related performance measures include the following:

Critical Success Factor	Key Performance Indicator (KPI)
New customer acquisition	No. of new customers acquired during period
	% sales to new customers
Overall customer satisfaction	Customer satisfaction index
Delivery on time	% of on-time deliveries (OTD)
Quality, including overall hygiene	% rejects by customers
	No. of hygiene violations
Cost competitiveness	Cost per unit; relative price index with competitors
Innovation, including new products	No. of new products introduced
	% sales from new products
Dispatch efficiency	Cost per unit shipped
Productivity	No. of chickens processed per employee

(**Note:** students will only be expected to provide four critical success factors and related key performance indicators.)

2. Apportionment of Costs of Jointing Process

The apportionment of jointing costs can be done in a number of ways. I have prepared calculations on the basis of the physical number of units involved. This quick calculation gives a joint cost of 50c per unit, as shown below:

Total Joint Costs to be Apportioned		
Chickens (*used*)	35,000 chickens @ 60c each	21,000
Storage and other jointing costs (given)		70,000
Disposal costs (given)		14,000
		105,000

Product:	Units	%	Joint Costs	Joint Costs (per unit)
Breasts	70,000	33.3%	€35,000	50c
Wings & legs	140,000	66.7%	€70,000	50c
Total	210,000	100%	€105,000	

The main limitation of the physical output, i.e. units method of apportioning joint costs, is that each joint product is assigned the same cost per unit. This method is not realistic in the context that all costs are incurred to create value. Thus, it would make much more sense to apportion costs in relation to their net realisable value.

3. Separate Process Accounts

I detail below my calculations regarding the cost of your three main processes, i.e. jointing, breast fillets and finishing of wings/legs.

Jointing (of carcass) Process Account

	Chickens	€		Chickens	€
Purchases	40,000	24,000	WIP (breasts)	35,000	35,000
Bank	N/a	70,000	WIP (wings/legs)	*	70,000
Bank (disposal)	N/a	14,000	Balance	5,000	3,000
	40,000	108,000		40,000	108,000

Work in Progress Account (Filleting of Breasts)

	Units	€		Units	€
Transferred in	70,000	35,000			
Conversion costs	N/a	32,500	T/f to COGS	70,000	67,500
	70,000	67,500		70,000	67,500

Work in Progress Account (Finishing of Wings/legs)

	Units	€		Units	€
Transferred in	140,000	70,000			
Conversion costs	N/a	31,000	T/f to COGS	140,000	101,000
	140,000	101,000		140,000	101,000

* Equivalent to 140,000 wings/legs

4. Overall Cost/Income Statement

Based on the information provided to me, which I did not verify, the following is my summarised cost/income statement, as requested.

Summarised Income Statement for Year xxxx

	Breasts	Wings/legs	Total
No. of units sold	70,000	140,000	210,000
Sales revenue (see working below)	140,000	102,000	242,000
Less: Cost of goods sold:	(67,500)	(101,000)	(168,500)
= Gross profit margin	72,500	1,000	73,500
Selling, distribution and admin. Costs (25k + 60K)			(85,000)
Net loss for year			(11,500)

Working: Schedule of Sales

	Buns	Mossgo	Superdim	Total
Breasts (70,000)	€60,000	€38,000	€42,000	€140,000
Wings/legs (140,000)	€48,000	€36,000	€18,000	€102,000
	€108,000	€74,000	€60,000	€242,000

5. Breakeven Point

A crucial target for any business is to reach, at least, its breakeven point. As detailed below, I estimated that the breakeven point is represented by sales of about €255,000 per annum. It should be noted that overall sales in the current year amounted to €242,000. Thus an overall increase in gross revenue of about 5% is required. This additional revenue can be generated either by selling additional output or increasing prices to existing customers, introducing new products and/or acquiring new customers.

Calculation of BEP (in €)
Summarised income statement for year:

		€
Sales revenue		242,000
Less: Cost of goods sold:	168,500	
Selling and administration expenses	85,000	
Total costs	253,500	
Less: variable costs (chickens used)	(21,000)	(21,000)
Total fixed costs	232,500	
Contribution		221,000
Less: fixed costs		(232,500)
Net loss for year		(11,500)
Contribution/sales ratio		0.913
BEP (€)	€232,500/ .913	€255 K ®
Alternatively:		
Average selling price per unit	€242,000/210,000	€1.15
Less: Variable costs (€21,000/210,000)		(0.10)
Average unit contribution		€1.05
BEP (units)	€232,500/ 1.05 =	221,429 units
BEP (revenue)	221,429 × €1.15 =	€255 K ®

6. Relevant Costs of Accepting Special Disposal Offer

Currently your company is paying €14,000 per annum to dispose of waste from your operations. This is an important issue due to the range of health and safety legislation which prevails, and also environmental concerns by the public at large. Compliance with such legislation would be an important element in complying with the firm's Corporate Social Responsibility obligations.

By my provisional calculations, the proposal to 'sell' waste to the local pet food manufacturer is attractive in financial terms, as detailed below, as it reduces the company's overall costs to €5,000 – generating an overall cost saving of €9,000:

(i) Current disposal cost payable by company	(14,000)
(ii) Revenue from Pet Food manufacturer	3,000
Less: Additional storage costs	(8,000)
Estimated future cost of selling to Pet Food manufacturer	(5,000)
Net financial benefits of 'outsourcing'	9,000

However, there are a number of other issues to be considered.

- Is the pet food manufacturer reliable in terms of collection of waste and payment?
- The additional storage time (three weeks on average) may create additional problems, e.g. smell and appearance.
- It is possible that the current 'waste' has other commercial possibilities. For example, it may be useful to other outlets that are now using the carcasses to produce chicken stock for cooking purposes. Alternatively, the company could use the waste in order to expand its product range, e.g. manufacture its own brand of pet food. Also, there is an increasing tendency to produce 'Mechanically Removed Meat' or MCM. As the term suggests, this meat is removed from the carcass by special machines and the produce is used to manufacture products for human consumption – sold mainly through fast-food outlets! However, a fuller analysis needs to be undertaken before a final decision is made.

In conclusion, I hope you find this memorandum of benefit to you. Should you have any queries or require any additional information, please do not hesitate to contact me.

Case 10
Solution to Newtown Manufacturing Limited
Tom Kennedy, University of Limerick

Pedagogical Objective

The case is intended to make students aware of the circumstances in which more refined product-costing models are appropriate in informing managerial decision-making in terms of product pricing and product profitability. It facilitates comparison between a traditional product-costing model and the more contemporary ABC approach. The case content is categorised under the full costing element of managerial accounting.

Question 1
Prepare Revised Product-costing Models for the Components Product Group

As there are real concerns that the current, traditional costing system distorts the cost of product lines, it is appropriate to prepare revised models using methods which are deemed to be better able to represent the demands made by each product line on Newtown's resources.

The current practice of using a method based on direct labour is likely to provide biased product cost information and lead to significant cross-subsidisation. Direct labour, as a basis for assigning general overheads, is becoming increasingly irrelevant, as it generally bears no relationship to how they were incurred. Direct labour is being replaced by sophisticated machinery and becoming a much smaller component of total product cost. Therefore, a more appropriate measure that could better reflect the new technological environment is machine-hours. Appendix 1 presents the revised product-line performance report for January–March 2XX6, using machine-hours as an allocation base.

In recognition of the fact that general overheads in the modern business environment are not homogeneous in terms of being primarily influenced by volume and in order to capture the increasing complexity of business activity, the ABC method could be used. This method is based on two basic principles, namely:

(a) that all costs (resources) are perceived as a result of the activities performed, such as mould design/manufacture, manufacturing operations, quality inspection etc.;
(b) that all costs are first related to activities and then to cost objects, depending on how much each cost object draws on the activities.

Appendix 2 presents the revised product-line performance report for January–March 2XX6, using the major activities and associated cost drivers identified as part of the pilot study and presented in Appendix 2 of the case.

Question 2

Comment on the Outcome of the Revised Costing Models

The aim of the pilot study was to critically review the components product group cost structure and see if Newtown could or should revise its pricing policy. A review of Appendix 1 of the case study shows that Newtown is achieving a healthy mark-up on its costs of 18% versus a target of approximately 20%. However, the results are not consistent across the three product lines. Alpha is reporting a mark-up of 14%, Beta 21% and Gamma 18%. This suggests that Alpha is the product line that is underperforming, Beta is overperforming and Gamma is in a relatively strong position to address the competitive threat from the Malaysian supplier.

However, a traditional costing system, using direct labour hours as an allocation base, has the potential to give unreliable product cost data and lead to significant product cross-subsidisation. This type of broad averaging, or cost smoothing, is an expected outcome of the system currently used by Newtown. Its consequences are particularly critical for companies that place great reliance on mark-up as a pricing basis and/or strategy. Therefore, 'more appropriate and refined' allocation methods, such as machine hours and ABC, should be used in order to better inform managerial decision-making.

Appendix 1 shows a revised product-line performance report, using machine hours as the allocation base. This allocation base better reflects the greater complexity and automation associated with the individual product lines. It shows that both Alpha and Beta are overperforming at 25% and 23%, respectively, and that Gamma is only barely profitable with a mark-up of 3%.

Appendix 2 incorporates the results of the pilot study and shows a revised product-line performance report, using ABC data as the allocation base. This methodology further reflects the greater complexity and automation associated with the individual product lines. It shows that Alpha is performing well with a mark-up of 20%, Beta is the jewel in the business at 34% and Gamma is not even covering its costs at a minus 2% mark-up.

These outcomes should come as a major surprise to the senior management team and are likely to be seriously challenged. Questions will be asked about the integrity and reliability of the process that gave rise to this information. Reference should be made to the principles underpinning the model and the input of the various parties in activity and cost-driver identification. Some caution should be expressed as to the claims of absolute accuracy, but ultimately the debate should focus on what model best reflects the consumption of resources in the organisation. In effect, do the revised models better capture the underlying complexity and variety of tasks as identified by Appendix 2 (of the case) by product line and are they consistent with reasonable expectations? In other words, are they intuitively sound and rational? If so, management should, therefore, concentrate their efforts in using the 'new' information to make the appropriate decisions and continue their search for further refinement of the process.

Further, at a micro level, Appendix 2 presents powerful information in terms of resource usage, efficiency and the potential for greater economies by identifying a cost-driver rate. For example, it shows the impact of Gamma using more moulds and having higher distribution and order-processing costs relative to the other product lines. This information should focus the attention of individual managers for corrective action. Serious consideration needs to be given to initiating greater efficiencies in the areas clearly identified by the magnitude of the individual cost-driver rates.

Appendix 3 and 4 present a comparison by product line and allocation base. They suggest that Newtown should look seriously at its pricing strategy for both Alpha and Beta, with a view to generating more volume in both cases. This potential re-balancing of its product mix may offer some possibilities of protecting or improving its overall profitability while it is dealing with the specific Gamma product line competitive threat. In the absence of the pilot study and the insights gained by the activity analysis, management action would be likely to compound the current problem by making the wrong decision. Appendix 3 and 4 clearly show that Gamma is not operationally efficient and a knee-jerk reaction in reducing the price is not the solution. Newtown is typical of a lot of firms that place 'blind' faith in championing a product line that is strategically driven, technologically rich and resource intensive, but cost poor relative to its other products.

In summary, the current traditional costing system appears to mask serious undercosting in the Gamma product line and some overcosting in both the Alpha and Beta product lines. Consequently, as currently manufactured and delivered, Newtown is not in a position to address the competitive threat to Gamma from the Malaysian supplier through price competitiveness. In the short-term, it may have to address the threat by focusing on the non-price attributes, such as functionality, reliability, service quality, flexibility, after-care service, etc. This is due to the fact that it would take some time to implement the operational decisions identified by the activity identification exercise. Obviously, the option to do nothing is not sustainable, as the competitive threat is real and potentially could be very damaging. A combination of serious market re-evaluation of all product lines, better informed and more focussed operational action has to be undertaken with some urgency.

Question 3

Advise on Whether Newtown Should Adopt ABC

ABC has generally proved highly successful in firms that have implemented it. Product costs and profitability have been shown to be significantly different and overhead cost causality has been better understood. There is evidence to suggest that cost-driver measures can have strong motivational effects on those in contact with them (Jones and Wright, 1987). With careful selection of cost drivers, the dysfunctional consequences of ill-considered measurement systems could be reduced. Ultimately, the utility of ABC will be dependent on how well the system fits the circumstances of the organisation.

Adopting a fully customised ABC system would represent a significant strategic decision by Newtown and would require the full support of all management in order to be successful. The pilot project could be seen as a first step in improving the quality and integrity of the management information and should continue. The process could be further refined by critically reviewing the choice of activities and cost drivers on an ongoing basis. It could be embellished by further classification of the cost categories and an attempt at constructing a cost hierarchy under four levels: unit, batch, product and facility. It could attempt to increase the degree of costs directly traceable to individual products or product lines. Attention should also be brought to bear on the direct costs and the need for ongoing competitiveness in these areas. The appropriate level of sophistication adopted would be subject to the cost/benefit test and the contingency theory perspective.

In effect, the process should be seen as a continual search for a greater understanding of the link between resource spending and consumption and confidence in the choice of activities and drivers. The financial analyst, Mick Dowd, should continue to champion the process and engage with all the functional department heads and other relevant personnel. Newtown would benefit greatly from the deepening interaction between operational managers and accounting staff and the availability of relevant non-financial data.

In the short to medium term, the process could be mapped and supported using Excel. It is unlikely that the investment in technology and intellectual capital necessary for the installation of a fully customised system would be feasible at this time. The process could, in time, be expanded to include budgeting, cost modelling and performance measurement.

Finally, a refined costing model using machine hours or ABC is not a panacea for all the problems associated with the provision of costing information to management. Like any conventional system, they are concerned with yesterday's costs. However, it is fair to suggest that a better understanding of the past is a prerequisite for enhancing the ability of management to better predict the future.

Question 4

Circumstances in Which ABC Would be Most Beneficial

Circumstances in which you would expect ABC to be most beneficial:

- high overhead costs that are not proportional to the unit volume of individual products;
- significant automation that has made it more difficult to assign overhead to products using the traditional approach;

- the production of a wide variety of products or services;
- profit margins that are difficult to explain; and
- hard-to-make (complex) products that show profits and easy-to-make products that show losses.

Key Attributes of ABC

- New technology/new way of thinking with potential to offer new insights (Friedman & Lyne, 1995);
- evolutionary rather than revolutionary (*Bromwich & Bhimani v Kaplan & Cooper*);
- a more equitable allocation of overheads (determines underlying 'driver' of the activities);
- an ability to deal with a complex and opaque cost structure (range of measurement and calculative routines);
- an ability to integrate the non-accounting aspects – transaction costing (process of activity identification – minutiae of production process);
- characteristics of diversity and enrichment versus conservatism and uniformity of traditional systems; and
- a control device – disciplinary technique, enabling 'managing of managers', depersonalises act of control.

Essential Features

- Activity analysis;
- enlarged concept of cost variability – treat as many costs as is possible as variable;
- flexibility;
- compatibility with general process approach to organisations, i.e. business process engineering; and
- diversity in use and wider application than a traditional volume-based costing system.

Appendix 1: Components Group – Revised Product-Line Performance Report

(Traditional Job Costing System using Machine Hours): January – March 2XX6

	Product Lines (Gross)				Rate per machine hour*1	Product Lines (Unit)		
	Alpha €	Beta €	Gamma €	Total €		Alpha €	Beta €	Gamma €
Sales Value	1,600,000	1,650,000	1,150,000	4,400,000		80.00	110.00	115.00
Direct Costs								
Direct Material	400,000	255,000	250,000	905,000		20.00	17.00	25.00
Direct Labour	220,000	225,000	135,000	580,000		11.00	15.00	13.50
Total Direct Costs	620,000	480,000	385,000	1,485,000		31.00	32.00	38.50
General Overhead								
Manufacturing	221,964	291,327	249,709	763,000	11.10	11.10	19.42	24.97
Engineering	82,327	108,055	92,618	283,000	4.12	4.12	7.20	9.26
Sales & Distribution	161,018	211,336	181,146	553,500	8.05	8.05	14.09	18.11
Administration*2	189,673	248,945	213,382	652,000	9.48	9.48	16.60	21.34
Total General Overhead	654,982	859,663	736,855	2,251,500	32.75	32.75	57.31	73.68
Total Product Cost per Traditional System (Machine Hours)				3,736,500		63.75	89.31	112.18
Profit by product line/unit	325,018	310,337	28,145	663,500		16.25	20.69	2.82
(Before inventory adjustments)			Mark-up	18%		25%	23%	3%

*1 Total machine hours 20,000 26,250 22,500 68,750
*2 Includes contribution of €130,000 to corporate head office
Volume (units) 20,000 15,000 10,000 45,000

Case 10: Solution to Newtown Manufacturing Limited

Appendix 2: Components Group – Revised Product-Line Performance Report (ABC System): January – March 2XX6

	Product Lines (Gross)						Unit Product Cost €		
	Alpha €	Beta €	Gamma €	Total €	Dept	Rate per Cost Driver	Alpha €	Beta €	Gamma €
Sales Value	1,600,000	1,650,000	1,150,000	4,400,000			80.00	110.00	115.00
Direct Costs									
Direct Material	400,000	255,000	250,000	905,000			20.00	17.00	25.00
Direct Labour	220,000	225,000	135,000	580,000			11.00	15.00	13.50
Total Direct Costs	620,000	480,000	385,000	1,485,000			31.00	32.00	38.50
General Overhead Activities									
Mould design/manufacture	72,222	126,389	126,389	325,000			3.61	8.43	12.64
Manufacturing operations	67,782	88,964	76,254	233,000	Manf	3,611.11	3.39	5.93	7.63
Supervision of direct labour	41,739	46,957	31,304	120,000	Manf	3.39	2.09	3.13	3.13
Quality inspection	23,448	29,310	32,242	85,000	Mnfg	2.09	1.17	1.95	3.22
Plant engineering/utilities	66,105	41,316	49,579	157,000	Mnfg	586.21	3.31	2.75	4.96
Process and test engineering	47,547	42,792	35,661	126,000	Eng	5.51	2.38	2.85	3.57
Distribution	131,250	131,250	175,000	437,500	Eng	2,377.36	6.56	8.75	17.50
Sales & marketing expenses	29,455	30,375	21,170	81,000	S/D	4,375.00	1.47	2.03	2.12
Invoicing	10,938	13,125	10,937	35,000	S/D	810.00	0.55	0.88	1.09
Materials management	42,681	32,638	42,681	118,000	S/D	437.50	2.13	2.18	4.27
Procurement	57,459	36,630	35,911	130,000	Adm	502.13	2.87	2.44	3.59
Order processing	13,103	22,931	58,966	95,000	Adm	1,300.00	0.66	1.53	5.90
Customer administration	15,758	19,697	29,545	65,000	Adm	655.17	0.79	1.31	2.95
Information systems support	18,667	10,667	9,666	39,000	Adm	1,969.70	0.93	0.71	0.97
General administration	71,304	80,217	53,479	205,000	Adm	333.33	3.57	5.35	5.35
Total general overhead	709,458	753,258	788,784	2,251,500		3.57	35.48	50.22	78.89
Total product cost per ABC system				3,736,500			66.48	82.22	117.39
Profit by product line/unit	270,542	416,742	−23,784	663,500			13.52	27.78	−2.39
			Mark-up	18%			20%	34%	−2%

Data from ABC Process

	Activities	Cost Drivers	Alpha	Beta	Gamma	Total	Dept.
				Cost Driver Volume			
1.	Mould design/manufacture	No. of parts-square foot	20	35	35	90	Manf.
2.	Manufacturing operations	No. of machine hours	20,000	26,250	22,500	68,750	Manf.
3.	Supervision of direct labour	No. of direct labour hours	20,000	22,500	15,000	57,500	Mnfg
4.	Quality inspection	No. units audited	40	50	55	145	Mnfg
5.	Plant engineering/utilities	Square feet	12,000	7,500	9,000	28,500	Eng.
6.	Process and test engineering	No. of eng. change revisions	20	18	15	53	Eng.
7.	Distribution	% traced directly to customers	30	30	40	100	S/D
8.	Sales & marketing expenses	% of sales revenue	36	38	26	100	S/D
9.	Invoicing	No. of invoices	25	30	25	80	S/D
10.	Materials management	No. of stock transactions	85	65	85	235	Adm.
11.	Procurement	% of direct material	44	28	28	100	Adm.
12.	Order processing	No. of orders	20	35	90	145	Adm.
13.	Customer administration	No. of customers	8	10	15	33	Adm.
14.	Information systems support	No. of desktop units	56	32	29	117	Adm.
15.	General administration	No. of direct labour hours	20,000	22,500	15,000	57,500	Adm.

Relevant Additional Data

	Product Lines			
	Alpha	Beta	Gamma	Total
		Cost Driver Volume		
Production volume (units)	20,000	15,000	10,000	45,000
Direct material (unit) €	20	17	25	
Direct material	400,000	255,000	250,000	905,000
Direct material %	44	28	28	100
Machine hours (unit)	1.00	1.75	2.25	
Total machine hours	20,000	26,250	22,500	68,750
Direct labour hours (unit)	1.00	1.50	1.50	
Total direct labour hours	20,000	22,500	15,000	57,500
Direct labour rate per hour	11.00	10.00	9.00	
Direct labour hours €	220,000	225,000	135,000	580,000
Sales price (unit)	80.00	110.00	115.00	
Sales revenue €	1,600,000	1,650,000	1,150,000	4,400,000
Sales revenue %	36	38	26	100

Appendix 3: Components Group – Product Profitability Comparison: Overview by Product Line

	Alpha			Beta			Gamma			Overall
Sales Value €	80.00	80.00	80.00	110.00	110.00	110.00	115.00	115.00	115.00	
	DL	MH	ABC	DL	MH	ABC	DL	MH	ABC	
	Allocation Base			Allocation Base			Allocation Base			
Direct Costs €										
Direct Material	20.00	20.00	20.00	17.00	17.00	17.00	25.00	25.00	25.00	
Direct Labour	11.00	11.00	11.00	15.00	15.00	15.00	13.50	13.50	13.50	
Total Direct Costs €	31.00	31.00	31.00	32.00	32.00	32.00	38.50	38.50	38.50	
General Overhead €										
Manufacturing	13.27	11.10	10.26	19.90	19.42	19.44	19.90	24.97	26.62	
Engineering	4.92	4.12	5.68	7.38	7.20	5.61	7.38	9.26	8.52	
Sales & Distribution	9.63	8.05	8.58	14.44	14.09	11.65	14.44	18.11	20.71	
Administration	11.34	9.48	10.96	17.01	16.60	13.52	17.01	21.34	23.04	
Total General Overhead €	39.16	32.75	35.48	58.73	57.31	50.22	58.73	73.68	78.89	
Total Product Cost €	70.16	63.75	66.48	90.73	89.31	82.22	97.23	112.18	117.39	
Profit by Product: Unit €	9.84	16.25	13.52	19.27	20.69	27.78	17.77	2.82	-2.39	
Profit by Product: Gross €	196,868	325,018	270,542	288,979	310,337	416,742	177,653	28,145	-23,784	663,500
Mark-up	14%	25%	20%	21%	23%	34%	18%	3%	-2%	18%
Production Volume (units)	20,000	20,000	20,000	15,000	15,000	15,000	10,000	10,000	10,000	45,000

Appendix 4: Components Group – Product Profitability Comparison: Overview by Allocation Base

	Product Lines Labour Hours				Product Lines Machine Hours				Product Lines ABC			
Allocation Base	Alpha	Beta	Gamma	Total	Alpha	Beta	Gamma	Total	Alpha	Beta	Gamma	Total
Sales Value	80.00	110.00	115.00		80.00	110.00	115.00		80.00	110.00	115.00	
Direct Costs €	DL	DL	DL		MH	MH	MH		ABC	ABC	ABC	
Direct Material	20.00	17.00	25.00		20.00	17.00	25.00		20.00	17.00	25.00	
Direct Labour	11.00	15.00	13.50		11.00	15.00	13.50		11.00	15.00	13.50	
Total Direct Costs €	31.00	32.00	38.50		31.00	32.00	38.50		31.00	32.00	38.50	
General Overhead €												
Manufacturing	13.27	19.90	19.90		11.10	19.42	24.97		10.26	19.44	26.62	
Engineering	4.92	7.38	7.38		4.12	7.20	9.26		5.68	5.61	8.52	
Sales & Distribution	9.63	14.44	14.44		8.05	14.09	18.11		8.58	11.65	20.71	
Administration	11.34	17.01	17.01		9.48	16.60	21.34		10.96	13.52	23.04	
Total General Overhead €	39.16	58.73	58.73	288,979	32.75	57.31	73.68	310,337	35.48	50.22	78.89	270,542
Total Product Cost €	70.16	90.73	97.23		63.75	89.31	112.18		66.48	82.22	117.39	
Profit by Product: Unit €	9.84	19.27	17.77		16.25	20.69	2.82		13.52	27.78	-2.39	
Profit by Product: Gross €	196,868	288,979	177,653	663,500	325,018	310,337	28,145	663,500	270,542	416,742	-23,784	663,500
Mark-up	14%	21%	18%	18%	25%	23%	3%	18%	20%	34%	-2%	18%
Production Volume (units)	20,000	15,000	10,000	45,000	20,000	15,000	10,000		20,000	15,000	10,000	45,000

Case 11
Solution to Lennon Department Store Ltd.
Bernard Pierce and Barbara Flood, Dublin City University

**REPORT ON PROJECTED INCOME FOR YEAR ENDING
31 DECEMBER 2XX7**

**PROPOSALS FOR REVISION OF ALLOCATION OF
STORE FLOOR SPACE AND RELATED
STRATEGIC ISSUES**

MCF Consultants
November 2XX6

Introduction

This report addresses a number of issues recently raised by the Board. Financial projections and a related commentary are presented for year ending 31 December 2XX7 and detailed analysis and commentary are provided regarding two proposals for revisions to the allocation of store floor space. The report concludes by addressing longer term strategic issues.

Projected Profit Statement

The projected profit statement is shown in Appendix 1. Calculations are based on assumptions regarding cost and revenue behaviour patterns which the company has been using in the preparation of financial projections. Although these assumptions have been confirmed as being valid for the projected level of activity, it is important to point out that it would be inappropriate to apply them to other proposed levels of activity and care should be exercised in interpreting the resulting projections.

In particular, the projections facilitate only limited assessment of the projected performance and do not provide a useful basis for assessing strategic options of the type currently under consideration.

Projected turnover is €607 million, generating a projected gross profit of €177 million which represents a gross margin of 29% for the company. Gross profit margins vary from 40% for hardware down to 25% for supermarkets, while the average concessions commission is 20%. These figures should be benchmarked against industry statistics and any shortfall should be fully investigated. There may be a need to review company policy in areas such as pricing, purchasing, discounts and store layout. The rationale behind floor-space allocation also needs to be carefully examined.

Projected net profit of €2.37 million represents 0.4% of turnover. Again, this should be benchmarked against industry norms. The figures shown for Product Group Profit are not reliable for comparison purposes across product groups, across different store sizes or with external benchmarks. This is because the information on which the projections are based does not permit an analysis of payroll and overhead costs between fixed and variable components. Fixed costs, by their nature, do not change within a specified range of activity and it is therefore necessary that such costs be identified and removed from the analysis before any attempt is made to draw comparisons in situations of varying activity levels. Therefore, while the overall accuracy of the estimates has been confirmed for the given level of activity, the figures do not provide a reliable basis either for assessing projected performance or evaluating alternatives.

In order to complete a full evaluation of the projected net profit figure, it would be necessary to obtain a complete analysis of payroll and overhead figures, analysed by product group and store category, where appropriate. Some further analysis of cost behaviour patterns is included in later sections of the report, based on additional details provided by the consultants.

Depreciation and Head Office costs combined amount to €17.5 million. While it is appropriate that these costs should be allocated to stores, it is important to recognise the arbitrary nature of such allocations and the fact that these costs are not controlled at store level. Accordingly, there is a need to conduct an evaluation of these costs using appropriate benchmarks and to carry out a review of related decision-making and control procedures at Head Office.

Proposal 1

Proposal 1 involves the possibility of discontinuing the supermarket business and devoting the space currently occupied by supermarkets to increasing the space available for group 1 business. Clearly, this proposal only affects category A stores and the analysis is therefore confined to the five stores in this category. References to the analysis below all relate to Appendix 2.

Schedule 1 shows the current projections for category A stores, generating a combined Product Group Profit of €6,526,860. Schedule 2 repeats these projections, using the additional information provided by the consultants to analyse payroll and overheads between fixed and variable components. This information forms the basis of contribution calculations shown in Schedule 3. Those calculations show that if current sales levels could be maintained, then closing the supermarkets and transferring the additional 30,000 sq. ft. per store to hardware would increase combined category A stores profits by 24% to €8,122,360.

However, it is expected that closing the supermarkets may result in some reduction in footfall, although there is some uncertainty regarding what the impact of this will be. Schedule 3 shows that if proposal 1 is implemented, then the combined category A stores profit could vary between €5.76 million and €7.83 million. These projections are based on management's estimates varying from a possible decrease of 1% in projected turnover (probability 15%) to a decrease of 3% (probability 60%) or, in a worst-case scenario, to a decrease of 8% (probability 25%). The projections indicate that there is a 25% chance that implementation of proposal 1 will result in a lower profit than is currently projected. If this occurs, then category A store profits will fall €764,558 below current projections, thereby reducing overall projected company net profit of €2,374,557 by 32%.

The range of possible profits for the combined category A stores, taking into account the uncertainty regarding footfall, is shown in Schedule 4. Expected value of profits represents an average of the likely outcomes, weighted according to probability of occurrence. Although this analysis seems to suggest that the overall outcome will be an increase in combined category A stores profits of €430,221 or 6.6%, it is important to point out that the expected value is a term used for a notional average and does not represent a likely out-turn. The analysis is totally dependent on estimates of footfall and on the subjective probabilities of those estimates materialising.

Because of the difficulties in predicting how the proposed action would affect footfall, the directors have requested a calculation of what could be termed a 'breakeven' footfall, i.e. what level of footfall would be required after implementing proposal 1 in order to maintain the existing level of combined category A store profits? The analysis shows that as long as any reduction in category A store sales is less than 5.4% of current projected turnover, the implementation of proposal 1 would result in an increase in profits. If turnover drops below this level, it will result in decreased profits (Schedule 5).

In making a decision in relation to proposal 1, management may wish to consider closely the estimates that form the basis of the analysis. In particular, estimates of drop in footfall, probabilities, and cost and revenue functions clearly have a major impact on the projected outcome. Management's attitude to risk is also an important consideration. Given such a low company net profit margin, it may be considered too risky to implement a proposal with a 25% likelihood of reducing profits further.

A further consideration relates to the allocation of space to product groups that would arise from implementation of proposal 1. Half of the entire space in a category A store would then be allocated to hardware. While hardware is clearly a profitable line of business and is successful in all store categories, management should consider whether this is an appropriate long-term strategic emphasis. Current estimates of the anticipated impact on footfall seem to be based on the likely drop in customer traffic due to the fact that the stores will no longer incorporate a supermarket. Any adverse effect on the company's image could result in a further reduction in footfall. For example, would category A stores be viewed as predominantly hardware and DIY stores by some customers and would this have a negative impact on demand for women's, men's and children's clothing? Would it compromise possible opportunities for profitable concession arrangements? Is it in keeping with the kind of image and reputation that management wishes to build for the company? It is also questionable as to whether sales performance in hardware can be maintained in terms of sales per sq. ft., in circumstances where such a large proportion of the store is allocated to one product group. Some additional fixed costs and capital investment may also be necessary in those circumstances.

Proposal 2

Proposal 2 requires that floor space in every store be allocated to product groups in a way that maximises the company's annual profits, subject to 25% of the space in every store being devoted to concessions and a maximum of 25,000 sq. ft. being allocated to any one product group. A further requirement is that a minimum of 10% of space in each store will be allocated to each product group, except that category B stores will not have supermarkets and category C stores will only have hardware and concessions. An evaluation of this proposal is presented below, based on analyses shown in Appendix 3.

Schedule 1 shows a calculation of the contribution margin per sq. ft., which is an appropriate basis for establishing the optimum space allocation. Contribution is calculated based on Gross Profit less variable payroll and overhead costs. Accepting the assumptions regarding sales per sq. ft. as valid, the driver of turnover (and contribution) in any product group is therefore the number of sq. ft. allocated to that product group. The key to optimising space allocation with a view to maximising profits is therefore to identify the product group that generates the highest contribution for every sq. ft. of floor space allocated to that product group.

Using this criterion, hardware is clearly the most attractive product group in all store categories. Supermarkets represent the next most profitable group for A stores, while women's wear is the next most profitable for B stores.

Based on these rankings and recognising the various conditions that have been set, the optimum space allocation is set out in Schedule 2. For example, for category A stores, concessions are allocated 25% of space or 22,500 sq. ft. and all other product groups are allocated 10% of space or 9,000 sq. ft. Remaining space is allocated 16,000 sq. ft. to hardware and 6,500 sq. ft. to supermarkets, thereby allocating a total of 25,000 sq. ft. to hardware and 15,500 sq. ft. to supermarkets. The revised allocations show a turnover figure for the company of €566 million, representing a 7% reduction on the original projected turnover. Despite this, the revised projections show an increase of 5.1% in total contribution and an increase of €3.7 million or 156% in overall net profit. These increases reflect the fact that the revised plan prioritises those product groups that generate the highest contribution (and therefore net profit) per sq. ft. of floor space.

Cost and revenue estimates need to be carefully examined before making a final decision on proposal 2. For example, will there be a need for increased fixed costs where there is a very large increase in floor allocation? Are the concession estimates realistic, especially for C stores where there are no existing concessions? Will it be possible to secure concessions for small stores? As for proposal 1, are GP estimates realistic, especially where a significant increase or decrease in floor allocation and sales are predicted and suppliers' terms and conditions may be affected?

Before proceeding with a decision on proposal 2, management should consider longer-term strategic issues, such as those set out below. A fundamental issue concerns the long-term vision for the company and the possible tension between a desire to carry a broad range of product groups on the one hand, and the need to generate an acceptable level of profits and cash-flow on the other, in order to finance growth and expansion and secure the company's long-term future.

Longer-term Strategic Issues

Management may wish to consider a number of issues regarding longer-term strategic planning. The view expressed by Deirdre Lennon is to some extent supported by the analysis. Appendix 3, Schedule 1 shows that, for every product group, the rate of contribution earned per sq. ft. of floor space is higher in the larger stores. The growth strategy pursued by the company has therefore had some success, but it may not be appropriate to pursue this for all stores, given that local conditions regarding population patterns, level of competition, etc. need to be considered for each individual store.

The policy regarding allocation of floor space needs to be carefully considered. The analysis has shown that profitability can be improved by re-allocating space to product groups that yield the highest return, in terms of sales less all variable costs, per sq. ft. of floor space. This may present some options for enhancing profitability and cash-flow, thereby providing an improved return to the shareholders and potential for growth and re-investment. However, this needs to be carefully managed in order to ensure consistency with the long-term vision for the company and its image and reputation among its customers. If it is desired to maintain the original Lennon policy of carrying the full range of products, then this clearly places constraints on allocation of floor space.

The policy of allocating the same space to product groups in stores of equal size also needs to be reconsidered. As the number of stores has expanded over the years, local conditions are likely to show wide variations, despite the fact that the areas chosen for store location have similar characteristics. It may be appropriate to allow for some flexibility in terms of space allocation in individual stores in response to local conditions. Again, this will need to be done in the context of overall guidelines, which will need to be developed in order to maintain consistent long-term strategic focus.

Decision making in the company is highly centralised. Consideration needs to be given to allowing an appropriate amount of decentralised decision making, particularly where quick decisions are needed in response to local competition. If implemented, this needs to be done in the context of appropriate guidelines and suitably tailored control and information systems in order to ensure appropriate levels of coordination and control are maintained. Linked to this is the possibility of introducing some form of incentive scheme for local management. This would need to be based on a suitable set of performance indicators, both financial and non-financial, that reflect the company's key priorities. Suitably tailored and accompanied by appropriate information and control systems, these measures could provide enhanced motivation and job satisfaction for managers, help improve company performance and develop management potential.

Profitability for product groups varies widely. Hardware is clearly very profitable in all stores. Supermarkets also appear to be highly profitable and have a positive effect on footfall in stores where they are located. Children's wear is the least profitable product, irrespective of store size. This needs to be investigated and perhaps the policy of stocking children's wear needs to be reconsidered. Concessions also appear less profitable than most other product groups, in all three types of store. This needs to be examined, particularly in the context of the requirement put forward in proposal 2, whereby 25% of floor space in the revised allocations will be allocated to concessions. For example, the allocation of 25% of C stores to concessions, as envisaged in proposal 2, would result in lost contribution of €1.64 million for the combined C stores. The company should conduct a detailed examination of its use of concessions, including the rate of commission charged compared to industry norms, the likely impact of concessions on the company's own sales and the possibility of fixed cost savings in the longer term if use of concessions is increased.

Conclusion

The scope of this report is restricted by the information made available and confined to the two specific proposals put forward. Given the range of activities and the complexities of the company's operating environment, a more comprehensive analysis would be necessary in order to provide a sound basis on which to determine future strategic direction.

Appendix 1 Projected Profit Statement Year ending 31 Dec 2XX7

Category A (5) 90,000 sq. ft.

	Group 1A Hardware	Group 2A Women's	Group 3A Men's	Group 4A Children's	Group 5A Concessions	Group 6A Supermarkets	TOTAL A
Sq. ft.	15,000	10,000	7,500	7,500	20,000	30,000	90,000
Sales/sq. ft.	500	450	425	400	600	1,000	
VAT rate	1.21	1.21	1.21	1.1	1.21	1.08	
Excl. VAT	413.22	371.90	351.24	363.64	495.87	925.93	
Sales per store	6,198,347	3,719,008	2,634,298	2,727,273	9,917,355	27,777,778	52,974,059
No. stores	5	5	5	5	5	5	5
Total Sales	30,991,736	18,595,041	13,171,488	13,636,364	49,586,777	138,888,889	264,870,294
GP Margin	0.4	0.35	0.34	0.3	0.2	0.25	
Gross Profit	12,396,694	6,508,264	4,478,306	4,090,909	9,917,355	34,722,222	72,113,751
Payroll %	0.13	0.15	0.14	0.15	0	0.15	
Payroll	4,028,926	2,789,256	1,844,008	2,045,455	0	20,833,333	31,540,978
Overhead %	0.16	0.16	0.16	0.16	0.16	0.1	
Overheads	4,958,678	2,975,207	2,107,438	2,181,818	7,933,884	13,888,889	34,045,914
Prod. Group Profit	3,409,091	743,802	526,860	−136,364	1,983,471	0	6,526,860
Depreciation (Note 1)							2,142,857
Category Profit (Note 2)							4,384,002
Head Office							4,361,084
Net Profit							22,918

Note 1. €15,000,000 ÷ 7
Note 2. €10,000,000 × 43.61%

Projected Profit Statement Y/E 31 December 2XX7

	Group 1B Hardware	Category B (12) 50,000 sq. ft.				TOTAL B
		Group 2B Women's	Group 3B Men's	Group 4B Children's	Group 5B Concessions	
Sq. ft.	10,000	7,500	5,000	5,000	22,500	50,000
Sales/sq. ft.	500	450	425	400	600	
VAT rate	1.21	1.21	1.21	1.1	1.21	
Excl. VAT	413.22	371.90	351.24	363.64	495.87	
Sales per store	4,132,231	2,789,256	1,756,198	1,818,182	11,157,025	21,652,893
No. stores	12	12	12	12	12	12
Total Sales	49,586,777	33,471,074	21,074,380	21,818,182	133,884,298	259,834,711
GP Margin	0.4	0.35	0.34	0.3	0.2	
Gross Profit	19,834,711	11,714,876	7,165,289	6,545,455	26,776,860	72,037,190
Payroll %	0.13	0.15	0.14	0.15	0	
Payroll	6,446,281	5,020,661	2,950,413	3,272,727	0	17,690,083
Overhead %	0.18	0.18	0.18	0.18	0.18	
Overheads	8,925,620	6,024,793	3,793,388	3,927,273	24,099,174	46,770,248
Prod. Group Profit	4,462,810	669,421	421,488	−654,545	2,677,686	7,576,860
Depreciation (Note 3)						3,771,429
Category Profit						3,805,431
Head Office (Note 4)						4,278,174
Net Profit						−472,743

Note 3. €26,400,000 ÷ 7
Note 4. €10,000,000 × 42.78%

Case 11: Solution to Lennon Department Store Ltd.

	Category C (8) 25,000 sq. ft.		
		Group 1C **Hardware**	**COMPANY**
Sq. ft.		25,000	
Sales/sq. ft.		500	
VAT rate		1.21	
Excl. VAT		413.22	
Sales per store		10,330,579	
No. stores		8	
Total Sales		82,644,628	607,349,633
GP Margin		0.4	
Gross Profit		33,057,851	177,208,792
Payroll %		0.13	
Payroll		10,743,802	59,974,862
Overhead %		0.2	
Overheads		16,528,926	97,345,087
Prod. Group Profit		5,785,124	19,888,843
Depreciation	(Note 5)	1,600,000	7,514,286
Category Profit		4,185,124	12,374,557
Head Office	(Note 6)	1,360,742	10,000,000
Net Profit		2,824,382	**2,374,557**

Note 5.   €11,200,000 ÷ 7
Note 6.   €10,000,000 × 13.61%

Appendix 2 – Proposal 1 – Schedule 1 – Current Projections

			Category A (5) 90,000 sq. ft.				
	Group 1A Hardware	Group 2A Women's	Group 3A Men's	Group 4A Children's	Group 5A Concessions	Group 6A Supermarkets	TOTAL A
Sq. ft.	15,000	10,000	7,500	7,500	20,000	30,000	90,000
Sales/sq. ft.	500	450	425	400	600	1000	
VAT rate	1.21	1.21	1.21	1.1	1.21	1.08	
Excl. VAT	413.22	371.90	351.24	363.64	495.87	925.93	
Sales per store	6,198,347	3,719,008	2,634,298	2,727,273	9,917,355	27,777,778	52,974,059
No. stores	5	5	5	5	5	5	5
Total Sales	30,991,736	18,595,041	13,171,488	13,636,364	49,586,777	138,888,889	264,870,294
GP Margin	0.4	0.35	0.34	0.3	0.2	0.25	
Gross Profit	12,396,694	6,508,264	4,478,306	4,090,909	9,917,355	34,722,222	72,113,751
Payroll %	0.13	0.15	0.14	0.15	0	0.15	
Payroll	4,028,926	2,789,256	1,844,008	2,045,455	0	20,833,333	31,540,978
Overhead %	0.16	0.16	0.16	0.16	0.16	0.1	
Overheads	4,958,678	2,975,207	2,107,438	2,181,818	7,933,884	13,888,889	34,045,914

Schedule 2 – Current Projections Showing Analysis of Payroll and Overheads

	Group 1A Hardware	Group 2A Women's	Group 3A Men's	Group 4A Children's	Group 5A Concessions	Group 6A Supermarkets	TOTAL A
Sq. ft.	15,000	10,000	7,500	7,500	20,000	30,000	90,000
Sales/sq. ft.	500	450	425	400	600	1000	
VAT rate	1.21	1.21	1.21	1.1	1.21	1.08	
Excl.VAT	413.22	371.90	351.24	363.64	495.87	925.93	
Sales per store	6,198,347	3,719,008	2,634,298	2,727,273	9,917,355	27,777,778	52,974,059
No. stores	5	5	5	5	5	5	5
Total Sales	30,991,736	18,595,041	13,171,488	13,636,364	49,586,777	138,888,889	264,870,294
GP Margin	0.4	0.35	0.34	0.3	0.2	0.25	
Gross Profit	12,396,694	6,508,264	4,478,306	4,090,909	9,917,355	34,722,222	72,113,751
Fixed Payroll %	0.3	0.3	0.3	0.3	0.3	0.3	
Fixed Payroll	1,208,678	836,777	553,202	613,636	0	6,250,000	9,462,293
Payroll %	0.13	0.15	0.14	0.15	0	0.15	
Variable Payroll	2,820,248	1,952,479	1,290,806	1,431,818	0	14,583,333	22,078,685
Total Payroll	4,028,926	2,789,256	1,844,008	2,045,455	0	20,833,333	31,540,978
V Payroll/Sales	0.09	0.11	0.10	0.11	0	0.11	
Fixed Overhead %	0.35	0.35	0.35	0.35	0.35	0.35	
Fixed Overhead	1,735,537	1,041,322	737,603	763,636	2,776,860	4,861,111	11,916,070
Overhead %	0.16	0.16	0.16	0.16	0.16	0.1	
Variable Overheads	3,223,140	1,933,884	1,369,835	1,418,182	5,157,025	9,027,778	22,129,844
Total Overheads	4,958,678	2,975,207	2,107,438	2,181,818	7,933,884	13,888,889	34,045,914
V Overhead/Sales	0.10	0.10	0.10	0.10	0.10	0.07	
Prod. Group Profit	3,409,091	743,802	526,860	–136,364	1,983,471	0	6,526,860

68 Solutions to Cases in Management Accounting and Business Finance

Schedule 3 – Assuming Current Sales Level

	Group 1A Hardware	Group 2A Women's	Group 3A Men's	Group 4A Children's	Group 5A Concessions	TOTAL A
		Category A (5) 90,000 sq. ft.				
Sq. ft.	45,000	10,000	7,500	7,500	20,000	90,000
Sales/sq. ft.	500	450	425	400	600	
VAT rate	1.21	1.21	1.21	1.1	1.21	
Excl. VAT	413.22	371.90	351.24	363.64	495.87	
Sales per store	18,595,041	3,719,008	2,634,298	2,727,273	9,917,355	37,592,975
No. stores	5	5	5	5	5	5
Total Sales	92,975,207	18,595,041	13,171,488	13,636,364	49,586,777	187,964,876
GP Margin	0.4	0.35	0.34	0.3	0.2	
Gross Profit	37,190,083	6,508,264	4,478,306	4,090,909	9,917,355	62,184,917
V Payroll/Sales	0.09	0.11	0.10	0.11	0	
V Payroll	8,460,744	1,952,479	1,290,806	1,431,818	0	
V Overhead/Sales	0.10	0.10	0.10	0.10	0.10	
V Overhead	9,669,421	1,933,884	1,369,835	1,418,182	5,157,025	
Total V Cost	18,130,165	3,886,364	2,660,640	2,850,000	5,157,025	32,684,194
Contribution	19,059,917	2,621,901	1,817,665	1,240,909	4,760,331	29,500,723
Fixed Payroll						9,462,293
Fixed Overhead						11,916,070
Total F Cost						21,378,363
Prod. Group Profit						8,122,360

Assuming 8% Decrease

Contribution	27,140,665
Total F Cost	21,378,363
Prod. Group Profit	5,762,302

Assuming 3% Decrease

Contribution	28,615,701
Total F Cost	21,378,363
Prod. Group Profit	7,237,338

Assuming 1% Decrease

Contribution	29,205,716
Total F Cost	21,378,363
Prod. Group Profit	7,827,353

Schedule 4 – Expected Value of Profits

Sales	Profit	Probability	EV
8% Decrease	5,762,302	0.25	1,440,576
3% Decrease	7,237,338	0.6	4,342,403
1% Decrease	7,827,353	0.15	1,174,103
Total EV of Profit			6,957,081

Schedule 5 – 'Breakeven' Decrease in Sales

Current Profit	6,526,860
Fixed Costs	21,378,363
Current Contribution	27,905,223
Proposal 1 at 100%	29,500,723
B/E Sales	0.945
B/E Decrease	0.054

Assuming 5.4% Decrease

Contribution	27,905,223
Total Fixed Cost	21,378,363
Prod. Group Profit	6,526,860

Appendix 3: Proposal 2 – Schedule 1 – Contribution per sq. ft. Based on Current Projections

Category A (5) 90,000 sq. ft.

	Group 1A Hardware	Group 2A Women's	Group 3A Men's	Group 4A Children's	Group 5A Concessions	Group 6A Supermarkets	TOTAL A
Sq. ft.	15,000	10,000	7,500	7,500	20,000	30,000	90,000
Sales/sq. ft.	500	450	425	400	600	1,000	
VAT rate	1.21	1.21	1.21	1.1	1.21	1.08	
Excl. VAT	413.22	371.90	351.24	363.64	495.87	925.93	
Sales per Store	6,198,347	3,719,008	2,634,298	2,727,273	9,917,355	27,777,778	52,974,059
No. stores	5	5	5	5	5	5	
Total sales	30,991,736	18,595,041	13,171,488	13,636,364	49,586,777	138,888,889	264,870,294
GP Margin	0.4	0.35	0.34	0.3	0.2	0.25	
Gross Profit	12,396,694	6,508,264	4,478,306	4,090,909	9,917,355	34,722,222	72,113,751
Payroll/Sales	0.13	0.15	0.14	0.15	0	0.15	
Total Payroll	4,028,926	2,789,256	1,844,008	2,045,455	0	20,833,333	31,540,978
Fixed Payroll %	0.3	0.3	0.3	0.3	0	0.3	
Fixed Payroll	1,208,678	836,777	553,202	613,636	0	6,250,000	9,462,293
Variable Payroll	2,820,248	1,952,479	1,290,806	1,431,818	0	14,583,333	22,078,685
Overhead/Sales	0.16	0.16	0.16	0.16	0.16	0.10	
Total Overheads	4,958,678	2,975,207	2,107,438	2,181,818	7,933,884	13,888,889	34,045,914
Fixed Overhead %	0.35	0.35	0.35	0.35	0.35	0.35	
Fixed Overhead	1,735,537	1,041,322	737,603	763,636	2,776,860	4,861,111	11,916,070
Variable Overhead	3,223,140	1,933,884	1,369,835	1,418,182	5,157,025	9,027,778	22,129,844
Prod. Group Profit	3,409,091	743,802	526,860	-136,364	1,983,471	0	6,526,860
Fixed Payroll	1,208,678	836,777	553,202	613,636	0	6,250,000	9,462,293
Fixed Overhead	1,735,537	1,041,322	737,603	763,636	2,776,860	4,861,111	11,916,070
Prod. Group CM	6,353,306	2,621,901	1,817,665	1,240,909	4,760,331	11,111,111	27,905,223
Sq. ft. per store	15,000	10,000	7,500	7,500	20,000	30,000	90,000
Stores	5	5	5	5	5	5	5
Total sq. ft.	75,000	50,000	37,500	37,500	100,000	150,000	450,000
CM per sq. ft.	84.71	52.44	48.47	33.09	47.60	74.07	62.01
Ranking	1	3	4	6	5	2	

70 Solutions to Cases in Management Accounting and Business Finance

Case 11: Solution to Lennon Department Store Ltd. 71

Category B (12) 50,000 sq. ft.

	Group 1B Hardware	Group 2B Women's	Group 3B Men's	Group 4B Children's	Group 5B Concessions	TOTAL B
Sq. ft.	10,000	7,500	5,000	5,000	22,500	50,000
Sales/sq. ft.	500	450	425	400	600	
VAT rate	1.21	1.21	1.21	1.1	1.21	
Excl.VAT	413.22	371.90	351.24	363.64	495.87	
Sales per Store	4,132,231	2,789,256	1,756,198	1,818,182	11,157,025	21,652,893
No. stores	12	12	12	12	12	12
Total sales	49,586,777	33,471,074	21,074,380	21,818,182	133,884,298	259,834,711
GP Margin	0.4	0.35	0.34	0.3	0.2	
Gross Profit	19,834,711	11,714,876	7,165,289	6,545,455	26,776,860	72,037,190
Payroll/Sales	0.13	0.15	0.14	0.15	0	
Total Payroll	6,446,281	5,020,661	2,950,413	3,272,727	0	17,690,083
Fixed Payroll %	0.3	0.3	0.3	0.3	0	
Fixed Payroll	1,933,884	1,506,198	885,124	981,818	0	5,307,025
Variable Payroll	4,512,397	3,514,463	2,065,289	2,290,909	0	12,383,058
Overhead/Sales	0.18	0.18	0.18	0.18	0.18	
Total Overheads	8,925,620	6,024,793	3,793,388	3,927,273	24,099,174	46,770,248
Fixed Overhead %	0.35	0.35	0.35	0.35	0.35	
Fixed Overhead	3,123,967	2,108,678	1,327,686	1,374,545	8,434,711	16,369,587
Variable Overhead	5,801,653	3,916,116	2,465,702	2,552,727	15,664,463	30,400,661
Prod. Group Profit	4,462,810	669,421	421,488	−654,545	2,677,686	7,576,860
Fixed Payroll	1,933,884	1,506,198	885,124	981,818	0	5,307,025
Fixed Overhead	3,123,967	2,108,678	1,327,686	1,374,545	8,434,711	16,369,587
Prod. Group CM	9,520,661	4,284,298	2,634,298	1,701,818	11,112,397	29,253,471
Sq. ft. per store	10,000	7,500	5,000	5,000	22,500	50,000
Stores	12	12	12	12	12	12
Total sq. ft.	120,000	90,000	60,000	60,000	270,000	600,000
CM per sq. ft.	79.34	47.60	43.90	28.36	41.16	48.76
Ranking	1	2	3	5	4	

	Category C (8) 25,000 sq. ft. Group 1C Hardware	COMPANY
Sq. ft.	25,000	
Sales/sq. ft.	500	
VAT rate	1.21	
Excl. VAT	413.22	
Sales per Store	10,330,579	
No. stores	8	
Total Sales	82,644,628	607,349,633
GP Margin	0.4	
Gross Profit	33,057,851	177,208,792
Payroll/Sales	0.13	
Total Payroll	10,743,802	59,974,862
Fixed Payroll %	0.3	
Fixed Payroll	3,223,140	17,992,459
Variable Payroll	7,520,661	41,982,404
Overhead/Sales	0.2	
Total Overheads	16,528,926	97,345,087
Fixed Overhead %	0.35	
Fixed Overhead	5,785,124	34,070,781
Variable Overhead	10,743,802	63,274,307
Prod. Group Profit	5,785,124	19,888,843
Fixed Payroll	3,223,140	17,992,459
Fixed Overhead	5,785,124	34,070,781
Prod. Group CM	14,793,388	71,952,082
Sq. ft. per store	25,000	
Stores	8	
Total sq. ft.	200,000	1,250,000
CM per sq. ft.	73.97	57.56

Case 11: Solution to Lennon Department Store Ltd. 73

Schedule 2 – Profit Projection Based on Optimum Space Allocation

	Group 1A Hardware	Group 2A Women's	Category A (5) 90,000 sq. ft.		Group 5A Concessions	Group 6A Supermarkets	TOTAL A
			Group 3A Men's	Group 4A Children's			
Sq. ft.	25,000	9,000	9,000	9,000	22,500	15,500	90,000
Sales/sq. ft.	500	450	425	400	600	1000	
VAT rate	1.21	1.21	1.21	1.1	1.21	1.08	
Excl.VAT	413.22	371.90	351.24	363.64	495.87	925.93	
Sales per Store	10,330,579	3,347,107	3,161,157	3,272,727	11,157,025	14,351,852	45,620,447
No. stores	5	5	5	5	5	5	5
Total Sales	51,652,893	16,735,537	15,805,785	16,363,636	55,785,124	71,759,259	228,102,234
GP Margin	0.4	0.35	0.34	0.3	0.2	0.25	
Gross Profit	20,661,157	5,857,438	5,373,967	4,909,091	11,157,025	17,939,815	65,898,493
V Payroll/Sales	0.091	0.105	0.098	0.105	0	0.105	
V Payroll	4,700,413	1,757,231	1,548,967	1,718,182	0	7,534,722	17,259,516
V Overhead/Sales	0.10	0.10	0.10	0.10	0.10	0.07	
V Overhead	5,371,901	1,740,496	1,643,802	1,701,818	5,801,653	4,664,352	20,924,021
Contribution	10,588,843	2,359,711	2,181,198	1,489,091	5,355,372	5,740,741	27,714,956
Fixed Payroll							9,462,293
Fixed Overhead							11,916,070
Depreciation							2,142,857
Store Fixed Cost							23,521,220
Store net profit							4,193,735

74 Solutions to Cases in Management Accounting and Business Finance

	Category B (12) 50,000 sq. ft.					
	Group 1B Hardware	Group 2B Women's	Group 3B Men's	Group 4B Children's	Group 5B Concessions	TOTAL B
Sq. ft.	22,500	5,000	5,000	5,000	12,500	50,000
Sales/sq. ft.	500	450	425	400	600	
VAT rate	1.21	1.21	1.21	1.1	1.21	
Excl. VAT	413.22	371.90	351.24	363.64	495.87	
Sales per Store	9,297,521	1,859,504	1,756,198	1,818,182	6,198,347	20,929,752
No. stores	12	12	12	12	12	12
Total Sales	111,570,248	22,314,050	21,074,380	21,818,182	74,380,165	251,157,025
GP Margin	0.4	0.35	0.34	0.3	0.2	
Gross Profit	44,628,099	7,809,917	7,165,289	6,545,455	14,876,033	81,024,793
V Payroll/Sales	0.091	0.105	0.098	0.105	0	
V Payroll	10,152,893	2,342,975	2,065,289	2,290,909	0	16,852,066
V Overhead/Sales	0.12	0.12	0.12	0.12	0.12	
V Overhead	13,053,719	2,610,744	2,465,702	2,552,727	8,702,479	29,385,372
Contribution	21,421,488	2,856,198	2,634,298	1,701,818	6,173,554	34,787,355
Fixed Payroll						5,307,025
Fixed Overhead						16,369,587
Depreciation						3,771,429
Store Fixed Cost						25,448,040
Store net profit						9,339,315

Category C (8) 25,000 sq. ft.

	Group 1C Hardware	Group 5C Concessions	TOTAL C	COMPANY
Sq. ft.	18,750	6,250	25,000	
Sales/sq. ft.	500	600		
VAT rate	1.21	1.21		
Excl. VAT	413.22	495.87		
Sales per Store	7,747,934	3,099,174	10,847,107	
No. stores	8	8	8	
Total Sales	61,983,471	24,793,388	86,776,860	566,036,119
GP Margin	0.4	0.2		
Gross Profit	24,793,388	4,958,678	29,752,066	176,675,352
V Payroll/Sales	0.091	0		
V Payroll	5,640,496	0	5,640,496	39,752,078
V Overhead/Sales	0.13	0.12		
V Overhead	8,057,851	2,900,826	10,958,678	61,268,071
Contribution	11,095,041	2,057,851	13,152,893	75,655,204
Fixed Payroll			3,223,140	
Fixed Overhead			5,785,124	
Depreciation			1,600,000	
Store Fixed Cost			10,608,264	59,577,525
Store net profit			2,544,628	16,077,679
Head Office				10,000,000
Company Net Profit				**6,077,679**

Case 12
Solution to Autoparts SA
Tony Brabazon and Tony O'Dea, University College Dublin

Question 1

		Varin €	Yatese €
ROCE	(900/2800 = 32.14%)	30,000	
	(1400/6600 = 21.2%)		Nil
Bonus Pool		90,000	200,000
Total		120,000	200,000

If the revaluation is put through, there are affects on both the asset base and the reported profit figures.

		Varin	Yatese
Current net assets		2,800,000	6,600,000
Asset adjustment	(Buildings)	500,000	2,000,000
	(Machinery)	(20,000)	(200,000)
	(Debtors)	(105,000)	(130,000)
		3,175,000	8,270,000
Current profit figures:		900,000	1,400,000
Add back depreciation		35,000	200,000
Deduct adjusted depreciation		118,000	580,000
		817,000	1,020,000
ROCE on adjusted values:		25.7%	12.3%

Both ROCEs fall, but Varin still exceeds the 22% cut-off.

	Varin €	Yatese €
ROCE	30,000	
		Nil
Bonus Pool	81,700	200,000
Total	111,700	200,000

Question 2

A wide variety of solutions could be acceptable. The quality and flow of the argument is the critical factor. Points raised could include:

General Comments

Compensation systems attempt to achieve several (sometimes conflicting) objectives.

1. Assist goal congruence.
2. Be easy to administer.
3. Be perceived as 'fair'.
4. Balance incentives between short term and long term (strategic considerations).
5. Balance risk
   To worker: e.g. if incentive agreement imposes much uncontrollable risk on the employee could => significant risk premium will be sought (employee is most likely risk adverse);
   To firm: e.g. risk of major payout.
6. Attract and retain high-quality staff.

It is notable that the existing bonus scheme does not have a long-term component and that the bonus to be paid is determined solely by financial factors. This could motivate the manager to take a short-run perspective in decision making. Strategic and non-financial factors relating to customer satisfaction and internal process efficiency are missing (e.g. customer retention rate, on-time delivery %, breakages, complaints).

It is also noticeable that the compensation system of each manager is solely linked to the performance of his/her division. There is no linkage to 'group' performance. This would not encourage intra-divisional co-operation, although it is not clear from the scenario details whether significant intra-group trading does take place.

The answer should consider the potential benefits and shortcomings of a bonus pool system: no lower or upper cut-off; deferred payment acts as golden handcuff but weakens link between performance and reward; avoids 'hard-threshold' problem.

General comments would be expected on ROCE measure, its advantages and potential disadvantages. The solution should also recalculate the ROCE for each division based on the revalued asset figures.

Solution should note that bonus payments are substantial relative to the basic management salaries.

Question 3

Allocating general group administration costs makes the CEO of each subsidiary aware that these costs exist and must be covered by the individual subsidiaries for the company as a whole to be profitable. However, the CEOs of each subsidiary may feel that they are being asked to bear a share of costs over which they have no control.

Care must be taken to ensure that overheads are not allocated on an arbitrary basis between the divisions as this would create cross-subsidisation.

The greater the portion of a manager's salary which is linked to the profit figure, the greater is the potential for conflict. Heavy reliance on pay for short-term performance will increase the potential for dysfunctional behaviour.

A distinction can be drawn between the evaluation of the manager and the evaluation of the division. A strong argument can be made for not including uncontrollable costs when evaluating managerial performance, but for including them when evaluating the performance of the division.

Question 4

A wide variety of answers could be valid.

The key requirements are that the solution must demonstrate how the proposed system will overcome the shortcomings of the current scheme.

In general, better designed compensation systems attempt to achieve these objectives by taking a segmented approach and consist of three major components: a base salary, short-term incentives and long-term incentives. It is expected that the proposed schemes will contain all three components. Good answers may also discuss intrinsic versus extrinsic rewards. The proposed scheme should also take into account the strategic position of each subsidiary. Will the new scheme encourage entrepreneurial behaviour on the part of management of Yatese?

Case 13
Solution to IXL Limited
Joan Ballantine, University of Ulster

REPORT ON THE FINANCIAL ACCEPTABILITY OF THE SAP ERP AUTOMOTIVE SUPPLIER PACKAGE

Prepared by the Financial Controller
IXL Limited

Executive Summary

- The attached financial analysis indicates that the ERP/JIT project is financially viable in terms of all three criteria used, namely return on investment (ROI), net present value (NPV) and payback.
- The ROI of the project initially yields 23% in year one and this rises to an astonishing 380% in year five. For all years, the ROI achieved exceeds the company's target return of 22%.
- The ERP/JIT project yields a positive NPV of €6,640,109 when discounted at the company's cost of capital of 8%, which indicates that the project should be accepted.
- The undiscounted payback of the project is two years and two months, which is a relatively short period of time within which the initial investment is paid back. When the time value of money is taken into account, the payback period increases to two years and six months.
- The attached financial analysis does not take account of a number of important factors, namely taxation, inflation and risk. Before a final decision is made it is important that these factors are accounted for in the financial analysis.

- The ERP/JIT project is expected to generate additional sales volume. However, this is likely to exacerbate the problems currently being experience by the Dublin site in terms of managing accounts receivable. This report has highlighted a number of issues which should be addressed by the Dublin site to help alleviate this problem.

MAIN REPORT

Terms of Reference

Further to your request, please find attached my report on the financial acceptability of the ERP/JIT system within the Dublin site. The report contains a financial analysis of the project using a number of criteria: return on investment, net present value and payback. As requested, I have also considered a number of additional issues, including the incorporation of risk, inflation and taxation, and have outlined how the financial analysis presented might be adjusted to take these into account. Before making a final decision regarding the ERP/JIT project, these issues should be incorporated fully into the financial analysis. Additionally, a number of qualitative issues should also be considered.

This report addresses two further issues. First, it outlines the problems associated with using ROI and considers how the alternative methods of appraisal applied here, namely net present value and payback, help alleviate these problems. Secondly, the report outlines what actions need to be taken by the Dublin site to ensure effective management of accounts receivable, which has been identified as a potential problem area given the increased sales volumes that are expected to flow through following the implementation of the ERP/JIT system.

Recommendations to Management

1. Financial Analysis of the ERP/JIT Project

The financial analysis of the ERP/JIT project has been carried out using a number of criteria: return on investment, net present value and payback (additionally, internal rate of return could be calculated). In carrying out the analysis a number of assumptions have been made:

- the costs incurred to date of €50,000 for employing specialists to determine cost/revenue estimates are sunk and therefore irrelevant to the investment decision;
- the additional fixed operating overheads of €100,000 charged to the Dublin site are irrelevant as they will be incurred irrespective of whether the project is accepted or not;
- taxation and inflation have been ignored.

(a) ROI

The calculation of ROI is presented in Appendix 1. The ROI has been calculated for all five years of the project. ROI has been calculated using average annual profits (net cash-flows after adjusting for depreciation) divided by average investment (opening plus closing investment divided by two). The ROI for the first year of the project is 23%, which exceeds the current requirement of 22%. For all remaining years of the project the ROI obtained more than exceeds the company's target. On the basis of ROI then, the company should accept the project.

(b) Net Present Value

The NPV of the project has also been calculated, details of which can be found in Appendix 3. (Appendix 2 provides details of the calculation of contribution per unit that is used in Appendix 3.) The NPV alleviates some of the potential problems of ROI (see later) by taking into account the time value of money (i.e. money received in the future is worth less than that received today). In order to calculate NPV we use the company's cost of capital of 8%. When the cash-flows are discounted using 8%, the project yields a positive NPV of €6,640,109. On the basis of this financial analysis, the NPV indicates that the ERP/JIT project should be accepted.

(c) Payback

The payback, both discounted and otherwise, of the ERP/JIT project has also been calculated. Payback is one of the most frequently used methods of appraisal in practice and is defined as the length of time that is required for a stream of cash-flows from an investment to equal the original cash outlay required for the investment. Payback alleviates some of the problems of ROI by using cash-flows and, in the case of discounted payback, taking account of the time value of money. The payback of the current project is two years and two months, which is a relatively short period of time. This suggests that our initial investment is paid back fairly quickly. However, if we take into account the time value of money, the payback increases to two years and six months. This still represents a fairly short period within which the initial investment is recouped by the ERP/JIT project.

(d) Qualitative Issues

On the basis of the financial appraisal of the ERP/JIT project, IXL Limited would be advised to proceed with the project as it will enhance the company's long-term value. However, before a final decision is made, there are a number of qualitative issues which need to be considered. First, is the project in line with the long-term strategy of the company? Secondly, has IXL Limited got the expertise internally to implement the ERP/JIT project or will external help be required? If external support is required, how will this impact on the costs of the project? Thirdly, how reliable are the estimates of costs and benefits which are used to determine the ROI, NPV and payback calculations?

2. Discussion of ROI and its Appropriateness as an Appraisal Technique

Historically, capital investment decisions have been made by IXL Limited on the basis of Return on Investment (ROI), which is currently set at a level of 22%. Whilst ROI is a widely used technique of investment appraisal, it suffers a number of limitations that limit its usefulness. Each of these will be discussed below.

(i) ROI can lead managers to make sub-optimal investment and divestment decisions, that is, decisions which are not in the best interests of the company.

(ii) ROI is based on the measurement of profits as opposed to techniques such as NPV and IRR, which are based on cash-flows. Profit measures invariably suffer from the inclusion of non-cash items, such as depreciation and amortisation, and are affected by accounting policy choice.

(iii) ROI is a relative accounting ratio and therefore fails to reflect the absolute size of an investment.

(iv) ROI fails to take into account the time value of money.

(v) ROI can encourage managers to adopt a short-term perspective to decision making.

(vi) No standard measure of investment and profit exist for calculating ROI. As a result, huge variations can arise when calculating ROI based on, for example, opening values of investment as opposed to average or closing values, the use of historical asset costs as opposed to revalued amounts or replacement costs.

The use of NPV as an alternative method of appraisal alleviates many of the problems of ROI. It does this in a number of ways.

(i) It adopts a long-term perspective by selecting projects that increase shareholder value.

(ii) NPV uses cash-flows not profits.

(iii) NPV takes account of the time value of money.

(iv) NPV is an absolute measure.

3. Incorporation of Risk

Risk is an important element that should be considered when appraising capital projects. For example, it is entirely feasible that acceptance of a profitable but highly risky investment proposal may increase the perceived riskiness of the total business and result in a reduction in the long-term value of the firm.

Risk is defined as the set of unique consequences for a given decision which can be assigned probabilities. In the context of investment decisions, risk refers to the variability in the capital project's expected cash-flows. There are two ways of dealing with risk in relation to capital projects. The first method aims to incorporate the investor's perception of the risk of the project within the NPV formula. It does this by adjusting the discount rate by a risk premium. The higher the perceived riskiness of a project, the greater the risk premium which should be added to the discount rate used to discount cash-flows. The second method of dealing with risk aims to describe the riskiness of a given project. This can be done, for example, by carrying out sensitivity analysis, which aims to identify the factors or variables that are potentially risk-sensitive. Sensitivity analysis aims to provide the decision maker with answers to a whole range of 'what if' questions. For example, what would the NPV be if sales volumes were 10% lower than expected or variable costs increased by 5% per annum?

The ERP/JIT project should be assessed for risk. If the project is considered to have a higher than average level of risk, then a risk premium should be added to the discount rate before the net cash-flows are discounted. This would have the effect of increasing the discount rate, which in turn would reduce the NPV. Sensitivity analysis should also be performed by adjusting some of the key variables. These are likely to include sales volumes, the cost savings from holding stock and the initial investment in the ERP system. Sensitivity analysis can be carried out by adjusting the key variables one at a time or, alternatively, by adjusting a number of variables simultaneously.

4. Treatment of Taxation and Inflation

The exclusion of taxation from a NPV calculation is likely to either overstate the value of a capital project or understate it where generous capital allowances are relevant. For these reasons, taxation is generally taken into account in arriving at the NPV of a capital project.

The tax implications of the ERP/JIT project would be accounted for as follows.

(i) The taxation payable is first calculated by adjusting the accounting profit for non-allowable expenses, such as depreciation.
(ii) If capital allowances exist (which is likely to be the case for the production machinery), these are also deducted from accounting profits.
(iii) The corporation tax payable is arrived at by multiplying the taxable profits arrived at after adjusting for (i) and (ii) above by the current corporation tax rate.
(iv) The tax payable is then included as a cash outflows in the year to which it relates.

Inflation can be ignored where all cash inflows and outflows are affected by the same inflation rate. If this is the case for the ERP/JIT project, then real cash-flows (i.e.

unadjusted for inflation) can be discounted by the real discount rate. In practice, however, different elements of cash-flow will be affected by different inflation rates. For example, cash outflows related to material costs might rise by 2% during a particular period, whereas cash inflows related to sales revenue might rise by 3% during the same period. In this situation, inflation cannot be ignored. Rather, individual cash-flows need to be adjusted by their respective inflation rates to produce nominal cash-flows, which should then be discounted by a nominal (i.e. money) discount rate. A further complication arises when both taxation and inflation are present and need to be accounted for in the investment appraisal. Since capital allowances are not affected by inflation (i.e. they are based on nominal values), cash-flows are required to be adjusted for inflation (i.e. nominal cash-flows) and discounted using a nominal (i.e. money) rate.

The effect of inflation on the ERP/JIT project should be assessed before a final decision is taken. It should also be noted that we are not told if the current cost of capital of 8% represents a real or a nominal discount. This would also need to be clarified.

5. Management of Accounts Receivable

As you are aware the Dublin site has in the past found it difficult to effectively manage its accounts receivable. The implementation of the ERP system provides the Dublin site with a timely point at which to assess its management of accounts receivable. There are a number of issues which the management of the Dublin site should pay particular attention to at this point in time. These include the following.

(i) Custom and practice within the industry – the Dublin site should have regard to what is considered to be normal practice within the industrial sector in which it operates. For example, it should attempt to understand what is normal practice with respect to credit periods, the operation of cash settlement discounts and the likely or acceptable level of bad debts. The Dublin site needs to compare normal practice with its own current practice to ascertain if it is giving sufficient credit terms to attract new customers. Alternatively, it may be offering very generous cash settlement discounts that are detrimental to the company as a whole.

(ii) Credit-rating procedures – having determined basic credit terms, the Dublin site needs to set up procedures aimed at identifying those customers to whom it is willing to offer credit. This involves an assessment of the likelihood of the potential customer defaulting on the debt. A wide range of sources of information can be used to assess the credit-worthiness of potential customers, including bank and trade references and the use of credit agencies.

(iii) An effective credit management system should also be set up to ensure that, as far as practicable, all credit customers adhere to the terms of credit which were offered to them. In the case of the Dublin site, this would involve: ensuring that new customers have been given adequate credit checks; ensuring that invoices are generated and dispatched to the customer as soon as possible after the goods have been delivered; ensuring that customers are monitored in terms of their adherence to credit terms; setting up effective debt-collection procedures to ensure, for example, that statements are set out at the end of accounting periods, reminder letters are sent to customers who fail to make payment on time and that appropriate action is taken to deal with customers who are in default of their debt.

Appendix 1: Calculation of ROI

Year	1	2	3	4	5
Net Cash-flows	3,220,000	3,572,500	3,550,625	3,695,406	3,762,877
Less Depreciation:					
Production Machinery	1,200,000	1,200,000	1,200,000	1,200,000	1,200,000
Software	500,000	500,000	500,000	0	0
Average Annual Profits	1,520,000	1,872,500	1,850,625	2,495,406	2,562,877
Average Investment					
Investment at beginning of year	7,500,000	5,800,000	4,100,000	2,400,000	1,200,000
Depreciation	1,700,000	1,700,000	1,700,000	1,200,000	1,200,000
Investment at end of year	5,800,000	4,100,000	2,400,000	1,200,000	150,000
Average Investment	6,650,000	4,950,000	3,250,000	1,800,000	675,000
ROI	23%	38%	57%	139%	380%

Appendix 2: Calculation of Contribution per Component

	€	€
Selling Price		380
Direct Labour	107	
Direct Materials	85	
Variables Manufacturing Overheads	50	
Variables selling and distribution costs	30	272
Contribution per unit		108

Appendix 3: Calculation of Net Present Value

Relevant Cash-flows

Year	0	1	2	3	4	5
Outflows						
Investment in ERP System	1,500,000					
Investment in Production Machinery	6,000,000					
Volume of Components		40,000	45,000	50,000	52,000	48,000
Fixed Manufacturing Costs		900,000	900,000	1,150,000	1,150,000	900,000
Fixed Selling & Distribution Costs		250,000	250,000	375,000	460,000	375,000
Opportunity Cost of Rental		200,000	400,000	600,000	600,000	600,000
Total Cash Outflows	**7,500,000**	**1,350,000**	**1,550,000**	**2,125,000**	**2,210,000**	**1,875,000**
Inflows						
Cost savings from stock-holding		250,000	262,500	275,625	289,406	303,877
Contribution		4,320,000	4,860,000	5,400,000	5,616,000	5,184,000
Resale of production machinery						150,000
Total Cash Inflows		4,570,000	5,122,500	5,675,625	5,905,406	5,637,877
Net Cash Flows	(7,500,000)	3,220,000	3,572,500	3,550,625	3,695,405	3,762,877
8% NPV Factors	1	0.9259	0.8573	0.7938	0.7350	0.6806
NPV	(7,500,000)	2,981,481	3,062,843	2,818,601	2,716,234	2,560,951
Overall NPV	**6,640,109**					

Payback 2 year 2 months
Discounted Payback 2 years 6 months

Section B

Solutions to Cases in Business Finance

Case 18
Solution to The Corner Café
Jill Lyttle, Queen's University Belfast

1. (a) General Financing Options

Long-term Sources of Finance:

- share capital – private and public companies;
- debenture loans – public companies;
- leasing or hire-purchase of equipment;
- bank loan (secured).

Medium-Term Sources of Finance:

- leasing or hire-purchase of equipment;
- bank loan (secured).

Short-Term Sources of Finance:

- invoice discounting or factoring (credit sales);
- bank overdraft (unsecured).

Other:

- business angels – funding for start-up/early stage/developing/innovative businesses;
- government sources – from time to time government schemes are available to help small businesses, including short courses for business start-ups and grants for creating employment.

Sam's Situation:

- Sam needs start-up funding rather than a short-term overdraft;
- as a sole trader his options are restricted from the start;
- support from government should be investigated; although it is unlikely to provide finance, he may be able to access business advice;
- given the size of investment required, medium-term funding (bank loan) would be ideal in theory, but as he has no catering or business experience and no guarantee of income as it is a cash business, this is unlikely to appeal to the bank;
- a short-term loan might be a possibility, but there are no significant business assets so a personal guarantee will be required as security;
- an unsecured overdraft is unlikely despite cash-flow projections.

1. (b) Sam's Financing Options

- 100% bank overdraft / loan – in theory this is an option, depending on the terms offered by the bank, but in practice is unlikely to be available.
- 100% redundancy money – this would require at least one-third of his capital, which would not be replaced for some time; if he is planning to use some of this for living expenses as well, the capital sum could be eroded quite quickly. If the business needs more money in the future, the bank may not extend further credit and he may have to use some of his redundancy money at that time.
- Part bank overdraft/loan and part redundancy money – this could represent the best of both worlds, allowing Sam to invest as much of his money as he can to offset the interest charged on the overdraft/loan. He will not be over-exposed to the bank and there should be enough capital to repay the overdraft/loan if business does not turn out as planned.

Recommendation

Probably the best option is to use as much bank overdraft / loan as possible and top it up with some of the redundancy money; even if he invested €10k, Sam would lose just €150 in interest per year [(5% – 3.5%) × €10k]. Alternatively, leasing at least some of the new equipment may also be a possibility.

2. (a) Projected P&L accounts for three years and monthly cash-flow projections for 12 months

	Forecast Sam – Year 1		Forecast Sam – Year 2		Forecast Sam – Year 3	
	€	€	€	€	€	€
Sales	106,250		111,563		117,141	
Cost of Sales	31,875		31,238		29,285	
Gross Profit		74,375		80,325		87,855

(Continued)

Wages *	28,340		29,474		30,653
Rent	15,000		15,750		16,538
Rates and Insurance	2,344		2,438		2,535
Electricity and Gas	3,744		3,894		4,050
Sundry	2,808		2,920		3,037
Bank fees	832		865		900
Bank interest	500		520		541
Legal fees	1,000		–		–
Accountancy fees	1,040		1,082		1,125
Depreciation	2,500		1,875		1,406
		58,108		58,817	60,784
Net Profit		16,267		21,508	27,072
Drawings	1,000 pmth	12,000	1,250 pmth	15,000 1,500 pmth	18,000

* Naoimh: 5 hours × 5 days × €11 × 52 weeks
* Junior Staff: [(4 hours × 5 days × €9) + (10 hours × €9)] + 52 weeks

Revised Financing Recommendation:

Initial investment is €10k for equipment, but an additional €3.5k – probably better €5k – is needed to keep the cash-flow positive in the first few months. Sam could ask if the bank would give him a €15k loan instead or (probably better) he could use some of his redundancy money. The rest of the answer assumes €10k overdraft and €5k redundancy money; different assumptions are also valid.

2. (b) Issues to Consider

- he is moving from employment to self-employment and also becoming an employer;
- he carries full responsibility for the business;
- he will have to register with the relevant authorities;
- he will have to comply with relevant employment legislation;
- he will have to comply with general health and safety legislation as well as relevant food standard regulations;
- at this income level, he will have to register for VAT, which will impact on prices and cash-flow;
- he will have to pay employment taxes on his employees' wages;
- if he borrows money from the bank, he will probably have to give a personal guarantee;
- it may not work out: he will lose some or all of his redundancy money and will still have to look for another job;
- he should consider this move thoroughly; he is committing himself very quickly in an unfamiliar work environment.

Monthly cash-flow for first 12 months

	Apr Mth 1 €	May Mth 2 €	Jun Mth 3 €	Jul Mth 4 €	Aug Mth 5 €	Sep Mth 6 €	Oct Mth 7 €	Nov Mth 8 €	Dec Mth 9 €	Jan Mth 10 €	Feb Mth 11 €	Mar Mth 12 €
Cash Inflows												
Initial capital	10,000											
Sales	8,854	8,854	8,854	8,854	8,854	8,854	8,854	8,854	8,854	8,854	8,854	8,854
Total cash inflow	18,854	8,854	8,854	8,854	8,854	8,854	8,854	8,854	8,854	8,854	8,854	8,854
Cash outflows												
Bernie – F&F	4,000											
Refurbishment	6,000											
Purchases / Cost of sales	2,656	2,656	2,656	2,656	2,656	2,656	2,656	2,656	2,656	2,656	2,656	2,656
Wages	2,362	2,362	2,362	2,362	2,362	2,362	2,362	2,362	2,362	2,362	2,362	2,362
Rent	3,750			3,750			3,750			3,750		
Rates and insurance	2,344											
Electricity and Gas (1)			736			736			1,136			1,136
Sundry	234	234	234	234	234	234	234	234	234	234	234	234
Bank fees			208			208			208			208
Bank interest			125			125			125			125
Legal fees		1,000										
Accountancy			260			260			260			260
Drawings	1,000	1,000	1,000	1,000	1,000	1,000	1,000	1,000	1,000	1,000	1,000	1,000
Total cash outflow	22,346	7,252	7,581	10,002	6,252	7,581	10,002	6,252	7,981	10,002	6,252	7,981
Net cash inflow / (outflow) (2)	(3,492)	1,602	1,273	(1,148)	2,602	1,273	(1,148)	2,602	873	(1,148)	2,602	873
Balance b/fwd	0	(3,492)	(1,890)	(617)	(1,765)	837	2,110	962	3,564	4,437	3,289	5,891
Balance c/fwd	(3,492)	(1,890)	(617)	(1,765)	837	2,110	962	3,564	4,437	3,289	5,891	6,764

Note (1) Electricity and gas are likely to vary according to the quarter.
Note (2) More cash is needed at the start for working capital, say €5,000.

3. (a) Price-Setting Strategies

Price Takers:

- businesses that have little or no influence over the prices of their products;
- prices set by general market supply and demand – commodity markets or industries with dominant market leaders;
- must look at competitors and price accordingly;
- this approach implies some form of *target costing* (sales price less target profit margin equals target cost).

Price Makers or Price Setters:

- businesses that have customised or specialised products or otherwise have a unique selling point;
- market leaders can set own price based on own costs or profit targets (perhaps tempered by competitor prices);
- businesses may adopt a *cost-plus* strategy (total cost plus required mark-up equals selling price).

Recommendation

Sam is in a small, localised market and is unlikely to be able to influence prices. Unless he is offering a significantly different menu or significantly higher quality than surrounding competition, he is likely to have to pitch his prices at a similar level; to increase profit he will therefore have to drive costs down. His main costs are purchases of food supplies and staff wages.

3. (b)

	P&L 3 months			P&L 6 months		
	Budget	**Actual**	**Variance**	**Budget**	**Actual**	**Variance**
	€	€	€	€	€	€
Sales	26,563	21,400	5,163A	53,125	39,600	13,525A
Cost of Sales	7,969	7,490	479F	15,938	14,915	1,023F
Gross Profit	18,594	13,910	4,684A	37,187	24,685	12,502A
Wages	7,086	7,086		14,170	14,757	587A
Rent	3,750	3,750		7,500	7,500	
Rates and Insurance	586	586		1,172	1,172	
Electricity and Gas	936	700	236F	1,872	1,400	472F
Sundry	702	690	12F	1,404	1,380	24F
Bank fees	208	208		416	466	50A

(Continued)

Bank interest	125	188	63A	250	388	138A
Legal fees	250	250		500	500	
Accountancy fees	260	260		520	520	
Depreciation	625	625		1250	1,250	
	14,528	14,343	185F	29,054	29,333	279A
Net Profit / (Loss)	4066	(433)	4,499A	8,133	(4,648)	12,781A

3. (b)

	Cash Flow 3 mths			Cash Flow 6 mths		
	Budget	Actual	Variance	Budget	Actual	Variance
Cash Inflows						
Initial capital	10,000	15,000	5,000F	10,000	18,000	8,000F
Sales	26,562	21,400	5,162A	53,124	39,600	13,524A
Total cash inflow	36,562	36,400		63,124	57,600	
Cash outflows						
Bernie – F&F	4,000	4,000		4,000	4,000	
Refurbishment	6,000	6,000		6,000	6,000	
Purchases / Cost of sales	7,968	7,490	478F	15,936	14,915	1,021F
Wages	7,086	7,086		14,152	14,757	522A
Rent	3,750	3,750		7,500	7,500	
Rates and insurance	2,344	2,344		2,344	2,344	
Electricity and Gas	736	700	36F	1,472	1,400	72F
Sundry	702	690	12F	1,404	1,380	24F
Bank fees	208	208		416	466	50A
Bank interest	125	188	63A	250	388	138A
Legal fees	1,000	1,000		1,000	1,000	
Accountancy	260	260		520	520	
Drawings	3,000	2,000	1,000F	6,000	2,000	4,000
Total cash outflow	37,179	35,716		61,014	56,670	
Net cash inflow / (outflow)	(617)	684	1301F	2110	930	1180A
Balance b/fwd	0	0		0	0	
Balance c/fwd	(617)	684		2,110	930	

3. (c) Major Variances / Possible Reasons for Cash-flow Difficulty/ How to Improve Income / Management of Working Capital

This is urgent as Sam has already used quite a lot of his redundancy money: assuming €5k initially, €3k in July and probably a further €3k in September, offset by just €2k drawings; presumably he has also used more of this capital for living expenses – and maybe the holiday, too.

Income

- Main variance/reason for cash-flow difficulty is the level of sales income, which was apparent even in June.
- Initial over-optimism about increased income, based on additional opening hours and on the assumption that income arises evenly throughout the day.
- The average weekly sales level is similar to Bernie's usual sales level, not higher.
- The café was shut for two weeks in August, which has had a big impact (this was not included in the initial projections).
- Pricing should be reviewed – can he cost his menu more keenly or differentiate at least some of his menu items?
- The menu itself should be reviewed and updated and Sam should consider what other products/services he could offer, for example a carryout service or sandwich deliveries to local businesses.
- Must increase footfall and/or spend per customer.

Purchases/Cost of Sales

- Disproportionate decrease in CoS: Sam expected this to be 30% of sales income, but it is nearly 38%.
- No details are given about waste, particularly of perishable items; these may not have not been monitored closely enough and waste has increased.
- No details are given about stock levels of non-perishable items; these may not have not been monitored closely enough and stock has built up.
- Costs of ingredients for items made on the premises may have increased – could these be substituted by lower cost items?
- Bought-in food for resale may have increased in price – could these items be bought for less?
- Are there other suppliers or could Sam negotiate a discount with his current suppliers?

Wages

- Wages should have been 27% of sales, whereas they are over 37%; even if budgeted sales had been achieved, wages would have represented 28%.
- Naoimh is now working slightly longer hours than budgeted – she used to work 4.5 hours but is now working five hours; perhaps she would be prepared to drop to

four hours; however, she appears to be a key employee so this should be discussed tactfully.
- Sam has not spent as much time in the café each day as he intended, therefore he is paying the junior staff for more hours – he could cut back on their hours and work more hours himself.
- Opening hours could be cut back to Bernie's level without significant loss of income, but it would save on staff costs.

Other Expenses

- Electricity and gas appears to be much lower than expected – but these are the warmer, lighter months; in autumn and winter these costs will be higher.
- Bank interest rates appear to have increased.
- Most of the other costs are fixed, although sundry expenditure should be investigated further.

General

- There should be no more drawings until the cash situation has improved dramatically.
- Sales, purchases, waste and stock levels should be monitored weekly and monthly, not quarterly.
- Sam should discuss the possibility of a small overdraft to cover the quarterly jumps in his costs; however the bank may not be prepared to do this as he has not been able to build up the business – or the cash levels – sufficiently to engender confidence.
- Are there franchised outlets nearby? Managing a well-known franchised brand might be a more attractive prospect.
- It is worth questioning how serious Sam is about this project – is he really committed to making it work in the medium to long term?

Case 19
Solution to Calvin plc
Peter Green, University of Ulster

REPORT ON UTILISATION OF SURPLUS FUNDS

Prepared by: A. Student
Management Consultant

For: Calvin plc

1. Terms of Reference

Further to our discussions of xx/xx/xx, I present the report requested. With respect to the two main suggestions forwarded by the board of directors with regard to utilising surplus funds, that is redeeming the €20 million secured loan or increasing the dividend payment to shareholders by €20 million, given the other data you have supplied, I must advise that neither of these suggestions would appear to be desirable when compared with the option to expand operations into the Republic of Ireland. Although I must emphasise that the calculations included in the report are based upon figures which have been supplied by the market research commissioned by your company and which I have not verified.

2. Executive Summary/Recommendations

(a) The current cash surplus has derived from volume expansion due to an increased demand for housing. The building industry suffers from volatile fluctuations in housing demand. Hence, in future years cash shortages may be experienced, rather than the current cash surplus.

(b) The company's gearing level in 2XX3/4 is well below the industry average (see Appendix 1). The proposed redemption of the secured loan stock may result in a reduction in interest payments over the next 10 years, but if the reasons for redemption are not properly explained to the market, it may be interpreted by shareholders as a sign that the management of the company believe that future prospects are poor and this may result in a drop in share price (see section 3.3 of the report). Furthermore, if additional financing is needed within the next 10 years, which is possible given the volatile nature of the market in which the company operates, it may cost more to borrow in the future than the current 7% payable on the loan stock.

(c) The company's dividend payout ratio for the year 2XX3/4 was 53%, which, although above the industry average (41%), is in-line with the overall UK average payout of 56%. The proposed increase for 2XX4/5 of €20 million would represent an increase to 87% (see Appendix 1). Such a significant increase may signal to shareholders, if not adequately explained, that management is unable to identify beneficial investment opportunities and may not be welcomed by some shareholders depending upon their current tax status (see section 4.2 of the report).

(d) Despite the high transportation costs, based upon the data supplied, exporting to the Republic of Ireland is beneficial. However, an even more attractive option would appear to be the acquisition of the existing company in Dublin and the relocation of excess capacity from Belfast to Dublin, thus avoiding additional transportation costs to service the entire Republic of Ireland market. This will require the investment of more than the €20 million surplus funds, but will increase the value of the company by between €19 and €23 million. Although it must be noted that this calculation is heavily dependent upon the assumption that the operating performance in the Republic of Ireland continues at the estimated level indefinitely.

3. Issues Relating to the Redemption of the Secured Loan Stock

3.1 Return to Shareholders

The redemption of the loan stock will result in a reduction in interest payments of €1.4 million per year for the next 10 years. As interest payments are a tax-deductible expense, the net saving would be €938,000 (1,400,000 × €0.67) per year, assuming that the company has sufficient taxable profits to fully utilise tax savings. This should result in an increase in the value of the shareholders' wealth of €4,707,822 (5.019 × € 938,000), assuming that the required return from shareholders remains at 15% per annum and that the net saving can be invested at this rate.

3.2 Risk to Shareholders

Theoretically, eliminating debt will result in a reduction of financial risk to shareholders. That is, there will be a reduction in the volatility of earnings attributable to shareholders and a decrease in the probability of liquidation and/or costs of financial distress being incurred. However, currently, due to the conservative financial policy pursued by the company, the gearing level of the company is very low compared with the industry average. This implies that bankruptcy risk is not significant. The gearing of the company is at present 5%, compared with the industry average of 45%, whilst interest cover is 17.9 compared with the industry average of 6.5 (see Appendix 1).

3.3 Signalling Considerations

As noted above, loan interest is a tax-deductible expense and the return to shareholders is increased by this tax reduction. This is technically referred to as a 'tax shield'. This benefit will be lost if the loan is redeemed, and if not properly explained to investors the repayment of the loan may be interpreted as a signal that there are difficult times ahead, resulting in a fall in share price.

3.4 Future Interest Rate

An important issue with regard to the redemption of a current fixed interest rate loan is the level of interest rates expected in the future. For example, if the loan is redeemed now at par but to borrow in the future would cost more than 7%, then redemption would probably not be worthwhile.

4. Issues Relating to the Proposed Increase in Dividends

4.1 Overview

The payment of a dividend represents a distribution of the wealth generated by a company. It is generally accepted that wealth is created by investing in assets that are worth more than they cost and financing those investments at the lowest possible cost (that is, identifying investment opportunities with a positive net present value). As such, it is argued that dividend policy is irrelevant. However, most finance directors would appear to be of the opinion that dividend policy should be managed so that dividend payments follow a steady rate of increase over time. That is, the dividend decision is independent rather than the residue of investment and financing decisions. This positive management of dividend policy is said to increase investor confidence, though the matter is far from proven.

Due to the differential tax treatment of dividend payments and capital gains from increases in share prices, the desired level of dividend return may be different for certain classes of shareholder. For example, those individuals who pay income tax at a higher rate may prefer their return from an equity investment in the form of a capital gain, so that they can utilise their capital gains tax allowance before incurring any personal tax liability. Whereas, those individuals paying basic rate tax or no tax may prefer their return in the form of a dividend, in order to minimise any transaction costs associated with selling their equity investment to obtain cash. In other words, tax clienteles may exist for a particular level of dividend payout.

4.2 Views of the Company's Shareholders

This proposal may be preferred by those shareholders who want a large, immediate cash distribution and will not suffer any adverse tax consequences if it is received as a dividend. In your company's case, this may be tax-exempt institutions, such as Pension Funds, which are the majority shareholders, and possibly some retired employees and current employees, who pay basic rate income tax.

4.3 Dividend Signalling

The main problem with the proposed increase in dividend is that the payout ratio would increase from 55% to 87% (see Appendix 1), which is very large in comparison with both the industry average and the national average. Unless the reasons for this dramatic increase are carefully explained, this may send a negative signal to current and potential investors. Specifically, some investors may assume that the level of dividends in future years will continue to increase at the same rate, whilst others may interpret the large payment as a sign that the management of the company cannot identify investment opportunities, thus questioning their competence. It is best to avoid confusion of this sort, as it can have a negative impact upon the company's share price. Companies wishing to pay large increases in cash to shareholders have historically avoided such confusion by either announcing a 'one-off' special dividend or by making a share buy-back. The latter has the advantage of being subject to capital gains tax (for higher tax rate investors), rather than income tax, but does result in a change in the disposition of shareholdings.

5. Issues Relating to Expansion into the Republic of Ireland

5.1 Exporting Option

Despite the high level of transportation costs, on the assumption that operations continue indefinitely in accordance with the data supplied, this option is financially viable, with a net present value of approximately €2.5 million (see Appendix 2).

5.2 Takeover Option with Purchase of New Machinery

On the assumption that operations continue indefinitely in accordance with the data supplied, this option may be viable, provided that the purchase price is approximately €19 million. However, at the very least I would like to inspect the most recent audited accounts of the potential target firm and conduct further investigations to determine the extent to which the data supplied is reliable. Further, you should seriously consider the associated problems of integration and control with regard to the establishment of a wholly owned subsidiary in Dublin. As this is a horizontal takeover these problems may not be severe, but any financial implications should be factored into the numerical analysis.

5.3 Takeover with Transfer of Machinery from Belfast

Of the possible options investigated in this report, this would appear the most desirable, based upon the data supplied. Appendix 2 provides the relevant calculations and demonstrates that this option is preferable largely as a result of the elimination of the transportation costs of finished goods between Belfast and Dublin, together with an expansion into new markets in the Republic.

As this option is a combination of the latter two, the points noted above also apply. In addition, however, this will require the investment of more than the €20 million surplus funds, but will increase the value of the company by between €19 and €23 million. Given the company's current capital structure, the optimal financing policy may be to borrow any additional funds required, to take advantage of the 'tax shield' that debt provides, over the medium to long term.

5.4 Other Issues

It must be noted that the analysis above is heavily dependent upon the assumption that the operating performance in the Republic of Ireland continues at the estimated level indefinitely, and on the other data supplied from the market research report, neither of which I have verified. Further analysis should therefore be performed with regard to the reliability of this data. In particular, the analysis presented has largely focused upon return, with little or no consideration of risk. At the very least, sensitivity analysis should be performed to identify which estimates the decision to invest is most sensitive to.

Appendix 1: Dividend Payout Ratio (Assuming Surplus Paid as Dividend)

		2XX4	2XX5
Earnings before interest and tax		25,000,000	50,000,000
Interest	(20,000,000 × 0.07)	1,400,000	1,400,000
Earnings before tax		23,600,000	48,600,000
Tax @ 33%		7,788,000	16,038,000
Earnings after tax		15,812,000	32,562,000
Dividend	(560,000,000 × 0.015)	8,400,000	28,400,000
Dividend payout (%)		53.12%	87.22%
Interest cover		17.86	
Book value of debt		20,000,000	
Book value of equity		400,000,000	
Gearing (%)		5.00%	

Appendix 2: Exporting Option

	Year					
	0	1	2	3	4	5
Sales		1,000,000	2,000,000	4,000,000	8,000,000	20,000,000
Variable costs:						
Operating		700,000	1,400,000	2,800,000	5,600,000	14,000,000
Transportation		250,000	500,000	1,000,000	2,000,000	5,000,000
Legal fees	500,000					

Corporate tax rate 0.33 (Payable in current year)
Required return 0.15

Exporting Option

DCF Analysis

	Year					
	0	1	2	3	4	5
Pre-tax contribution	−500,000	50,000	100,000	200,000	400,000	1,000,000
Tax	165,000	−16,500	−33,000	−66,000	−132,000	−330,000
Post-tax contribution	−335,000	33,500	67,000	134,000	268,000	670,000
PV year 5 onwards (670,000/0.15)					4,466,666.7	
Total net cash-flows	−335,000	33,500	67,000	134,000	4,734,666.7	
DCF		1	0.869565	0.756144	0.657516	0.5717532
Present Values	~335,000	29,130.43	50,661.63	88,107.18	2,707,061	
Net Present Value						€2,539,960.27

Takeover Data

	Year					
	0	1	2	3	4	5
Cost of acquisition			16,000,000 to 20,000,000			
Initial working capital	8,000,000 (Not to be increased with inflation)					
New machines	4,000,000					
Transportation of existing machinery	500,000					
Post-tax cash-flows		3,000,000	5,000,000	5,000,000	5,000,000	5,000,000
Capital allowances		0.25 (Reducing balance)				

Takeover Option with Purchase of New Machinery

DCF Analysis

	Year			
	0	1	2	3
Post-tax contribution		3,000,000	5,000,000	5,000,000
Working capital	−8,000,000			
New machines	−4,000,000			
PV year 3 onwards (5,000,000/0.15)				33,333,333
Total net cash-flows	−8,335,000		3,000,000	38,333,333
DCF		1	0.869565	0.756144
Present values	−8,335,000		2,608,696	28,985,507
Net Present Value		Purchase price =	16,000,000	**€3,594,202.90**
		Purchase price =	20,000,000	**−€405,797.10**

Takeover Option with Transfer of Machinery

DCF Analysis

	Year					
	0	1	2	3	4	5
New RoI Market						
Sales		1,000,000	2,000,000	4,000,000	8,000,000	20,000,000
Operating costs		−700,000	−1,400,000	−2,800,000	−5,600,000	−14,000,000
Legal fees	−500,000					
Pre-tax contribution	−500,000	300,000	600,000	1,200,000	2,400,000	6,000,000
Tax	165,000	−99,000	−198,000	−396,000	−792,000	−1,980,000
Post-tax contribution	−335,000	201,000	402,000	804,000	1,608,000	4,020,000

PV year 5 onwards (4,020,000/0.15)					26,800,000
Net cash-flows exporting	−335,000	201,000	402,000	804,000	28,408,000
DCF	1	0.869565	0.756144	0.657516	0.5717532
Present values	−335,000	174,782.6	303,969.8	528,643.1	16,242,366
Net Present Value					€16,914,761.61

Takeover (Acquiring Target Company's RoI Market)

DCF Analysis

	0	1	2	3
Post-tax contribution		3,000,000	5,000,000	5,000,000
Lost tax benefit on capital allowances				
Capital allowance	1,000,000	−330,000		
	750,000		−247,500	
	562,500			−185,625
Working capital	−8,000,000			
Transportation costs (existing machinery)	−500,000			
Tax on transportation costs	165,000			
Net post-tax contribution	−8,335,000	2,670,000	4,752,500	4,814,375
PV year 3 onwards (4,814,375/0.15)			32,095,833	
Total net cash-flows	−8,335,000	2,670,000	36,848,333	
DCF		1	0.869565	0.756144
Present values	−8,335,000		2,321,739	27,862,634
Net Present Value:	Purchase price = 16,000,000			€5,849,373.03
	Purchase price = 20,000,000			€1,849,373.03

Case 21
Solution to Sun Shine Limited
John Cotter, University College Dublin

REPORT ON ISSUES FACED BY SUN SHINE LIMITED AND ITS TRADING DECISIONS

Prepared by: John Oglewski (consultant)

For: CEO of Sun Shine Limited

1. Terms of Reference

Further to our discussions on xx/xx/xx, I present the report requested. With respect to the expansion we use three different types of analysis and discuss the associated findings. We first look at the projected cash-flows supplied by Sun Shine and value these by calculating the present values of the inflows and outflows. We also calculate the net present value and related ratios to support our findings. The numerical analysis of the cash-flows in the report relates to a set of figures provided by the chief financial officer (CFO) of Sun Shine and are taken on good faith, having not been independently verified for the purposes of this report. We also, independently, gathered macro-economic forecasts from various sources, such as the IMF and the respective countries' industrial development organisations. We have analysed this macro-economic information to aid the decision-making process. Furthermore, we gathered, and did analysis on, exchange rate data in dollars and Euro. This third form of analysis on foreign exchange data uses calculations of foreign exchange exposure by looking at average changes and the level of risk in the changes. Using summary statistics we discuss the likely foreign exchange exposure facing Sun Shine from setting up in Ireland, and comment on ways of minimising the foreign exchange exposure.

2. Recommendations

Ireland dominates Scotland as the preferred location from all available data and its associated analysis.

(a) All the net present value analysis supports choosing Ireland as the preferred location for expansion. Ireland has a higher positive net present value and associated profitability index than Scotland.
(b) These findings hold true even if the discount factor were to change (assuming that the discount factor for both Irish and Scottish investments were to remain equal).
(c) The analysis of the macro-economic forecasts suggests choosing Ireland as the preferred location for expansion. This recommendation is driven in particular by the corporate tax rates available in Ireland for the foreseeable future.
(d) Overall the analysis of the past exchange rate changes suggests choosing Ireland as the preferred location for expansion. This recommendation is driven in particular by the volume of trade it currently does in Euro compared to sterling.
(e) Our final recommendation is that Sun Shine should consider going a step further than locating its future expansion in Ireland and that it should transfer the existing production facilities there. The main criterion for this recommendation is the fact that it would eliminate much of the exchange rate uncertainty associated with a large proportion of its trade in the Eurozone.

3. Summary of Issues Relating to the Expansion of Sun Shine Limited

Much of the analysis of this report is based on the time value of money and converting cash-flows (inflows and outflows) into present values. In Appendix 1, positive cash-flows are presented in their future value form as they are given as projected future cash-flows but, in contrast, negative cash-flows are given as present values. We also complete analysis of macro-economic forecasts of Ireland and Scotland's attributes in terms of location for the expansion. Our third type of analysis is the foreign exchange exposure Sun Shine is likely to face in trading from Scotland or Ireland. In order to assess the relative merits of each location for Sun Shine Limited, we will examine the three different types of analysis separately and comment on the respective findings.

Analysis 1: Projected Cash-flow Analysis

We use net present value and related analysis to discuss the importance of the cash-flows. The current value of the outflows can be obtained directly from Appendix 1 and are £1,000 million. However, projected inflows are given in the context of their future values and must be discounted by the time value of money. We use the US cost of capital as the discount factor of 5% and the timeframe of the analysis is five years. We are assuming the projected cash-flows will actually evolve as forecasted. Given these assumptions and the timeframe involved, we suggest that a reasonable estimate of the present value of locating in Ireland and Scotland is given in Appendix 1. For example, the present value of the fifth year's contribution to Scotland is:

$400m/(1.05)^5$ = $313.41 million

And the present value of the fourth year's contribution to Ireland is:

$600/(1.05)^4$ = $493.62 million

Having calculated each year's present value, we now proceed to calculate the net present value. This will allow us make a recommendation based on the projected cash-flows. Thus, to obtain the net present values we need to sum the individual present values for each economy; the findings are given in Appendix 1. For example, for Scotland, we find the net present value is:

−1000 + 476.19 + 181.406 + 259.151 + 329.081 + 313.41 = +559.239

As we find that the net present value for Scotland is positive, then it is a worthwhile investment, which is very encouraging for the expansion of Sun Shine. However, if we compare the value to that of Ireland, we find Ireland's net present value is even higher (+854.745). Thus, on this basis of net present value, we would choose Ireland over Scotland.

A simple but effective way of reporting the relative superiority of Ireland over Scotland is through a profitability index. Again, we illustrate our findings for one economy and find that the profitability index of choosing Ireland is:

854.745/1000 = 0.854.

Relative to a dollar (or thousand million dollar) investment, locating in Ireland has a profit of 85.4 cent (or 854 million dollars); this shows how profitable and lucrative expanding in Ireland really is. In comparison, Scotland represents an excellent investment opportunity, but does have a lower profitability index of 0.559, so would be ranked lower than Ireland as the preferred investment location.

Another way to analyse the figures using present value approaches is to calculate the respective internal rate of return for each location. The internal rate of return is the interest rate corresponding to a zero net present value. This allows us to confirm the earlier findings from the net present value analysis. Again the results for each economy are reported in Appendix 1. However, to illustrate the findings for Ireland we see:

$1000 = 300/(1 + r)^1 + 200/(1 + r)^2 + 400/(1 + r)^3 + 600/(1 + r)^4 + 700/(1 + r)^5$

And by solving by trial and error we find: r = 27%. Comparing this to the calculated IRR for Scotland, we report a lower value of 24%, suggesting that the rate of return on the Irish expansion is higher than that of Scotland. Again this would support the recommendation of choosing Ireland over Scotland as the preferred location for Sun Shine's expansion.

All the analysis supports choosing Ireland as the preferred location for expansion. These findings hold true even if the discount factor were to change (assuming that the discount factor for both Irish and Scottish investments were to remain equal). However, if interest rates or the discount factor were to increase beyond 27%, then both economies would have a negative net present value and neither should be chosen. If the discount factor were to increase beyond 24% but less than 27%, then Scotland would have a negative net present value and Ireland would have a positive net present value and, thus, only the latter would be an attractive option.

Analysis 2: Macro-economic Forecasts

Turning to the second type of analysis for determining the best location for Sun Shine to expand in, we examine some macro-economic forecasts on the respective economies. Our indications are summarised in Appendix 2. Overall the findings are very positive for both economies, as they perform well for all measures. Thus, they are both desirable destinations. However, overall we find that Ireland tends to have a more favourable set of macro-economic forecasts, in that it dominates Scotland in more categories than *vice versa*. Also, Ireland tends to perform well in those categories that are critical to expansion.

Let us go through each of these headings and comment on the relative performance of Ireland and Scotland. First, price changes tend to be more stable in Ireland, as exhibited by a lower inflation rate, although we must note that this proxy of price changes is very general and may not reflect price stability in software products and services. Secondly, the cost of capital is lower in Ireland and this is a very important plus for domestic firms trading there in comparison to Scotland. Given that Sun Shine is an international firm, it will source its capital in an international context, so the benefit of Ireland for this factor may not be a driving force in recommending that the company expands here. Nevertheless, assuming that the company does expand in Ireland and builds up good relationships with local organisations, such as banks, then the lower cost of capital may be a plus when Sun Shine comes to obtaining further capital in the future.

The next forecast is vital for the decision relating to expansion. The Profit Opportunity Rankings (POR) for Ireland is slightly higher than that of Scotland, which would indicate that Ireland offers a more attractive business climate to new enterprises. As these measures are subjective, the main finding that one should take from both rankings is that they are high and reasonably similar. If we had found low rankings for either or both economies, this would have been a strong signal not to expand in the location(s). Thus both economies are attractive places for Sun Shine to expand to. Sentiment is not (and should not be) part of any decision on expansion, but this analysis suggests that Sun Shine has identified two countries that would be top of any league table of countries to relocate to, with Ireland just shading Scotland on this criterion.

The next forecast, of infrastructure, is the only one in which Scotland has a clear advantage over Ireland. This factor examines the support network for a typical business, including road network and telecommunication facilities. From further analysis, it is suggested that Ireland's relative poor performance in this area is due to a relative lack of investment in this area historically compared to that of Scotland.

It must be noted that this is a generic measure that does not specifically relate to any company's infrastructural needs and, as such, may or may not be relevant to Sun Shine. Our discussions with Sun Shine and similar companies suggest that telecommunications is an important issue, but that these types of companies are not well served, given their requirements, in any economy; not even in Silicon Valley. Many software companies thus rely on privately developed telecommunication systems that build on their own expertise and avoid being totally reliant on the locally provided systems that are in place.

The quality of labour in both economies is excellent and we cannot separate the economies for this factor. Both economies have well-educated workforces that fit perfectly for the high-value production in which Sun Shine is involved. However, for another vital raw material of relevance to where the company should expand we find a clear indication of the suitability of Ireland over Scotland. In the area of grants and support, Ireland's industrial bodies are willing to give $22 million to support Sun Shine expanding there, in comparison to only $6 million being provided by their Scottish counterparts.

This brings us to another factor of relevance (and some might say the main factor) to help decide where Sun Shine should expand to. We note that Ireland's corporation tax is less than half that of Scotland (10% versus 21%). Thus, for any level of profits, the net figure at the disposal of Sun Shine will be much higher in Ireland. Given that this is a key factor (profit maximisation) for any company, the favourable tax rate in Ireland is the driving factor in recommending Ireland over Scotland. Also, it must be noted that Sun Shine will be able to use transfer pricing between its US and Irish subsidiary (assuming Ireland is chosen) that will further enhance its net profits. Here Sun Shine could report its profits in Ireland and thus be taxed there at the relatively low rate (10% versus 16% in the US), resulting in higher net profits.

The last two factors affecting the decision of where to expand are the measures of fiscal responsibility and of monetary stability. Scotland scores higher (just) on the first, and Ireland scores higher on the second. The main finding for these factors, however, is that both economies offer very attractive monetary and fiscal arrangements. The overall package for both economies is quite similar, although Scotland has some uncertainty associated with it due to the UK remaining outside the Eurozone; we will address this issue in more detail shortly.

Thus, overall the analysis of the macro-economic forecasts suggests choosing Ireland as the preferred location for expansion. This recommendation is driven in particular by the corporate tax rates available in Ireland for the foreseeable future.

Analysis 3: Projected Exchange Rate Uncertainty

Turning to the third type of analysis for determining the best location for Sun Shine to expand in, we examine six-month exchange rate changes over the past five years for the dollar in terms of Euro, sterling and yen. These are the currencies that represent Sun Shine's main markets, making up 80% of its current turnover. Some summary findings are given in Appendix 3. Overall, our analysis here indicates that the preferred location for Sun Shine's expansion is Ireland.

We use summary statistics (average changes and risk of exchange rate change) to discuss the importance of exchange rate changes. Let us first look at the calculations and explain their relevance. We find that the lowest average exchange rate change (2.07%) occurs for sterling, based on the following:

$$(1.8 + 1.6 + 3 + 2.3 + 2.1 + 1.7 + 2 + 3.2 + 1.2 + 1.8) = 2.07.$$

We find that the risk in exchange rate changes is lowest for the yen, based on the following:

$$\frac{1}{n-1}\sum_{x=1}^{n}\sqrt{(x_i - \bar{x})^2}$$

Where n is the number of six-month values (10 in this case).
Thus the risk for the yen exchange rate changes is:

$$\frac{1}{9}\sqrt{\left[(2.8 - 3.45)^2 + \cdots + (4 - 3.45)^2\right]} = 0.575$$

We also report the largest (maximum) and smallest (minimum) exchange rate changes and note that sterling is associated with the smallest exchange rate change and the yen is associated with the largest rate change. Now let us interpret the figures. The dollar-sterling is the rate with the least level of uncertainty associated with it – it has a lower average value and reports the lowest minimum value. The dollar-Euro has the next lowest level of uncertainty associated with it, and the dollar-yen has the highest level of uncertainty associated with it.

If Sun Shine was deciding which market to export its products to, then the analysis suggests that exporting to the UK has lower foreign exchange exposure associated with it compared to the EU (including Ireland) and Japan. However, the issue at hand is where Sun Shine should expand to. On this basis, if Sun Shine chooses Ireland, it would avoid higher exchange rate risk compared to choosing Scotland, because it would avoid the requirement of converting its currency from Euro back to dollars. Furthermore – and the main reason for choosing Ireland over Scotland in this regard – the largest volume of trade that Sun Shine has is in Euro and, by locating there, the company will eliminate all uncertainty associated with its Euro trade. In contrast, its current volume of trade in sterling is only 25% (compared to 45% for the Euro trade), thus if Scotland were chosen, the amount of turnover associated with exchange rate uncertainty that would be eliminated would be smaller than if Ireland were chosen.

Thus, overall the analysis of the past exchange rate changes suggests choosing Ireland as the preferred location for expansion. This recommendation is driven in particular by the volume of trade it currently does in Euro compared to sterling.

Further Analysis: Expansion of Revenues

Relating to the previous analysis on the exchange rate changes, we noted that Sun Shine has a very heavy concentration of revenues being sourced from the

Eurozone (and from the UK). Given that we are recommending that Sun Shine makes its expansion in Ireland, we are now going to look at a related issue: would it be worthwhile for the company to move its production entirely to Ireland at the expense of its current headquarters in Silicon Valley? Although, it would maintain its headquarters and research and development facilities in Silicon Valley.

Let us assume that each market is equally profitable on all considerations, with the exception of exchange rate uncertainty. In order to investigate this we gather further exchange rate data in Euro and do some analysis. The values are given in Appendix 4, which details summary statistics for monthly exchange rates for the dollar, sterling and yen all in terms of Euro. Results are given for a 14-year period between 1992 and 2005, encompassing seven years before and after the introduction of the Euro.

We also note that Sun Shine's current trade is concentrated in, with descending order of importance: the EU, the UK, the US and Japan. In fact, only 20% of its current trade is domestic (US-based). Further analysis has suggested that this is due to the highly competitive nature of the US market and, in particular, to other companies that are also based in Silicon Valley specialising in similar products. In fact, our analysis suggests that this domestic market will continue to be competitive and it may be difficult for Sun Shine to increase its market share in the US. However, increased market share and turnover in its main markets is possible given our analysis. Thus we expect that the proportion of sales in the UK and the EU will increase and that these markets represent strong growth opportunities for Sun Shine in the future. Given this, and the fact that all markets are equally profitable, we would suggest that Sun Shine would not only expand in Ireland but would actually relocate its current facilities there. It would then eliminate foreign exchange exposure for 45% of its current trade (that, we project, will actually increase in the future) in comparison to its current domestic trade of 20% (that, we project, will be constant or fall due to increasing competitive pressures).

Also, we note from Appendix 4 that the uncertainty associated with trading with its second most important market, the UK, is actually lower than that of the US for the full period between 1992 and 2005. This lower level of exchange rate exposure is further enhanced in more recent times since the introduction of the Euro, as the volatility of sterling-Euro exchange rate changes has actually decreased on a monthly basis from 2.10% to 1.91% (in comparison, volatility in the dollar-Euro has actually increased). Also, the company would be able to obtain the grants and support as a minimum noted in Appendix 2, and may actually be able to bargain for further support given that it is moving the majority of its existing staff there. Finally, by keeping its US headquarters, Sun Shine can continue to exploit transfer pricing arrangements between the US and Ireland, while at the same time being able to reverse the transfer decision by keeping its intellectual capital in the US through maintaining its research and development facilities there.

Thus, our final recommendation is that Sun Shine should consider going a step further than locating its future expansion in Ireland and that it should transfer the existing production facilities there. The main criterion for this recommendation is the fact that it would eliminate much of the exchange rate uncertainty associated with a large proportion of its trade in the Eurozone.

Appendix 1: Summary of Cash-flow Analysis for Sun Shine Limited

	Ireland	PV(IRL)	Scotland	PV(SCT)
Year 0	−1000	−1000	−1000	−1000
Year 1	300	285.714	500	476.19
Year 2	200	181.406	200	181.406
Year 3	400	345.535	300	259.151
Year 4	600	493.621	400	329.081
Year 5	700	548.468	400	313.41
	NPV	854.745	NPV	559.239
	IRR	27%	IRR	24%
	Profitability index	0.85475	Profitability index	0.55924

Appendix 2: Summary of Macro-economic Forecasts for Sun Shine Limited

	Ireland	Scotland	Winner
Inflation rates	3%	3.8%	IRL
Interest rates	3.5%	5.0%	IRL
POR	86/100	84/100	IRL
Infrastructure	81/100	93/100	SCT
Employees	91/100	91/100	–
Grants and support	$22m	$6	IRL
Taxation	10%	21%	IRL
Fiscal responsibility	96/100	97/100	SCT
Monetary stability	95/100	91/100	IRL

For each macro-economic forecast a 'winner' is given between Ireland (IRL) and Scotland (SCT).

Appendix 3: Summary of Six-Monthly Exchange Rate Analysis for Sun Shine

	Euro		Sterling		Yen
Mean	2.71	Mean	2.07	Mean	3.45
St.deviation	0.648845	St.deviation	0.620125	St.deviation	0.575905
Minimum	1.9	Minimum	1.2	Minimum	2.8
Maximum	4	Maximum	3.2	Maximum	4.5

The results reported deal with sample values. As well as the measure of risk (standard deviation), other summary measures of exchange rate changes are given.

Appendix 4: Summary Statistics of Monthly Exchange Rate Changes for Euro

	Minimum	Maximum	Average	Deviation
Full sample				
Dollar	−9.37	6.97	−0.09	2.86
Sterling	−4.52	10.69	−0.04	2.01
Yen	−11.23	7.89	−0.12	3.26
Pre-Euro				
Dollar	−9.37	5.53	−0.20	2.82
Sterling	−4.52	10.69	−0.05	2.10
Yen	−11.23	7.89	−0.12	3.26
Post-Euro				
Dollar	−5.62	6.97	0.01	2.92
Sterling	−3.93	6.46	−0.03	1.91
Yen	−7.24	5.68	−0.16	3.25

Values are given as monthly percentage changes. All currencies are quoted in Euro. Deviation represents standard deviation of monthly values. The full sample is 1992–2005 inclusive with the pre-Euro sample encompassing 1992–1998 and the post-Euro period encompassing 1999–2005.

Case 22
Solution to Blackwater Hotel Group plc
Peter Green, University of Ulster

REPORT ON THE PROPOSED NEW LUXURY HOTEL IN BELFAST

Prepared by: A. Student
Management Consultant

For: Blackwater Hotel Group plc

1. Executive Summary/Recommendations

Further to our discussions of xx/xx/xx, I present the report requested. With respect to the financial viability of the proposed new luxury hotel group in the dockland area of Belfast, on the basis of the information that you have supplied to me it would appear that whilst the investment is viable with 100% occupancy, with a positive net present value of €14 million, on consideration of the occupancy rate required to 'breakeven', approximately 88%, this may be considered too high (see Appendix 1).

Of particular concern is the accuracy of the estimates made in the project evaluation, given both the long evaluation time horizon and the fact that the data supplied is based upon the popular seaside resort of Blackpool, using a fixed exchange rate. Whilst Belfast has certainly exhibited significant growth, both in infrastructure and tourism, it is highly unlikely that direct comparison with Blackpool is appropriate. Further, unless the UK government shortly agrees to join a single European currency, foreign exchange risk is likely to exist.

I would conclude that the proposal should be rejected at this time, but further consideration should be made in the future as the hotel's operations could change due to internal developments and external environmental factors. As a consequence, whilst additional independent analysis now is likely to be of limited use, it may be informative to perform sensitivity analysis to identify which input variables are the ones which cause most uncertainty in the evaluation of the breakeven occupancy rate.

2. Consideration of the Accuracy of the Analysis

2.1 Estimation of Revenues

There are a number of key factors to consider in the estimation of revenues. First, the hotel industry, particularly in the seaside resorts upon which the data has been gathered for this analysis, is highly seasonal. Obviously, the summer months may be expected to attract the most tourists, although given the nature of weather conditions, this may not be as big a factor for a hotel in Belfast as it would be for hotels located in a warmer climate. Secondly, and related to the first, is the need to reduce room charges to secure block bookings in 'off-peak' seasonal times. For example, Blackpool and other resorts are apparently successful in attracting conference bookings in autumn. Whether or not Belfast would attract such clienteles is uncertain, although Dublin has achieved some success in doing so.

Thirdly, luxury hotels, in particular, are influenced by the state of the economy. During periods of boom, with surplus residual income, luxury hotels generally may be expected to perform well. However, in recession a luxury hotel located in an area with historically low disposal income may not perform as well as those located in a relatively affluent location. Whether or not the dockland area of Belfast should be considered affluent or not is open to interpretation.

Finally, the residual value of the hotel has been estimated at €50 million after tax. There are no supporting calculations, nor any indication as to how this figure has been derived. Given that you are proposing to purchase a 100-year leasehold, it is not clear whether the hotel would be sold as a going-concern, including or excluding the leasehold. This clearly is a matter of fundamental importance, as is any restrictions on how the leasehold could be utilised, for example, is it possible to sell the leasehold for further housing development in the area?

2.2 Estimation of Costs

Similar to the above arguments, costs are also subject to inaccuracy. All of the calculations have been based upon average occupancy rates per room, and a standard gross-profit margin for each source of revenue. Whilst statistically it may be appropriate to calculate an average occupancy rate of 1.5, it cannot be guaranteed in advance that this figure will be achieved in practice, and gross profit margins may also vary in accordance with seasonality and the state of the economy. In addition, the cost estimates would appear somewhat 'ad hoc'. For example, no details of the way in which specific price level inflation might affect particular costs have been given and the cost models employed (the split between fixed and variable costs and the use of particular cost drivers) have not been clearly identified.

2.3 Estimation of the Cost-of-Capital

Appendix 2 outlines how the cost-of-capital may have been estimated.

In order to calculate the cost-of-equity, it would appear that the company has used the capital asset pricing model (CAPM). The CAPM produces a required return based upon the expected return of the market, expected project returns, the risk-free interest rate and the variability of project returns relative to the market return.

The CAPM is based upon a number of unrealistic assumptions, such as:

(i) all investors hold well-diversified portfolios and have homogeneous expectations with regard to future share price performance;
(ii) return, risk and correlation can be evaluated over a single time period;
(iii) risk is measured entirely by the variability of returns;
(iv) there is a perfect capital market.

As many of these assumptions are unrealistic, it is not surprising that there are numerous examples of inaccurate predictions made by the CAPM (technically known as empirical regularities). For example, when it is applied to small companies, companies with low equity betas, certain days of the week or months of the year. Further, the only feasible way of estimating a company's beta factor or the market risk premium is by examining historical data and making the assumption that the future will be the same as the past.

When applied to capital investment appraisal, which is the case here, the CAPM makes the additional assumption that companies make decisions on behalf of the shareholders only. This ignores the position of other stakeholders, such as employees, who have different attitudes to risk because they find it more difficult to diversify their position than shareholders do.

The greatest practical problems with the use of the CAPM in capital investment decisions are as follows:

(a) The beta factor represents the sensitivity of the company's shares to the risk of the economy. It is hard to estimate returns on projects under different economic environments, market returns under different economic environments and the probabilities of the various environments.
(b) The CAPM is a single period model. Few investment projects last for one year only and certainly not the one under consideration. To extend the use of the model to more than one time period would require both project performance relative to the market and the economic environment to be reasonably stable. This is highly unlikely over a 17-year period and historically beta factors are not stable through time.
(c) It may be difficult to determine the risk-free rate of return. Government debt (bonds) are usually considered risk-free, however the return (yield) on these securities varies according to their term to maturity.

In performing the discounted cash-flow analysis in Appendix 1, the weighted average cost of capital (WACC) has been employed. The WACC can be used in investment appraisal if the following assumptions are made.

(i) The project is small relative to the overall size of the company.
(ii) The WACC reflects the company's long-term future capital structure, i.e. the cost of capital to be applied to the project evaluation should reflect the marginal cost of new capital. If this were not so, the current WACC would become irrelevant because eventually it would not relate to any actual cost of capital.
(iii) The project has the same degree of 'business risk' as the company currently has.
(iv) New investments must be financed by new sources of funds: retained earnings, new share issues, new loans and so on.

The arguments against using the WACC as the cost of capital for investment appraisal are largely based on criticisms of the assumptions outlined above. Specifically:

(i) The project is relatively large. The company's current market valuation (debt and equity) is approximately €203 million and the proposed investment is approximately €92 million (including working capital at the end of year two). On the basis of these figures the investment would appear to be relatively large.
(ii) New investments undertaken by a company might have different business risk characteristics from the company's existing operations. From the information provided, although the proposed investment is in the same industry as the company's current investments, the financial director does consider the construction of a hotel in Belfast to be of a higher risk and, consequently, the hotel has been appraised over a 15-year operating time horizon, rather than their standard 20-year period. This method of dealing with the risk of the investment may be considered rather 'ad hoc', without any theoretical basis.
(iii) There is no information provided to indicate how the proposed investment is to be financed. However, as a general point, many companies raise floating-rate debt as well as fixed-interest-rate debt. Floating-rate debt is difficult to incorporate into a WACC computation, as the cost of this debt will fluctuate as market conditions vary.

Overall, the use of a required return of 12%, based upon the current weighted average cost of capital and the application of the capital asset pricing model to establish the cost of equity, is questionable.

3. Issues Relating to the Risk of the Proposed Investment

It is evident (as noted above) that the financial director perceives the proposed investment as having more risk than your current investments. Consequently, the analysis performed has been restricted to a 15-year operating time horizon. There are a number of ways in which risk can be formally incorporated within an appraisal.

For example: applying a higher discount rate than the current weighted average cost of capital (see section 2.3); probability analysis; the application of certainty equivalents; simulation analysis; and sensitivity analysis. Given my recommendation not to proceed with this investment at this time, I feel that risk should be further investigated via sensitivity analysis.

Probably, the area of greatest concern with regard to the proposed investment is the accuracy of the estimates made in the project evaluation, given both the long evaluation time horizon and the fact that the data supplied is based upon the popular seaside resort of Blackpool. Essentially sensitivity analysis identifies which key input variables (for example average occupancy rates, gross profit margins, required return, etc.) the decision to invest is most sensitive to, which can change by the least percentage before the net present value of the investment falls to zero. Further analysis can then be directed to these key input variables in order to determine the reliability of the estimates currently being employed.

Appendix 1: Net Present Value of New Hotel

				€		€
Hotel cost				90,000,000	**Tax allowable**	50,000,000
	0.1	Year 0		9,000,000		5,000,000
	0.5	Year 1		45,000,000		25,000,000
	0.4	Year 2		36,000,000		20,000,000
Capital allowances				0.04	Straight line	
Corporation tax rate				0.3275	Payable in the year it arises	
Working capital		Year 2		2,000,000		
Hotel capacity				320	Bedrooms	
Average occupancy				1.5	People per night	
Charge per night				140	Whether one or more people are in room	
Food and drink spend				60	Per person, per day	
GPM on Food, etc.				0.5		
Other facilities				25	Per person, per day	
GPM on other facilities				0.2		
Non-resident income				3,000,000	Food and drink	
				1,000,000	Other facilities	
Function room rental				1,000,000	Pre-tax	
Total Contribution				2,700,000	Pre-tax	

Annual Expected Outlays

	€	
Staff	5,000,000	
Gas, etc.	1,400,000	
Other	1,000,000	
Redecoration costs	12,000,000	Every five years allowable in the year incurred
Hotel evaluation period	15 years	Operating horizon
Residual	50,000,000	After tax, excluding end of period refurbishment and release of working capital.
No. of days in the year	365	
All estimates at current prices		
Rate of inflation	0.04	per year
Nominal cost of capital	0.12	

Real Contribution per Room

	€
Food per guest, per day	30
Other per guest, per day	5
	35
Per room	52.5
Room charge per day	140
Total	192.5
Less tax	−63.04
After tax	129.46
Per annum (365 days)	47,252

Annual Operating Cash-flows

	€
Staff	−5,000,000
Services	−1,400,000
Maintenance	−1,000,000
	−7,400,000
Income from non-residents	2,700,000
Total	−4,700,000
Add tax relief	1,539,250
After tax	−3,160,750

Summary

	€
Total PV nominal annual operating cash-flows	−23,772,237.12
Total PV redecoration costs	−8,120,080.816
Total PV hotel construction/sale	−66,667,180.08
Total PV working capital investment	−1,604,689.943
Total	100,164,187.96.
Contribution per room, per annum	355,382
Occupancy required to breakeven (annual estimate)	282
Occupancy rate per annum	88%
NPV 100% occupancy	13,558,148

Year	1	2	3	4	5	6	7	8	9
Rate of inflation	0.04	0.04	0.04	0.04	0.04	0.04	0.04	0.04	0.04
Nominal contribution per room, per annum (€)			53,152	55,278	57,489	59,788	62,180	64,667	67,254
DCF (12%)	0.89285	0.79719	0.71178	0.635518078	0.567426856	0.506631121	0.452349215	0.403883228	0.360610025
PV nominal contribution per room, per annum (€)			37,832	35,130	32,621	30,291	28,127	26,118	24,252
Nominal annual operating CF (€)			−3,555,414	−3,697,630	−3,845,536	−3,999,357	−4,159,331	−4,325,705	−4,498,733
DCF (12%)	0.89285	0.79719	0.71178	0.635518078	0.567426856	0.506631121	0.452349215	0.403883228	0.360610025
PV annual operating cash-flows (€)			−2,530,673	−2,349,910.994	−2,182,060.209	−2,026,198.765	−1,881,470.282	−1,747,079.548	−1,622,288.151

Year	10	11	12	13	14	15	16	17
Rate of inflation	0.04	0.04	0.04	0.04	0.04	0.04	0.04	0.04

Case 22: Solution to Blackwater Hotel Group plc

Nominal contribution per room, per annum (€)	69,944	72,742	75,651	78,677	81,824	85,097	88,501	92,041
DCF (12%)	0.321973237	0.287476104	0.256675093	0.22917419	0.204619813	0.182696261	0.163121662	0.145644341
PV nominal contribution per room, per annum (€)	22,520	20,911	19,418	18,031	16,743	15,547	14,436	13,405
Total PV nominal contribution per room				355,382				
Nominal annual operating CF (€)	−4,678,682	−4,865,829	−5,060,463	−5,262,881	−5,473,396	−5,692,332	−5,920,025	−6,156,826
DCF (12%)	0.321973237	0.287476104	0.256675093	0.22917419	0.204619813	0.182696261	0.163121662	0.145644341
PV annual operating cash-flows (€)	−1,506,410.426	−1,398,809.682	−1,298,894.704	−1,206,116.511	−1,119,965.332	−1,039,967.808	−965,684.3932	−896,706.9366
Total PV nominal annual operating cash-flows (€)								−23,772,237.12

Working Capital Investment

Year	0	1	2	3	4	5	6	7	8
Incremental (€)		-2,000,000		-80,000	-83,200	-86,528	-89,989	-93,589	-97,332
DCF (12%)		0.89285714	0.79719387	0.71178024	0.63551807	0.56742685	0.50663112	0.45234921	0.40388322
PV working capital investment (€)			-1,594,387.755	-56,942	-52,875	-49,098	-45,591	-42,335	-39,311

Redecoration costs €

Real cost	-12,000,000								
Less tax	3,930,000								
After tax	-8,070,000								
Nominal value redecoration cost (€)								-10,619,569	
DCF (12%)		0.89285714	0.79719387	0.71178024	0.63551807	0.56742685	0.50663112	0.45234921	0.40388322
PV redecoration costs (€)								-4,803,753.91	

Hotel construction and sale costs

Construction cost allowable (€)	-9,000,000	-45,000,000	-36,000,000						
Capital allowance (€)		-200,000	-1,200,000	-2,000,000	-2,000,000	-2,000,000	-2,000,000	-2,000,000	-2,000,000
Tax benefit (€)		65,500	393,000	655,000	655,000	655,000	655,000	655,000	655,000
Net construction costs (€)	-9,000,000	-44,934,500	-35,607,000	655,000	655,000	655,000	655,000	655,000	655,000
DCF (12%)	1	0.89285714	0.79719387	0.71178024	0.63551807	0.56742685	0.50663112	0.45234921	0.40388322
PV construction and sale (€)	-9,000,000	-40,120,089	-28,385,682	466,216.06	416,264.34	371,664.59	331,843.38	296,288.73	264,543.51

Case 22: Solution to Blackwater Hotel Group plc

Year	9	10	11	12	13	14	15	16	17
Incremental (€)	−101,226	−105,275	−109,486	−113,865	−118,420	−123,156	−128,083	−133,206	3,463,352
DCF (12%)	0.36061002	0.32197323	0.28747610	0.25667509	0.22917410	0.20461981	0.18269626	0.16312166	0.14564434
PV working capital investment (€)	−36,503	−33,896	−31,474	−29,226	−27,139	−25,200	−23,400	−21,729	504,418
Total PV working capital investment (€)									−1,604,689.943
Redecoration costs									
Nominal value redecoration cost (€)				−12,920,330					
DCF (12%)	0.36061002	0.32197323	0.28747610	0.25667509	0.22917410	0.20461981	0.18269626	0.16312166	0.14564434
PV redecoration costs (€)				−3,316,326.905					
Total PV redecoration costs (€)									−8,120,080.816
Hotel construction and sale costs									
Capital allowance (€)	−2,000,000	−2,000,000	−2,000,000	−2,000,000	−2,000,000	−2,000,000	−2,000,000	−2,000,000	−2,000,000
Tax benefit (€)	655,000	655,000	655,000	655,000	655,000	655,000	655,000	655,000	655,000
Net construction costs (€)	655,000	655,000	655,000	655,000	655,000	655,000	655,000	655,000	655,000
After-tax residual value (€)									50,000,000
DCF (12%)	0.36061002	0.32197323	0.28747610	0.25667509	0.22917410	0.20461981	0.18269626	0.16312166	0.14564434
PV construction and sale (€)	236,199.56	210,892.47	188,296.84	168,122.18	150,109.09	134,025.97	119,666.05	106,844.68	7,377,614.00
Total PV of hotel construction and sale costs (€)									−66,667,180.08

Appendix 2: Estimation of the Cost of Capital

Market value of debt		€37,800,000	
Market value of equity		€165,600,000	
Current price of debt		€114	per 100
Interest rate (%)		12%	
Equity beta	β	0.8	
Return on market	R_m	15%	
Risk-free rate	R_f	7%	
Cost of equity (using CAPM)		**13.40%**	
Cost of debt			
Interest rates (%)		6.00	
		7.00	
Annual interest (%) net of tax		8.07	

Year	Cash-flow €	DCF 7%	DCF 6%	€PV 7%	€PV 6%
0	−114	1	1	−114	−114
1	8.07	0.934579439	0.943396226	7.542056075	7.613207547
2	8.07	0.873438728	0.889996440	7.048650537	7.182271271
3	8.07	0.816297877	0.839619283	6.587523867	6.775727614
4	8.07	0.762895212	0.792093663	6.156564361	6.392195862
5	8.07	0.712986179	0.747258173	5.753798468	6.030373455
6	8.07	0.666342224	0.704960540	5.377381746	5.689031561
7	8.07	0.622749742	0.665057114	5.025590417	5.367010907
8	8.07	0.582009105	0.627412371	4.696813474	5.063217837
9	8.07	0.543933743	0.591898464	4.389545303	4.776620601
10	8.07	0.508349292	0.558394777	4.102378788	4.506245850
11	8.07	0.475092796	0.526787525	3.833998867	4.251175330
12	8.07	0.444011959	0.496969364	3.583176511	4.010542764
13	8.07	0.414964448	0.468839022	3.348763094	3.783530909
14	100	0.414964448	0.468839022	41.49644479	46.88390222
TOTAL				**−4.99**	**4.39**
By Interpolation		6 + [(4/4+5)] × 1			**6.47**

Weighted Average Cost of Capital

13.40%	×	165,600,000 / 203,400,000	=	10.91%
PLUS				
6.47%	×	37,800,000 / 203,400,000	=	1.20%
				12.11%

Case 23
Solution to Tannam plc
Louis Murray, University College Dublin

REPORT ON ISSUES RAISED BY TANNAM PLC

Prepared by: J Milkins
Consultant

For: Gloria Knight
Finance Director
Tannam Holdings plc
Date: xx/xx/xxxx

Terms of Reference

Further to our discussions of xx/xx/xx, I present the report requested. It is divided into separate sections, to cover the two major concerns raised by Gloria Knight. Section one relates to Tannam, the holding company, and issues regarding hurdle rates for subsidiary companies that may have different risk profiles. Section two concentrates on Fasnet, and covers issues relating to the impact that forecasting error of estimated cash-flows will have on individual appraisal decisions.

With respect to Tannam plc, it contains an analysis and discussion on the issue of company cost of capital, together with comments on related issues. Previous diversification policies of Tannam are considered, as is the question of whether this will lead to the stated objective of reducing exposure to the risk associated with operating in a particular business sector. A separate section of the report will address the stated objective of Tom Glover, of only acquiring companies trading on a lower P/E ratio than Tannam itself. Numerical examples are presented to review the impact of this type of policy, and to consider the possible outcomes. A further substantial section of this report will consider the current approach towards investment appraisal, the potential difficulties associated with adapting an appraisal technique in a large diversified organisation, and the approaches that might be adapted to deal with this. A final section will offer advice on how Tannam should evaluate the current proposals, and will suggest an approach that should be adapted for any future investment proposals.

In section two, issues regarding Fasnet are discussed. I include a discussion on forecast error, and possible approaches to deal with it. Various forms of sensitivity analysis are outlined, and their advantages and disadvantages are reviewed. A quantitative assessment of the proposed extra investment is presented, and an initial sensitivity analysis is also presented. This section concludes with a discussion both on whether this specific proposal should be adapted, and on what approach should be taken towards forecast error, and how to adjust for it.

Recommendations

Section 1

1. The Board of Tannam should review its policy regarding diversification. It is not clear that the policy that has been pursued has in itself been beneficial.
2. The policy of only acquiring companies trading on a lower P/E ratio than Tannam is also questionable and should be reconsidered. This policy may have generated a short-term improvement in share price, but the long-term benefit is very questionable.
3. When estimating a cost of capital or hurdle rate to apply to investment proposals, no account should be taken of the specific financial package used to finance the investment. The average re-balanced capital structure should determine cost of capital.
4. An individual hurdle rate for investments should be introduced for each firm in the Tannam Group. This will allow adjustments for the risk profile in each individual business.
5. Using appropriate beta measures for each firm, an after-tax hurdle rate will be the measure against which proposals should be evaluated. Using this measure, the recommendation is that only the following be proceeded with: New Fleet, Kenge Haulage; Warehouse Facility, Tress; New Office Building, Image Consultants; Computer Equipment, Cross Timber; Extra Storage, Laheen. The purchase of Lennox Distributors offers a highly marginal return, so after allowing for forecasting error, it may not be profitable. The recommendation therefore is that it not be purchased.

Section 2

1. The Board of Tannam should adapt a more quantitative approach towards the assessment of risk associated with individual proposed investments. At a

minimum, a sensitivity analysis should be required that is based on pessimistic, expected and optimistic outcomes. If realistically possible, probabilities might be assigned to these outcomes, so that an expected outcome can be determined.
2. Based on expected outcomes, the proposed extra investment by Fasnet is marginally profitable, as indicated by both net present value and internal rate of return. These conclusions are based on an after-tax hurdle rate of 12%.
3. If forecast revenues are 5% below expectations, and operating expenses rise to 50% of sales, a sensitivity analysis clearly indicates that the proposal will be unprofitable. As this indicates a strong possibility of sizeable losses, the recommendation is that the proposal by Fasnet should not be accepted.

1.1 Issues Relating to Diversification Policy Pursued by Tannam

For over 10 years, Tannam has actively pursued a policy of diversification; this was motivated by a desire to reduce risk exposure to an individual business sector. As the original business had acquired a market quotation, it proved a desirable partner to other businesses seeking the opening to get access to the funding opportunities associated with a market quotation. The original decision was based on the assumption that diversification was the best means to reduce exposure to the market, or market risk as measured by beta. Although this decision would radically alter the nature of the business and convert Tannam into a holding company, the belief was that diversification would reduce risk and cost of capital, and would therefore increase value.

Clearly, it is true that mergers and acquisitions do on occasions generate value, through either a reduction in costs, or an increase in earnings due to improved opportunities. Benefits may also be expected, however, if there is an opportunity to benefit from synergies as a result of a good fit between the businesses involved. Typically, benefits of this type will be achievable if one organisation has a particular strength in one management function, e.g. marketing, and the other has strengths in other functional areas, e.g. product or service design. In all of these cases, to achieve economic benefits the businesses involved will need to be related to each other in some way, so that they will be able to get the benefits associated with combination. Also, the merger or acquisition can be expected to lead to an amalgamation of the businesses into a single structure, to facilitate these benefits. The research evidence on mergers and acquisitions generally is positive, as an increase in value tends to accompany an announcement of merger or acquisition. The question of whether acquiring or victim shareholders will receive this benefit is separate, and will largely depend on the state of the acquisitions market. However, as available evidence relates to an initial response on announcement, it is unclear as to whether these benefits will be sustained into the long run. This is a much more difficult research question, as many other factors will impact on longer-run performance, so it will be difficult to separate out the economic impact of an earlier decision to combine two or more businesses together.

In Tannam's case, the businesses combined together to form the holding company are not related to each other. The stated objective of company policy was to achieve potential benefits through diversification. As a result, it will not be possible to secure any wealth benefits that come with combining businesses that are in some way related to each other. The expectation of management is that diversification will in itself produce benefits, through a reduction in exposure to potential poor performance in an individual business sector. In effect, by combining unrelated companies into a single group, the risk associated with an individual business will be diversified away. Using the same logic as a fund manager who will hold shares in a range of different businesses, in order to eliminate or greatly reduce exposure to the unique risk of an individual business, the holding company will in itself become a diversified entity, also eliminating or greatly reducing exposure to individual company risk.

The benefit of a diversified business should be lower risk levels, and this should be delivered through a lower cost of capital, as investors respond by accepting lower rates of return. If this strategy does prove to be successful, lower cost of capital will result in an increase in company value.[1] An implication of this reasoning is that a single reduced cost of capital rate should be applied to all capital investments of the holding group, regardless of the business in which the investment is located. This was the approach that was adapted throughout Tannam Holdings. It is questionable, however, whether this reasoning is appropriate,[2] as it requires an assumption that all businesses that form part of a holding company can be viewed as part of a diversified single entity. If they actually continue to operate as separate entities, there must be some question as to whether a net benefit will be possible. There is considerable controversy regarding this point, and it is important because the expected benefits can only come if there truly is a single diversified entity, rather than a range of unrelated businesses that happen to be owned by the same holding company. The only remaining protection to shareholders of a diversified holding company could actually be a protection against bankruptcy costs and bankruptcy related costs, in the event of failure of a firm that is a wholly owned part of the group.

1.2 The Policy of only Acquiring Companies that Trade on a Lower P/E Ratio

The stated policy of Tom Glover has been to pursue a policy of rapid growth of the group, through a series of acquisitions. A series of mergers and acquisitions has delivered this outcome. The only stated criteria, when considering an acquisition of a publicly quoted company, has been that it is trading on a lower Price/Earnings (P/E) ratio than Tannam itself. In the case of both quoted and unquoted acquisitions that have been submitted for consideration, there is no stated policy regarding a strategic fit, or a connection with existing members of the group.

---

1 Company value can be viewed as expected future earnings, discounted at company cost of capital. A reduction in cost of capital will result in a reduced discount rate, and will therefore also result in an increase in value.
2 Please note section 1.3.

The policy of only acquiring companies trading on a lower P/E ratio is undertaken to ensure that there will be no immediate negative impact on Earnings per Share. The effect is that, by only purchasing company earnings at a multiple that is relatively lower, the number of new shares that must be issued to finance the acquisition will be minimised, so that Earnings per Share will not be reduced. If a company whose shares trade on a higher earnings multiple were acquired, Earnings per Share would decline. A worked example demonstrates this point in Appendix 1. In this case, acquisition terms are such that a company acquires a company trading on a P/E of 13, when its share price is trading at only 10 times earnings.

There is, however, an error in this analysis, as long-term implications have not been considered. First, Price/Earnings ratios provide a good indication of future potential, as investors will be prepared to pay a higher price for the earnings of a company that is considered to have better growth and development prospects. A decision to only consider acquiring companies that trade on a relatively lower ratio will limit Tannam to an acquisition of firms considered to have poor future growth prospects. Clearly, this could not be desirable. Secondly, the quantitative analysis on Earnings per Share and Price/Earnings assumes that, following acquisition, ABC will continue to trade on a P/E ration of 10. This may not be correct. For example, a decision to acquire XYZ, which trades on a higher P/E and is therefore well regarded by investors, may improve the prospects of ABC. This could enhance investor expectations, causing the P/E to increase above 10. As a result share price may actually increase. If, for example, following the acquisition the P/E of ABC were to increase to 11, a share price of €10.23 (*11 × €0.93*) could be expected.

1.3 An Assessment of the Current Policy towards Investment Decisions

With the establishment of Tannam Holdings, a budgetary control system was initiated throughout the group. Discounting-based appraisal methods were introduced. Before this, all appraisal decisions were evaluated using Payback Period. The senior management designated after-tax internal rate of return as the main criteria, however they also proposed that after-tax net present value also be used as a back-up criteria. Any investment proposal coming to the finance director of Tannam Holdings would be required to offer an after-tax internal rate of return that is in excess of the after-tax cost of capital for the group.

Considering that Tannam is the holding company of a diversified group of wholly owned firms, each operates as a separate business and has its separate financing structure of various forms of debt and equity capital. As the financing structure of the various businesses in the group does vary considerably, there are two issues that must be considered when determining the discount rate that should be applied to the evaluation process.

1. The balance between debt and equity capital is not the same in every firm in the Tannam Group. Also, it is likely that the form of debt capital that has been used will vary considerably across firms in the group. Some firms will have greater

concentrations of debentures or loan stock, whereas others will have greater concentrations of bank or term loans. New capital investments will be financed from various sources of either debt or equity capital that, again, will vary considerably across the firms in the group. The question that therefore arises is whether, when a hurdle rate is being determined for a particular proposal that will be situated in one of the firms, is it advisable to take account of how that proposal is financed? Also, is it advisable to take account of the particular financing structure of the firm itself? This is a complex question, but the generally accepted solution is to assume that the holding company will tend to continuously rebalance its financial structure towards an optimal balance of debt and equity capital. This rebalancing will also take account of an optimal combination of different forms of debt capital. As a result, the specific mix of financing used for a particular proposal will be irrelevant. The fact that a large or a small proportion of a certain debt source has been used is not relevant to the proposal. It is better to view all proposals as being financed by a combination of the overall financing mix of the group.

2. The risk exposure of each firm in the holding group is different. Individual proposals submitted by a particular firm will have risk characteristics similar to that firm, rather than to the overall group.[3] A general overall after-tax weighted average cost of capital value will therefore not be appropriate, as it takes no account of firm- or industry-specific risk characteristics. In some cases, if the firm risk profile is greater than the average profile of the group, an overall weighted average cost of capital will be too low, and vice versa. The recommendation therefore is that an adjustment must be made to allow for the risk profile of an individual firm in the holding group.

As a result, the cost of capital or hurdle rate that should be employed to assess a proposed investment should be determined by the following Weighted Average Cost of Capital Formula.

$$WACC = \left(D/V\right) Kd\left(1-T\right) + \left(E/V\right) Ke$$

Where: $WACC$ = After-tax weighted average cost of capital
D = Amount of Debt in Holding Company
E = Amount of Equity in Holding Company
V = Combined Value of Debt and Equity
Kd = Average Cost of Debt
Ke = Cost of Equity for individual firm
T = Company Tax rate

Cost of Equity for an individual firm should be determined using the Capital Asset Pricing Model. The level of beta or market exposure should depend on industry type for the individual firm.

---

[3] An assumption that the investment proposal is representative of company activities is required. If not, further adjustment to account for the risk profile of the individual proposal may be required.

$$Ke = Rf + Bi(Rm - Rf)$$

Where: Bi = Beta or Market Risk for the industry type
Rm = Rate of Return on Market Index
Rf = Risk-free Rate of Return

1.4 Recommended Technique for Estimating Hurdle Rate for Each Subsidiary

As discussed in the previous section, it is highly desirable to adjust project hurdle rates for the particular risk characteristics associated with projects undertaken by individual firms in the holding group. Using estimated beta values for each industry, and the formulae proposed in section 5, hurdle rates for each wholly owned subsidiary have been calculated. Calculations are presented in Appendix 2. An estimated hurdle rate for Lennox Distributors is also included, as one of the proposals under consideration is the purchase of this business. A discount rate that takes account of the risk profile of Lennox should be used when making an evaluation of the proposal to purchase the business.

Following the estimation of appropriate hurdle rates for each subsidiary company, each proposed investment should be evaluated against a risk-adjusted rate that is appropriate for the industry type. This further adjustment will ensure more accurate decision-making. The investment proposals, their appropriate hurdle rates and each recommendation are listed in Appendix 3.

2.1 The Problem with Forecast Error

Investment appraisal calculations are based on forecast annual net cash inflows that result from a proposed investment. Net cash inflows will normally result from an increase in sales revenue, less associated extra expenses. A typical expectation will be that a proposed investment will have an impact over a considerable number of years into the future. As a result, since the future cannot be forecast with certainty, there will always be a likelihood that forecast future net cash inflows will not be correct. Also, levels of uncertainty regarding forecast future inflows will probably increase, as it becomes necessary to estimate outcomes further into the future.

In practice, many businesses will initially estimate a Payback Period for every proposed investment, and will require all proposals to return the initial investment within a specified period before there can be a detailed evaluation of their suitability. It will be assumed that only forecast net cash inflows within this period can be regarded as being predictable with any degree of certainty. Cash-flows after this date are considered to be so unpredictable that they should not form part of the initial evaluation. By requiring payback within a stipulated period, the understanding is that a business can at least expect the return of its initial investment. Clearly, the Payback Period will not be a sufficient indicator of which investment proposals are suitable. It takes no regard of the yearly timing of net cash inflows within this period; it also takes no account of cash-flows after this date. As a result, it is generally accepted that net present value and/or internal rate of return are required when an appraisal is being conducted. However, as neither technique takes account of the potential inaccuracy of forecast net cash inflows, further, more detailed assessments are desirable.

A useful place to start is with a series of 'what if?' questions. This requires answering questions regarding what will happen to the proposed investment in various circumstances. Typical questions will include: 'what if costs are higher than expected?'; 'what if a competitor enters the market?'; and 'what if there is a decline in the overall market for this particular product or service?' An answer to any of these questions should determine whether a proposal is likely to remain profitable if unexpected negative outcomes influence predicted net cash inflows. As any proposal is based on estimates, and uncertainty is a concern, it may be possible to undertake further research to reduce uncertainty. For example, it may be possible to improve the accuracy of estimated sales levels through additional market research. Ultimately, there will be a trade-off between the value and the cost of any further analysis that is undertaken. But even though it will never be possible to remove all uncertainty, it is still desirable that reasonable attempts are made to reduce uncertainty regarding likely outcomes of a proposal through answering the 'what if' questions.

Sensitivity analysis provides the means to determine what might be the impact on profitability, should any 'what if' events occur. In order to do this, the components of each forecast annual net cash inflow are identified. Typically, it will be comprised of forecast cash in (normally sales revenues) and forecast cash out (normally a combination of fixed and variable costs). For each forecast, optimistic, expected and pessimistic forecast outcomes are identified. It is then possible to prepare a series of forecast annual net cash inflows, depending on the expected outcome. As a final stage, a net present value and/or an internal rate of return are estimated for each outcome. This allows the identification of a range of possible results, dependent on actual outcome. A final decision will then depend on the level of confidence with which a profitable outcome can be predicted.

Clearly, this approach will improve the quality of decision-taking. It does, however, still retain a number of drawbacks. An outcome can be somewhat ambiguous, as there is no clear definition of what is meant by pessimistic and optimistic. This difficulty may be reduced if probabilities can be attached to each. Another problem is that underlying inputs (forecast cash inflows and forecast cash outflows) may be interrelated. For example, if sales revenues are below expected levels, this may be because of reduced volumes, so that it is possible that costs will also change. Forecasts based on optimistic or pessimistic outcomes for all inputs are therefore likely to provide the most useful inputs to decision-making.

2.2 Evaluation of the Proposed Investment by Fasnet

Detailed calculations are presented in Appendix 4, based on forecast assumptions regarding expected sales revenues and operating costs. They also allow for estimated further working capital requirements, and for a projected sales value of the equipment, when it is disposed of at the end of the project life. A company tax rate of 15% is included, and tax payments are assumed to be made in the same year as estimated profits. Also, it is assumed that forecast project losses in any year can be allowed against other profits reported by the division. An after-tax hurdle rate of 12% is employed. The appropriate hurdle rate for Fasnet had previously been estimated as 11.66% (note Appendix 2). A slight upward adjustment is to account for any possible error in the estimation of cost of capital.

As is the normal convention, cash-flows are assumed to arrive at the end of each year. Estimated net present value is €18,790, and internal rate of return is 13.11%. A positive NPV is therefore forecast, and IRR is above the hurdle rate. Normally, the recommendation would be that this proposal is profitable, and that it should therefore be supported. It should be noted however that the forecast positive NPV is very small, and that project IRR is only marginally above the hurdle rate.

2.3 Sensitivity Analysis of the Proposed Investment by Fasnet

As there is a single set of alternative assumptions regarding future cash revenues and costs, they should be used to prepare an initial sensitivity analysis. It is therefore assumed that annual sales revenues are 5% lower than expected. Also, it is assumed that operating costs will represent 50% of sales.

Calculations based on these alternative assumptions are presented in Appendix 5. All other inputs to the calculation are assumed to remain unaffected. In this case, estimated net present value is -€52,240, and estimated internal rate of return is 8.82%. Based on these pessimistic assumptions, a negative NPV is forecast, and IRR is also forecast to be below the required hurdle rate. These results indicate an unprofitable investment proposal that should be rejected. It should also be noted that forecast negative NPV is sizeable and that IRR is considerably below the hurdle rate.

On balance, a correct recommendation is that this proposal should be rejected. Based on expected outcomes, it is only marginally profitable, however when calculations are based on the pessimistic forecast of sales revenues falling below projections, and of costs being higher than expected, a sizeable level of losses is predicted. A reasonable implication is that, even if forecast outcomes fall even slightly below expected levels, this proposal will be unprofitable. There is therefore a considerable risk of losses, and the proposal should be rejected.

A more complete sensitivity analysis is desirable, to take account of other possible outcomes. For example, an optimistic outcome is possible when sales revenues are above expectations. If, under these circumstances, a highly profitable outcome could be expected, this might impact on the recommendation not to invest. However, there would need to be a reasonably strong possibility of such an outcome before the recommendation should be altered. This is due to the fact that, if the pessimistic outcome were experienced, there is an exposure to considerable losses.

Ideally, if percentage probabilities could be attached to all expected outcomes, it might be possible to develop a more precise analysis of the likely result. Although this clearly is attractive, it must be remembered that the quantitative analysis is based on forecast outcomes that will always be subject to a degree of error. It may not be appropriate to assign quantitative values to what actually are no more than projected outcomes.

Appendix 1: Proposed Acquisition of Company XYZ by Holding Group ABC

Summary Data:

	Holding Group ABC	Company XYZ
Annual Earnings	€100m	€30m
No. of Shares Outstanding	100m	50m
Earnings Per Share	€1	€0.60
Price/Earnings	10	13
Share Price	€10.00	€7.80

Holding Group ABC makes offer for shares in Company XYZ.
The terms are a share-for-share exchange, based on current market values.
Transfer Ratio: €7.80 / €10.00, i.e. 0.78:1.00.
The number of new ABC Shares issued: 0.78 × 50m = 39m.

Workings:
The Impact on Earnings per Share, and possibly on Share Price.

Before:
E.P.S.: €100M / 100M = €1
Sh. Price: 10 X €1 = €10

After:
E.P.S.: €100M + €30M / 100M + 39M = €130M / 139M = €0.93
Sh. Price: 10 × €0.93 = €9.30

The implication is that if an acquisition of XYZ is made on these terms, ABC will suffer a decline in Earnings per Share, and may also experience a fall in share value.

Appendix 2: Estimation of Hurdle Rates for Individual Subsidiaries in the Tannam Group

Tannam Ltd (B =1.9)

$Ke = Rf = Bi(Rm - Rf)$, so
$Ke = 6 + 1.9(13-6) = 19.3$

$WACC = (D/V)Kd(1-T) + (E/V)Ke$, so

WACC = (0.175)8.5+(0.035)11.05+(0.09)7.65+(0.14)10.2+(0.56)19.3=14.9

The after-tax hurdle rate is 14.9%

Spollen Properties Ltd (B=2.2)

$Ke = Rf + Bi(Rm - Rf)$
$Ke = 6 + 2.2(13 - 6) = 21.4$

$$WACC = \left(D/V\right)Kd(1-T) + \left(E/V\right)Ke, \text{ so}$$
$$WACC = (0.175)8.5 + (0.035)11.05 + (0.09)7.65 + (0.14)10.2 + (0.56)21.4 = 15.97$$

The after-tax hurdle rate is 15.97%

CGU Distributors Ltd (B=0.7)

$$Ke = Rf + Bi(Rm - Rf), \text{ so}$$
$$Ke = 6 + 0.7(13 - 6) = 10.9$$

$$WACC = \left(D/V\right)Kd(1-T) + \left(E/V\right)Ke, \text{ so}$$
$$WACC = (0.175)8.5 + (0.035)11.05 + (0.09)7.65 + (0.14)10.2 + (0.56)10.9 = 10.09$$

The after-tax hurdle rate is 10.09%

Fasnet Media Services Ltd (B=1.1)

$$Ke = Rf + Bi(Rm - Rf), \text{ so}$$
$$Ke = 6 + 1.1(13 - 6) = 13.7$$

$$WACC = \left(D/V\right)Kd(1-T) + \left(E/V\right)Ke, \text{ so}$$
$$WACC = (0.175)8.5 + (0.035)11.05 + (0.09)7.65 + (0.14)10.2 + (0.56)13.7 = 11.66$$

The after-tax hurdle rate is 11.66%

Quirke Construction Ltd (B=1.8)

$$Ke = Rf + Bi(Rm - Rf), \text{ so}$$
$$Ke = 6 + 1.8(13 - 6) = 18.6$$

$$WACC = \left(D/V\right)Kd(1-T) + \left(E/V\right)Ke, \text{ so}$$
$$WACC = (0.175)8.5 + (0.035)11.05 + (0.09)7.65 + (0.14)10.2 + (0.56)18.6 = 14.4$$

The after-tax hurdle rate is 14.4%

Kenge Haulage Ltd (B=1.3)

$$Ke = Rf + Bi(Rm - Rf), \text{ so}$$
$$Ke = 6 + 1.3(13 - 6) = 15.1$$

$$WACC = \left(D/V\right)Kd(1-T) + \left(E/V\right)Ke, \text{ so}$$
$$WACC = (0.175)8.5 + (0.035)11.05 + (0.09)7.65 + (0.14)10.2 + (0.56)15.1 = 12.44$$

The after-tax hurdle rate is 12.44%

Tress Ltd (B=0.6)

$Ke = Rf + Bi(Rm - Rf)$, so

$Ke = 6 + 0.6(13 - 6) = 10.2$

$WACC = (D/V)Kd(1-T) + (E/V)Ke$, so

$WACC = (0.175)8.5 + (0.035)11.05 + (0.09)7.65 + (0.14)10.2 + (0.56)10.2 = 9.7$

The after-tax hurdle rate is 9.7%

Cross Timber Ltd (B=0.8)

$Ke = Rf + Bi(Rm - Rf)$, so

$Ke = 6 + 0.8(13 - 6) = 11.6$

$WACC = (D/V)Kd(1-T) + (E/V)Ke$, so

$WACC = (0.175)8.5 + (0.035)11.05 + (0.09)7.65 + (0.14)10.2 + (0.56)11.6 = 10.48$

The after-tax hurdle rate is 10.48

Image Consultants Ltd (B=1.7)

$Ke = Rf + Bi(Rm - Rf)$, so

$Ke = 6 + 1.7(13 - 6) = 17.9$

$WACC = (D/V)Kd(1-T) + (E/V)Ke$, so

$WACC = (0.175)8.5 + (0.035)11.05 + (0.09)7.65 + (0.14)10.2 + (0.56)17.9 = 14.01$

The after-tax hurdle rate is 14.01%

Laheen Refrigerators (B=1.0)

$Ke = Rf + Bi(Rm - Rf)$, so

$Ke = 6 + 1.0(13 - 6) = 13.0$

$WACC = (D/V)Kd(1-T) + (E/V)Ke$, so

$WACC = (0.175)8.5 + (0.035)11.05 + (0.09)7.65 + (0.14)10.2 + (0.56)13.0 = 11.27$

The after-tax hurdle rate is 11.27%

Lennox Distributors (B=0.9)

$Ke = Rf + Bi(Rm - Rf)$, so

$Ke = 6 + 0.9(13 - 6) = 12.3$

$WACC = (D/V)Kd(1-T) + (E/V)Ke$, so

$$WACC = (0.175)8.5 + (0.035)11.05 + (0.09)7.65 + (0.14)10.2 + (0.56)12.3 = 10.87$$

The after-tax hurdle rate is 10.87%

Appendix 3: The Investment Proposals, Hurdle Rates and Recommendations

	Hurdle Rate (%)	IRR (%)	Invest Y or N
Improved Retail Premises – Tannam	19.3	17	N
New Electrical Equipment – Tannam	19.3	15	N
New Fleet – Kenge Haulage	12.44	16	Y
Warehouse Facility – Tress	9.7	11	Y
New Office Building – Image Consultants	14.01	17	Y
Computer Equipment – Cross Timber	10.48	16	Y
Land Purchase – Spollen Properties	15.97	15	N
Expanded Storage – Laheen	11.27	14	Y
Head Office Building – Quirke Construction	14.4	13	N
Purchase of Lennox Distributors	10.87	12	Y*

* Internal rate of return on Lennox Distributors is only marginally above the estimated hurdle rate. As the estimation process will be subject to error, the decision to purchase this business must be highly marginal.

Appendix 4: Appraisal of Proposed Investment by Fasnet Services (Sales Revenues are Assumed to be as Expected)

All figures are €000s

Year	0	1	2	3	4	5
Revenue	0.0000	2.0000	3.4000	4.0000	4.0000	2.4000
Working capital	0.2000	0.3400	0.4000	0.4000	0.2400	0.0000
Change in Wk Cap	0.2000	0.1400	0.0600	0.0000	−0.1600	−0.2400
Revenue	0.0000	2.0000	3.4000	4.0000	4.0000	2.4000
Expense	0.0000	0.9000	1.5300	1.8000	1.8000	1.0800
Depreciation	0.0000	1.1700	1.1700	1.1700	1.1700	1.1700
Pre-tax profit	0.0000	−0.0700	0.7000	1.0300	1.0300	0.1500
Tax	0.0000	0.0105	−0.1050	−0.1545	−0.1545	−0.0225
After-tax profit	0.0000	−0.0595	0.5950	0.8755	0.8755	0.1275

Appendix 4: *(continued)*

CF from operations	0.0000	1.1105	1.7650	2.0455	2.0455	1.2975
Cash-flow						
CF: capital investments	−5.8500	0.0000	0.0000	0.0000	0.0000	0.4973
CF from Wk Cap	−0.2000	−0.1400	−0.0600	0.0000	0.1600	0.2400
CF from operations	0.0000	1.1105	1.7650	2.0455	2.0455	1.2975
TOTAL	−6.0500	0.9705	1.705	2.0455	2.2055	2.0348
Discount Factor (12%)	1.0000	0.8929	0.7972	0.7118	0.6355	0.5674
PV @ 12%	−6.0500	0.8665	1.3592	1.4559	1.4016	1.1546
Net present value	0.1879					
Internal rate of return	13.11%					

Appendix 5: Appraisal of Proposed Investment by Fasnet Services (Sales Revenues are Assumed to be 95% of Expected)

All figures are €000s

Year	0	1	2	3	4	5
Revenue	0.0000	1.9000	3.2300	3.8000	3.8000	2.2800
Working capital	0.1900	0.3230	0.3800	0.3800	0.2280	0.0000
Change in Wk Cap	0.1900	0.1330	0.0570	0.0000	−0.1520	−0.2280
Revenue	0.0000	1.9000	3.2300	3.8000	3.8000	2.2800
Expense	0.0000	0.9500	1.6150	1.9000	1.9000	1.1400
Depreciation	0.0000	1.1700	1.1700	1.1700	1.1700	1.1700
Pre-tax profit	0.0000	−0.2200	0.4450	0.7300	0.7300	−0.0300
Tax	0.0000	0.0330	−0.0667	−0.1095	−0.1095	0.0045
After-tax profit	0.0000	−0.1870	0.3783	0.6205	0.6205	−0.0255
CF from operations	0.0000	0.9830	1.5483	1.7905	1.7905	1.1445
Cash-flow						
CF: capital investments	−5.8500	0.0000	0.0000	0.0000	0.0000	0.49725
CF from Wk Cap	−0.1900	−0.1330	−0.0570	0.0000	0.1520	0.2280
CF from operations	0.0000	0.9830	1.5483	1.9705	1.7905	1.1445
TOTAL	−6.0400	0.8500	1.4913	1.7905	1.9425	1.8698
Discount Factor (12%)	1.0000	0.8929	0.7972	0.7118	0.6355	0.5674
PV @ 12%	−6.0400	0.7589	1.1888	1.2744	1.2345	1.0609
Net present value	−0.5224					
Internal rate of return	8.82%					

Case 24
Solution to Salmon Spray
Ray Donnelly, University College Cork

1. Criteria for Evaluation of the Project

Introduction

The correct criterion for the project's evaluation can only be determined in the light of the objectives of Salmon Spray. It is normal to assume that Salmon Spray wishes to maximise shareholder wealth. It is clear that Ms. Pitt is mindful of the Board's attitude. It is not unreasonable to assume that the latter will be determined, at least in part, by the shareholders to whom they must report on an annual basis. It may well be that the Board is interested in profits only insofar as they affect the share price.

Jack McBride is quite correct to use the net present value (NPV) analysis. The main reason for using the NPV criterion is that its use is entirely consistent with the objective of maximising shareholder wealth. If a firm with a value of €100 million takes on a project with an NPV of €10 million, it will then be worth €110 million. This should help keep the shareholders and the Board happy. Also, any positive NPV project will eventually yield enhanced profits as its cash-flows come to be recognised by the accounting system. Thus, if the project truly has a positive NPV, profits *will* be enhanced. As we will see below, profitability is a necessary but not a sufficient condition for a project to add value to a company.

Net Present Value

As well as being consistent with the objectives of the company, the NPV approach has the following advantages:

- it recognises the cost of capital and the time value of money;
- it has as clear decision rule: accept projects with NPV > 0 and if projects are mutually exclusive, choose the one with the highest NPV.

It is clear that the NPV is the theoretically correct investment appraisal criteria for firms whose objective is to maximise value and hence owners' wealth. This is the crucial point; its advantages over other methods also include the following:

1. It recognises the time value of money – unlike the accounting rate of return (ROR).
2. It is generally easy to use.
3. It can deal with multiple discount rates – unlike internal rate of return (IRR) or ROR.
4. It is not affected by differences of scale – unlike the Profitability Index, ROR or IRR.
5. The discipline of estimating future cash-flows makes for better capital budgeting decisions.

However, the NPV cannot deal with strategic options without adaptation. When using NPV everything is not as cut-and-dried as the calculations might lead one to expect. However, every complication that has been mentioned with regard to the use of NPV can also be attributed to ROR. Yet some of the problems with ROR do not apply to NPV. The latter is the most theoretically correct and versatile tool for the evaluation of investments.

NPV is difficult to use in later performance evaluation of managers – the ROR is easy to use (and misuse) in this regard. EVA® or residual income (RI) may be of use as an ex-post measure of whether managers are enhancing company value. This method adjusts accounting profits to reflect the fact that the capital used to generate them is not free. In particular, it levies a charge for capital used against profits. It can be reconciled with the NPV criterion since the PV of RI is the same as the NPV of the cash-flows.

Summary

In summary, the NPV rule is consistent with the objectives of maximising shareholder wealth. It imposes a good discipline in project evaluation in that it forces management to carefully consider the future in order to quantify the cash-flows arising from a project. But, using the NPV rule will never be a substitute for good business analysis, i.e. the manager must know his business. If someone cannot make informed estimates of future business conditions and their associated cash-flows, all the sophisticated techniques in the world will not prevent them making incorrect choices.

2. Evaluation of the Project

The first step here is to compute the appropriate cost of capital. This will be the project's cost of capital. For the Spanish project we estimate the project's cost of capital as the average cost of capital for the preserved fruit industry. The equity beta is 0.9, but this reflects both business and financial risk. The debt to equity ratio is 0.5, so debt to total value (D/V) is 0.33. Thus, letting E equal equity value, if we make the standard assumption that the beta of debt is zero, the asset beta is: E/V × 0.9 = 2/3 × 0.9 = 0.6. Applying the CAPM ($E(R_i) = R_f + \beta(R_m - R_f)$) gives 6 + 0.6(5) = 9%.

The same approach is taken to computing the cost of capital for the Polish project. The beta for fish processing is 1.3. This is unlevered to get 1.3 × 2/3 = 0.867. Using the Security Market Line, this gives an expected return equal to 6 + 0.867(5) = 10.33. This reflects the higher risk of the fish-processing industry.

The incremental cash-flows from the Spanish project are outlined in Appendix 1. When these cash-flows are discounted at the cost of capital, the project has an NPV of €54.75 million. This is the amount by which the value of the company should increase if the project is taken. Appendix 4 shows that, despite being profitable in every year, the NPV of the Polish project is negative. How this can come about is explained in the answer to 3: below.

3. Reconciliation of NPV and Profitability

It is not appropriate to evaluate projects solely on profits. To do so ignores that capital has to be invested to earn the profits and this capital, which is provided by shareholders, is not costless. After all, the shareholders could put their money into other investments which yield a rate of return. Thus, capital clearly has an opportunity cost. This fact has not escaped Penny. Rather than just focusing on profits, she has considered the accounting rate of return (ROR). This is simply the average annual profits, divided by the initial investment. It has the merit of taking cognisance of the fact that profits or returns must in some way be related to the level of investment required to generate them. However, the ROR has weaknesses. First, it ignores the time value of money, that is, cash today is worth more than the same amount of cash in the future. Since the current project spans several years, this is clearly a problem. Secondly, it is ambiguous with regard to the hurdle rate, that is, what is an acceptable ROR? If a firm wished to maximise its ROR, it would simply invest in one project – that with the highest ROR. It is axiomatic that this may lead to sub-optimal decisions since many projects which may fall short of the maximum ROR will be acceptable. An alternative is to compare the ROR with the company's cost of capital. It is demonstrated below that with some further modification to take account of the time value of money, this may be a reasonable way to adjust the ROR criterion. There is another problem with ROR in that its definition is ambiguous. If we are to reconcile it with NPV, we have to be very specific regarding how we compute it.

The Profitability of the Spanish Project

We have included the residual income for the Spanish project calculation for the benefit of Sir Rex, Penny and the Board (see Appendix 2). It is clear from Appendix 2 the present value of residual income is exactly the same as the NPV of the project.

Residual income (RI) is the net profit each year minus a capital charge. The capital charge is the book value of the project *at the beginning of the year (BVt-1)* multiplied by the cost of capital. Thus, RI is a measure of the profitability of the project. RI has the advantage that it is a better ex-post measure of managerial performance than cash flows.[4] An alternative way of computing RI is to compute the ROR as Earnings/BVt-1 and RI then becomes (ROR - Cost of Capital) × BVt-1. This is done in Appendix 3 and we observe that the residual income in each year is the same as in Appendix 2. Thus, assuming a positive opening book value, if ROR is higher than the cost of capital, residual income will be positive. Through residual income we see that there is a clear link between a project's profitability and its NPV. Provided the annual ROR, as computed above, is consistently greater than the cost of capital, the project will have a positive present value of residual income and a positive NPV. Thus, Penny is correct to focus on the rate of return for a project since this reflects the fact that capital is not free. However, annual ROR on its own does not mean a lot. A point that should be made is that the reduction in overall ROR of the company if this project is taken is not necessarily a bad thing. The project analysis should not be confused by considering the profitability of *independent* existing projects. It must be benchmarked against the cost of capital not the average rate of return of existing projects. We also notice that the average annual ROR is only 17.2%. Why, then, is a project with such a low rate of return desirable? Mainly because it has a lower risk that Salmon Spray's other business, as evidenced by the lower beta. Thus, the expected rate of return or cost of capital is lower for this project than for other projects in the company. In addition, in order to draw meaningful inferences annual residual income should be calculated and discounted to reflect the time value of money, as in Appendix 3.

Why the Polish Project is Not Viable

It is clear that the Polish project is profitable. However, it is also clear from Appendix 4 that profits are not of a sufficient size to justify the investment. This is because the cost of capital is greater than the ROR in every year. This is reflected in the residual income of the project, which is negative in each year. Accordingly, the present value of residual income (i.e. NPV) is negative and the project should not be accepted. Penny is correct: the profits from the Polish venture are not of sufficient size to justify the investment.

4. Assessment of Jack's Approach

Jack uses the NPV approach, which is theoretically the correct approach to take. He discounts nominal cash-flows at the nominal rate of interest and finds that the Spanish project has a positive NPV so indicates the correct decision to take.

By ignoring cash-flows after year five, Jack is implicitly assuming that these cash-flows provide a rate of return equal to the cost of capital and, thus, that their NPV

---

4 However, RI does suffer from the same allocation problems as accounting profit.

is zero. His assumption that the project will eventually only earn a return equal to the cost of capital is consistent with economic theory, but we would have preferred a more detailed analysis here.

We note that using the approach where RI is computed as (ROR - Cost of Capital) × BV_{t-1} makes it more explicit why Jack used a five-year horizon for a project that continues for far longer. He is suggesting that while the project will continue to be profitable from year six onwards, the rate of profitability will only compensate for the opportunity cost of capital, so from year six onwards the project does not add value to Salmon Spray. That is, ROR eventually declines to equal the cost of capital, presumably due to increased competition, and the RI falls to zero. Appendix 5 shows how a project can continue to be profitable and add no further value to the firm. The figures presented here illustrate that a project will have an NPV of zero when ROR is equal to the cost of capital.

One of the major difficulties of using the NPV rule is the estimation of the appropriate cost of capital. (This difficulty is also a facet of the use of ROR.) The correct discount rate is that which reflects the risk of the cash-flows that are being discounted. Jack has chosen the borrowing rate. This is not appropriate since it reflects the risk to a bank of lending money to Salmon Spray, not the risk of the cash-flows from the new project. Salmon Spray should use the project's, not the company's, cost of capital. The Capital Asset Pricing Model (CAPM) provides a method of calculating the project's cost of capital. However, it is not clear that *all* the shareholders are well diversified. Therefore, beta may not be the appropriate measure of risk for all the shareholders. A conflict may occur! The analysis in section (2), above, details the computation of the correct discount rate for the project on the assumption that Salmon Spray's shareholders are well diversified. However, it may well be that Penelope is not well diversified and will see the risk of the project in a different light from the other shareholders.

Consideration should also be given to the potential financing side-effects of the project (see answer to 5. below).

5. Investment and Financing Decisions

The capital structure aspects of the investment and their interaction with the investment itself need to be considered. Specifically, one needs to consider the impact of the project on the capital structure of the company. Note that one *cannot* attach a particular type of financing to a specific project. This is because a company needs a balance of debt and equity, so to suggest that one project is financed by debt and another by equity is totally incorrect. What is relevant, however, is the impact that a project has on the *company's* debt capacity, i.e. how does it affect the optimal capital structure? The project may allow some borrowing. It is clear that Salmon Spray is not geared at the moment, so is not exploiting the tax advantages of borrowing. The new Spanish plant may well provide some collateral to borrow against and a five-year loan might be considered. The tax shield provided by this loan would probably enhance the NPV of the project.

6. Sensitivity Analysis and Computation of IRR

The calculation of 9% for cost of capital is only an estimate of what the shareholders required rate of return is deemed to be. Estimating required rates of return is not a trivial matter and presents significant practical problems. Accordingly, there are two types of risk to take account of. First, the project's risk, which pertains to the fact that the cash-flows may not be as expected. This type of risk can be taken account of by adjusting the discount rate. The second type of risk relates to the fact that the discount rate itself is only an estimate. Interest rates and risk premia are not constant over time. Thus one would be tempted to establish how sensitive the project's NPV is to different discount rates. It must be stressed that this is entirely different from a scenario analysis where cash-flows would be low and interest rates high for the pessimistic scenario and vice versa for the optimistic scenario. The latter may be preferable if one is especially worried about downside risk. However, some sensitivity analysis has been done with respect to the interest rate and this is outlined in Appendix 6. This analysis does not give any cause for concern. It is clear that the project will have a negative NPV at a cost of capital of 21%, but it has a positive NPV if the discount rate is 20%. Accordingly, its IRR (the discount rate that makes NPV=0) is between 20% and 21%. It is actually 20.092% (see Appendix 6). Computing the margin between the IRR and the cost of capital is a shortcut method of establishing the sensitivity of a project to the discount rate (assuming the projected cash-flows are reasonably accurate). Salmon Spray needs to be confident that the cost of capital will not exceed 20% before proceeding. Since we estimate the project's cost of capital to be only 9%, which is far less than its IRR, there is a large margin for error in the computation of the discount rate. This sensitivity analysis confirms that the project is a good one from Salmon Spray's point of view.

7. Cash Surplus

If a company does not have sufficient cash, it has a problem. However, Penny seems to have a problem in that Salmon Spray has too much cash. It may be a problem for Penny, but it should not be a problem for the shareholders. If Salmon Spray cannot invest in positive NPV projects, it can return the cash to the shareholders either through a special dividend or a share repurchase. The problem from Penny's point of view is that a persistent excess of cash could be perceived as stemming from a paucity of ideas on her part regarding what to do with this capital. After all, shareholders can put money in the bank themselves; they do not need Salmon Spray to do this for them. Also, a company with a cash mountain may become a takeover target. This is a good scenario for the shareholders but not for management. The former can expect to receive a premium for their stock in the company and the latter might expect to lose their employment.

It is clear that if Salmon Spray did not have a project like the Spanish one, it should return the surplus cash to the shareholders. Penny, unlike the outside shareholders, does not appear to want the increased dividend. Thus, there is a potential conflict of interest here. Other conflicts are outlined in the next section.

8. Conflicts of Interest

The project here does *not* seem to be conglomerate diversification in that the technologies for canning seafood and fruit and vegetables should be similar. Thus, the project is probably not an opportunity that the shareholders could replicate themselves. Note also that while the CAPM would seem to suggest that conglomerate diversification is not in shareholders' interests, this model is derived assuming perfect capital markets. Accordingly, it precludes the possibility of bankruptcy costs. Thus, *some* diversification at firm level may be of benefit to well-diversified shareholders if it reduces that probability of bankruptcy and the associated costs. However, as discussed above, bankruptcy does not seem a likely scenario given the low financial risk of Salmon Spray.

There are also conflicts of interest between Penny, who is an insider, and the outside shareholders. The latter are only interested in maximising their wealth, whereas Salmon Spray means more to Penny than a mere investment. Furthermore, she has all of her human capital tied up in Salmon Spray. If she has not diversified her financial assets, she will have a very different perception of the risk of the project and beta will not be a good risk measure from her perspective.

Appendix 1: Calculation of NPV of Spanish Project

€ millions

Time	0	1	2	3	4	5
Capital Cost	−199.5					
Sale of Land		20				
Extension of Factory		−20				
Fruit Contribution		115	125	145	155	160
Olive Oil Contribution		83	73	53	33	33
Fixed Costs		−105	−100	−100	−120	−131
Legal fees	−0.5					
Salaries		−18	−18	−18	−18	−22
Rent		−5				
Net Cash Flow	−200	70	80	80	50	40
$(1+R)^t$		1.09	1.19	1.30	1.41	1.54
DCF	−200.00	64.22	67.33	61.77	35.42	26.00
Cumulative DCF		−135.78	−68.45	−6.67	28.75	54.75

The net present value is the cumulative DCF at the end of the five years, i.e. €54.75 million.

Appendix 2: Residual Income and NPV of Spanish Project

€ millions

Time	0	1	2	3	4	5
Net Cash Flow	−200	70	80	80	50	40
Depreciation (1000/5)		40.00	40.00	40.00	40.00	40.00
Profit		30.00	40.00	40.00	10.00	0.00
BV_{t-1}		200.00	160.00	120.00	80.00	40.00
Residual income		12.00	25.60	29.20	2.80	−3.60
$(1+R)^t$		1.09	1.19	1.30	1.41	1.54
DCF	−200.00	64.22	67.33	61.77	35.42	26.00
Cumulative DCF		−135.78	−68.45	−6.67	28.75	**54.75**
Discounted RI		11.01	21.55	22.55	1.98	−2.34
Cumulative Discounted Residual Income		11.01	32.56	55.10	57.09	**54.75**

The present value of residual income is the same as the NPV, i.e. €54.75 million.

Appendix 3: Residual Income and Rate of Return

€ millions

Time	0	1	2	3	4	5
Net Cash-flow	−200	70	80	80	50	40
Depreciation (1000/5)		40.00	40.00	40.00	40.00	40.00
Profit		30.00	40.00	40.00	10.00	0.00
Opening Book Value		200.00	160.00	120.00	80.00	40.00
ROR		0.15	0.25	0.333333	0.125	0
Cost of Capital		0.09	0.09	0.09	0.09	0.09
ROR − Cost of Capital		0.06	0.16	0.243333	0.035	−0.09
Residual Inc. BVt-1 × (ROR−COC)		12	25.6	29.2	2.8	−3.6
$(1+R)^t$		1.09	1.19	1.30	1.41	1.54
DCF		11.01	21.55	22.55	1.98	−2.34
Cumulative Residual Income		11.01	32.56	55.10	57.09	**54.75**

Appendix 4: Extension of Fish-processing to Poland

€ millions

Time	0	1	2	3	4	5
Cash-flows	−200.00	56.00	52.00	48.00	44.00	41.00
Depreciation (200/5)		40.00	40.00	40.00	40.00	40.00
Profit		16.00	12.00	8.00	4.00	1.00
BVt-1		200.00	160.00	120.00	80.00	40.00
Residual Income (Profit − COC × BVt-1)		−4.66	−4.53	−4.40	−4.26	−3.13
$(1+R)^t$		1.103	1.22	1.34	1.48	1.63
DCF	−200.00	50.76	42.72	35.74	29.69	25.08
Cumulative DCF		−149.24	−106.52	−70.78	−41.09	−16.01
ROR		0.080	0.075	0.067	0.050	0.025
Cost of Capital		0.103	0.103	0.103	0.103	0.103
ROR − COC		−0.023	−0.028	−0.037	−0.053	−0.078
RI = BVt-1 × (ROR−COC)		−4.660	−4.528	−4.396	−4.264	−3.132
Discounted RI		−4.224	−3.720	−3.273	−2.878	−1.916
Cumulative Discounted Residual Income		−4.224	−7.943	−11.217	−14.094	**−16.010**

The NPV is negative, so this project will destroy value despite being profitable. Note that the discount rate is higher here, reflecting a greater level of risk than the Spanish project.

Appendix 5: Earning a rate of return equal to the cost of capital from year six

This appendix illustrates how Jack's assumption of a project (company) earning a rate of return equal to the cost of capital adds nothing to value. Let us assume that after five years Salmon Spray needs to invest another €500 million to replace and update some equipment to keep the Spanish canning factories in operation for a further five years. The table below shows that the project continues to be profitable in each of years six to 10. However, the ROR is equal to the cost of capital and RI is therefore zero. This means that the project just earns a fair rate of return and its NPV is zero.

			€ millions			
Time	5	6	7	8	9	10
Cash-flows	−500.00	145.00	136.00	127.00	118.00	109.00
Depreciation (1000/5)		100.00	100.00	100.00	100.00	100.00
Profit		45.00	36.00	27.00	18.00	9.00
NPV of Cash-flows @ 9%	0.00					
BVt-1		500.00	400.00	300.00	200.00	100.00
ROI		0.09	0.09	0.09	0.09	0.09
Residual Income		0.00	0.00	0.00	0.00	0.00
NPV of RI @ 9%	0.00					
$(1+R)^t$		1.09	1.19	1.30	1.41	1.54
DCF	−500.00	133.03	114.47	98.07	83.59	70.84
Cumulative DCF		−366.97	−252.50	−154.44	−70.84	**0.00**
ROI		0.09	0.09	0.09	0.09	0.09
Cumulative ROI	0.45					
Average ROI per annum	0.09					
Discounted RI		0.00	0.00	0.00	0.00	0.00
Cumulative Discounted Residual Income		0.00	0.00	0.00	0.00	0.00

Appendix 6: Sensitivity Analysis

€ millions

		1	2	3	4	5	Cost of Capital
Cash-flows	−200	70.00	80.00	80.00	50.00	40.00	
$(1+R)^t$		1.09	1.19	1.30	1.41	1.54	0.09
DCF	−200	64.22	67.33	61.77	35.42	26.00	1.09
Cumulative DCF		−135.78	−68.45	−6.67	28.75	54.75	
Cash-flows	−200	70	80	80	50	40	
$(1+R)^t$		1.10	1.21	1.33	1.46	1.61	0.10
DCF	−200	63.64	66.12	60.11	34.15	24.84	1.10
Cumulative DCF		−136.36	−70.25	−10.14	24.01	48.84	
Cash-flows	−200	70	80	80	50	40	
$(1+R)^t$		1.11	1.23	1.37	1.52	1.69	0.11
DCF	−200	63.06	64.93	58.50	32.94	23.74	1.11
Cumulative DCF		−136.94	−72.01	−13.51	19.42	43.16	
Cash-flows	−200	70	80	80	50	40	
$(1+R)^t$		1.12	1.25	1.40	1.57	1.76	0.12
DCF	−200	62.50	63.78	56.94	31.78	22.70	1.12
Cumulative DCF		−137.50	−73.72	−16.78	14.99	37.69	
Cash-flows	−200	70	80	80	50	40	
$(1+R)^t$		1.16	1.35	1.56	1.81	2.10	0.16
DCF	−200	60.34	59.45	51.25	27.61	19.04	1.16
Cumulative DCF		−139.66	−80.20	−28.95	−1.33	17.71	
Cash-flows	−200	70	80	80	50	40	
$(1+R)^t$		1.20	1.44	1.73	2.07	2.49	0.20
DCF	−200	58.33	55.56	46.30	24.11	16.08	1.20
Cumulative DCF		−141.67	−86.11	−39.81	−15.70	0.37	
Cash-flows	−200	70	80	80	50	40	
$(1+R)^t$		1.21	1.46	1.77	2.14	2.59	0.21
DCF	−200	57.85	54.64	45.16	23.33	15.42	1.21
Cumulative DCF		−142.15	−87.51	−42.35	−19.02	−3.60	
20.092388%	= IRR						
Cash-flows	−200	70	80	80	50	40	
$(1+R)^t$		1.20092	1.44	1.73	2.08	2.50	0.20092
DCF	−200	58.29	55.47	46.19	24.04	16.01	1.20092
Cumulative DCF		−141.71	−86.24	−40.05	−16.01	0.00	

Case 25
Solution to Waterlife plc
Evarist Stoja, University of Bristol

REPORT ON FINANCING DECISIONS CONCERNING WATERLIFE PLC

Prepared by: M. H.
Consultant

For: Board of Directors
Waterlife plc

1. Terms of Reference

Further to our previous discussion on the financing matters concerning your company, I am pleased to offer my advice. This report includes a calculation and discussion of Waterlife's actual capital structure and cost of capital, along with remarks regarding other related matters. I have based my advice on the data and comments I was given by the senior management. The calculation of cost of capital and capital structure and the associated discussion relates to situations that your company had faced in the past, is facing now and/or may face in the future. Further, the calculation and discussion of these matters considers the underpinning theory as well as the practical issues.

2. General Recommendations for Future Reference

Although in practice it is very difficult to separate the financing decision and investment decision (as well as the dividend decision) as they are intrinsically linked, analysis of capital structure (and cost of capital) should start from the assumption that the two are separate.

Market imperfections should be assumed away. This will provide the management with a useful framework to initiate the analysis and understand the implications of capital structure and cost of capital on firm value.

Once a clear conclusion of the impact (or lack of impact) of capital structure on firm value has been established, the next step should be to 'bring into the picture' the elements which were assumed away. For example, analyse the impact of taxes, increased risk that comes with debt financing, types of asset that a firm employs, information asymmetry between the managers and investors and so on, on income and ultimately firm value.

Adjust the firm's capital structure while considering adjustment costs, such as transactions costs and the lumpiness of security issues, as well as the most likely movements of security markets in the foreseeable future.

3. Issues Relating to the Weighted Average Cost of Capital (WACC) of Waterlife

Cost of equity, and ultimately WACC, is calculated employing the capital asset pricing model (CAPM). It is important to note that this model relies on many assumptions that do not always hold in practice and hence it is important to remember the model does not yield a precise estimate of cost of equity.

Although the market risk premium of 8% (see Appendix 1(a) for detailed calculations) is not particularly high, a beta of 1.5 is very high and Waterlife's stock can be classified as aggressive. What this means is that Waterlife's share price is very sensitive to the market movement. Nick is right to say that they are in a very sensitive industry. This implies that recoveries in the economy which will be accompanied by stock market buoyancy will lead to an even higher percentage increase in Waterlife's share price. Recessions of the economy, however, which will be accompanied by stock market pessimism, will lead to even higher percentage decreases in the firm's share price. This is done through the effect that beta has on the cost of capital and ultimately share price.

In this case, the cost of equity is 16%. If the market risk premium increases by 2%, this will lead to a 3% increase in cost of equity of Waterlife. The opposite is also true: a 2% decrease in market risk premium will lead to a 3% decrease in the cost of equity (see Appendix 1(b) for detailed calculations).

With a cost of equity of 16% and a cost of debt of 8%, accounting for the tax rate, Waterlife's WACC is 14.36% (see Appendix 1(c)). This estimate is based on the following:

- equity capital is estimated in market values rather than book values. The reason for this is that if capital structure matters, it impacts upon the market value of the firm and book value is of little help when valuing a firm;
- equity capital includes retained earnings. Although, this source of funds is not originally contributed by shareholders, it belongs to them as they are the owners

- of the company and own everything that is left after the firm meets all of its obligations;
- debt book value is the equivalent of market value as they are essentially the same thing as long as the firm is not in financial distress, which Waterlife is not;
- we exclude the short-term loan from the calculation of the proportion of debt on capital employed. This source of funds constitutes a relatively small part of the financing for Waterlife and is not very likely that it will make a large impact on the estimates of WACC. Further, we are more interested in long-term firm value. I do recognise, that the decision to omit short-term loan is somewhat arbitrary. Short-term debt, however, has the potential to lead to bankruptcy and ultimately liquidation.

It is true that Waterlife's cost of capital is relatively high, due mainly to a high equity beta. With its current leverage ratio of 15.8%, its WACC is 14.4%. It may be possible to reduce the WACC by employing more debt, provided it does not significantly increase financial distress risk (see example in Appendix 2).

From a theoretical viewpoint, this would not be possible. As argued by Modigliani and Miller (1958) ("MM") and cited by one of the directors, the cost of equity of a levered firm increases in proportion to the leverage ratio so that the WACC remains constant. This implies that no combination of debt and equity is better than any other. Analytically this is expressed as:

$\gamma equity = \gamma assets + D/E(\gamma assets - \gamma equity)$

MM's analysis and conclusions relate to a 'perfect world' where there are no distortions and/or imperfections. They assume, among other things, that there are no taxes, that borrowing rates are the same for all market participants and that they can borrow as much as they like regardless of current debt levels. In this perfect world, the board director would be right and the junior finance manager would be wrong: changing the capital structure does not lead to changes in the cost of capital and the value of Waterlife would remain constant regardless of the debt level it employs. Therefore, the senior management/board of directors can ignore capital structure issues and concentrate exclusively on investment decisions, such as expanding production capacity to serve a wider market.

This theory ignores many distortions of the real world, however, one of which is tax. The government allows Waterlife (and all of the other companies) to deduct interest expenses from the tax bill. In the Income Statement of Waterlife, this is shown by the fact that interest payable is paid before taxes and the tax bill is calculated as a percentage of earnings after interest payments. The deductibility of interest expense from the tax bill provides debt financing with a clear advantage over equity. Analytically, the weighed average cost of capital of Waterlife is:

$ACC = \gamma debt(D/V)(1-tax) + \gamma equity(E/V)$

This equation clearly shows that by increasing the leverage ratio, Waterlife would be able to decrease the WACC and hence cash-flows are now discounted at a lower rate, creating some extra value for shareholders. Therefore, we may conclude that once we account for taxes that Waterlife pays, increases in the leverage ratio lead to decreases in WACC. Therefore, from this perspective the junior finance manager is right.

4. Issues Relating to the Negative Prospects of the Economy and the Impact upon Financing Commitments

Waterlife, like other firms, runs operational and financial risk. Operational risk, otherwise known as business risk, refers to variability of operating income (or earnings before interest and tax – EBIT) due to adverse economic conditions. Financial risk refers to variability of earnings per share (EPS) due to debt financing. Debt financing increases uncertainty and hence risk of share returns. If EPS of Waterlife change, this will have a valuation impact upon its share price. If, for example, EPS decrease, this might make it difficult for Waterlife to maintain the same dividend payout ratio. Waterlife may be forced to reduce its dividend payments, which most likely will lead to decreases in share price. While this is clearly undesirable and will lead to a decreased demand for Waterlife shares, shareholders cannot force Waterlife to pay any dividends until it recovers. Eventually Waterlife may recover and increase its dividend payments to the previous level. The point here is that while dishonouring equity, financing commitments will have an undesirable effect on share price and shareholders may be reluctant to contribute fresh equity capital, but Waterlife will still be able to survive.

However, when adverse economic conditions lead to a lower EBIT than interest payments or generally when interest payments are just too high to be covered by EBIT, then this would not just have a valuation impact (share price decrease in this case). Therefore, looking at the Income Statement, if EBIT is equal to or less than interest payable, then the company is on the brink of financial distress or bankruptcy (see Appendix 3(a) for detailed calculations). If this situation persists and the company cannot find the extra cash needed to pay the interest, it will have to declare bankruptcy. In Appendix 2 (of question), this happens in the first 35% probability scenario: EBIT is €320,000, well below the €599,000 interest payable. If this occurs and Waterlife cannot find the extra €279,000 (suppose the €1,200,000 of Cash and Marketable Securities is tied up), it may have to declare bankruptcy. The ratios EBIT-to-interest payable normally should be above 2 for the company to be considered financially safe and often is as high as 5.

The losses suffered by different companies during bankruptcy are different and depend to a large extent on the tangible assets (the proportion of fixed-assets to total-assets) employed. In the case of Waterlife, this ratio is around 64% (see Appendix 3(b)). While this ratio is not particularly low, we know that other firms in the industry employ a higher level of tangible assets. Waterlife, on the other hand, invests heavily on research and development and other intangible assets which have value only in Waterlife as a going concern. These intangible assets suffer great losses during bankruptcy and hence will reduce its value even further. Depending on the severity of the costs encountered and the length of time it remains insolvent, Waterlife might be forced into liquidation. From this perspective, although dishonouring financing commitments will have a valuation impact upon the share price, the inability of Waterlife to meet debt-financing obligations is far more critical for its long-term survival. It may lead to bankruptcy and, if quick recovery is not possible, even liquidation.

5. Issues Relating to Statements in the Financial Press regarding Efficiency

It is true that, other things being equal, the higher the debt level, the more efficient the management. High interest payments encourage management to work harder to meet financing obligations. Low debt levels, on the other hand, may lead to managers taking it easy and expanding their perks with cash that should be paid back to shareholders. This will ultimately lead to an inefficient firm because managers do not have contractual obligations to pay out cash and may even invest in projects that yield a return below the cost of capital. This type of agency problem is studied by Jensen (1986) and he argues that it is particularly severe for mature firms with a widely dispersed ownership structure where management owns few shares, if at all.

But does this theory apply to Waterlife? I do not have any data to comment on the ownership dispersion of Waterlife. However, it is a reasonably small firm with growth opportunities that are expected to generate a return above the cost of capital. Further, the EBIT-to-interest payable is under 2 in all three scenarios, classifying it as not safe financially. Additionally, Waterlife does not have the required asset structure (a significant proportion of tangible assets) to increase the debt level. However, even if it did have the required asset structure, increasing the leverage as a means to increase efficiency, particularly at this point in time when the prospects of the economy are not particularly optimistic, would be dangerous. If Waterlife has some financial slack, I think it would be better to save it for the future when quick access to debt financing might be essential for the company. I therefore agree with Nick, who thinks that a fast-growing firm with not as many tangible assets as other firms in the industry as Waterlife should not increase its leverage ratio to preserve flexibility as well as avoid financial distress costs.

6. Issues Relating to the Equivalence of Cost of Capital Minimisation and Firm Value Maximisation

The discussion relating to this issue is somewhat theoretical and is based on the assumption that Modigliani and Miller's Proposition I does not hold. This proposition states that the capital structure of a firm is irrelevant to its market value. If this is the case, then it will not be possible to change the value of the firm by changing its capital structure.

However, this proposition is based on the assumption that investment and financing decisions are totally different and do not interact. Other implicit assumptions are: the capital markets are perfectly competitive and securities are infinitely divisible; information is costless and available to all market participants; there are no transaction and bankruptcy costs or taxes; all market participants are price takers; investors can borrow on the same terms as firms; firms can be classified into homogeneous risk classes.

Many of these assumptions clearly do not hold in the real world. Waterlife is paying taxes and it incurs transactions costs every time it raises capital from the securities markets. Further, if Waterlife cannot honour its debt-financing commitments and bankruptcy occurs, this will not be costless. A large proportion of its asset value will be lost due to its particular structure (i.e. intangible assets). Hence, these violations (and others which I have not discussed for efficiency of presentation) of the assumptions upon which MM's Proposition I is based seriously challenge Proposition I. Whenever one adjusts the MM assumptions to allow for the 'tax shield' effect (discussed in section 3), the WACC of the firm declines as the proportion of debt financing increases. As the value of the firm is the present value of the future cash-flows attributable to it, this means that as gearing increases, so too does the value of the firm. However, in practice, as the level of gearing increases, so does the probability of the company facing liquidation or bankruptcy. This potential future cost must also be included in determining the present value of the firm; hence, there is a trade-off when increasing the level of gearing in a firm between the benefits of the reduced future tax bills and the cost of potential default on its debt commitments. This results in WACC decreasing with gearing up to a point (as the benefits of the tax shield are outweighing the possible bankruptcy costs), before increasing again, as the probability of bankruptcy becomes higher (see Appendix 4 for a graphical depiction of this). If this theory holds, then firm value *can* be maximised by adjusting the capital structure so as to minimise WACC.

7. Issues Relating to Financing with Retained Earnings as the Most Preferred Source of Funds

Clearly Waterlife, like all the other firms, has three main financing options: retained earnings, equity capital or debt capital. Retained earnings are an internal source of financing. Earnings that Waterlife has generated through trading have partly been paid to shareholders and partly been retained. Hence, access to this source of funds is transactions costs-free because they are already within the company.

If, however, Waterlife decides to raise external capital in the form of debt and /or equity, it will not just incur transactions costs. If it decides to raise debt, investors who do not have as much information about its future prospects and the probability of financial distress/bankruptcy might worry that a higher debt level might bring about bankruptcy and therfore might only be willing to buy the new bonds at a discount to compensate them for these potential costs. If, however, Waterlife decides to issue equity, investors might interpret this as a sign that senior management is not optimistic about the future and that current share price is overvalued and might again only be willing to buy the new shares at a discount. Hence, if Waterlife decides to finance the new project with retained earnings, it will save not only the transactions costs but also the signalling and information asymmetry costs. In this respect, retained earnings are the cheapest, quickest and most convenient form of financing and hence the most preferred one.

Joe is right to think that borrowing short-term and rolling it over could constitute a form of long-term financing, but this issue is important and requires particular attention. A large proportion of companies in practice appear to employ this technique to meet their financing needs. It is important, however, to respect the Maturity-Matching principle: long-term (fixed) assets are financed with long-term finance and current assets are financed with short-term finance. Adopting the alternative approach, where long-term (fixed) assets are funded with short-term finance, is generally considered as aggressive and dangerous. Waterlife might not have started to receive a return from its investment in long-term assets by the time short-term debt payments are due. This will cause serious liquidity problems, which are potentially as dangerous to Waterlife as defaulting on long-term debt finance and may lead to bankruptcy and ultimately liquidation.

8. Issues Relating to the Value of Waterlife Adopting the Trade-off Theory of Capital Structure

The main advantage of debt is that interest payments are tax deductible. If the current debt level is permanent, then the tax shield will be worth €600,000. If, however, Waterlife decides to increase its debt level to €7.3 million and roll it over on a permanent basis, then the tax shield is worth €1,590,000 + €600,000 = €2,190,000 (see Appendix 4(a)).

However, this strategy is not riskless. Increasing the leverage ratio means increased probability of default on interest payments given the current economic situation. In Appendix 2 (of question), we see that there is a 35% chance that Waterlife will not meet its interest obligations, in which case it will go bankrupt. If bankruptcy occurs, then due to Waterlife's particular asset structure bankruptcy costs will be €5 million. Therefore, the ex-ante bankruptcy costs are €1.75 million. It would appear that by increasing its leverage ratio from 15.8% to 40.6%, Waterlife might increase its market value by €440,000. How does this come about? Taking the MM Proposition I as the starting point and allowing for taxes, probability of bankruptcy and costs incurred, the value of Waterlife will be (see Appendix 4(b) for a graphical representation):

$$V_{levered} = V_{unlevered} + \text{Tax Shields} - \text{Possible Distress Costs}$$

Therefore the value of Waterlife, if it increases leverage from the current debt level (€2 million) to €7.3 million, will be:

$$V_l = 11{,}000{,}000 + 2{,}190{,}000 - 1{,}750{,}000 = 11{,}440{,}000.$$

The implied tax is 30% and is calculated as €1,590,000 / €5,300,000 = 0.3.

These calculations implicitly assume that the new debt level (€7.3 million) will be maintained for eternity and hence the tax shield will have a present value of €2.19 million. This is clearly a strong assumption. The tax rate might change in the future. For example, if it decreases to 25%, then the tax shields will only be worth €1.825 million. Further, Waterlife might decide to reduce or even pay off all of its debt in the future. Additionally, it is not certain that Waterlife will always be profitable and hence have income to shield from tax. If it makes losses, then the tax shields during this loss-making period will be gone forever. Therefore, the tax shield value of €2,190,000 is risky and may turn out to be much lower.

While the benefits of increasing the debt level are risky, we also need to consider the costs that a higher debt level will bring and how likely these costs are. In Appendix 2 (of question), it is shown that there is a 70% (35 + 35) chance that Waterlife will either not honour its debt commitments or will honour them with difficulty, and only a 30% chance that there will be something left for shareholders after interest and tax payments. These estimates are not very optimistic and we also need to allow for a margin of error. Once we allow for this possibility, then bankruptcy is more threatening to the market value of Waterlife because it lacks the required asset structure to increase leverage to such high levels. As already discussed, other firms in the industry can support the high leverage ratios with a large proportion of tangible (fixed) assets which retain most, if not all, of their value when sold should the company go bankrupt. If bankruptcy occurs, the intangible assets, such as research and development, patents, know-how and staff training, that Waterlife has been investing in will have little if any value. Therefore, raising debt in these circumstances is a risky strategy for Waterlife.

9. Issues Relating to the Reasons Why Equity is Safer than Debt and Options to Make Debt Payments Safer

Nick is right to think that equity is the safer option. However, in reaching this conclusion he is taking the firm's perspective, not an investor's. From the investor's perspective, the fact that interest payments are guaranteed but dividend payments are not makes debt the safer option. However, the fact that interest payments are guaranteed no matter what the level of operating income, and dividend payments are discretionary, makes debt a risky financing alternative and equity a safer one from the firm's perspective.

At the moment, given the economic situation and current market coverage, it appears that bankruptcy is not just a hypothetic or a remote situation. There is a 35% chance that Waterlife will go bankrupt and a 35% chance that it will meet its obligations with difficulty. Therefore, issuing debt is a very risky strategy unless Waterlife expands and enters the national market. Currently, there are one million young people and this group is predicted to increase by 4% each year. Further, one in 100 of them is likely to get involved in these sports and spend on average €500. Therefore, if Waterlife covers this market, the extra stream of income for the next three years would be: €5,000,000; €5,200,000; €5,408,000.

With this stream of extra income, Waterlife can comfortably meet its existing and new debt obligations with substantial amounts of earnings to retain and/or pay out to shareholders. It must be noted however, that these estimates ignore competition, i.e. the fact that this market might already be served by other companies and hence the actual extra stream of income would be less. However, even if the extra stream of income is half of the forecasted one, interest payments will still be relatively safe.

10. Issues Relating to the Possible Reasons for the Share Price Decrease Subsequent to the Potential Share Issue

It is a well documented fact that share issues are accompanied by a share price decrease. While the potential share issue might lead to a weaker position of the existing shareholders (they will own a smaller proportion of Waterlife compared to their current holding proportion), it is unlikely that the share price decrease is due to this dilution effect. The share price decrease is more appropriately attributed to agency relationships and information asymmetry. An agency relationship occurs when there is separation of ownership and control. In this case Waterlife shareholders have delegated control over the firm to managers (agents) who have expertise in running the business. The separation of ownership and control may lead to agency costs. Managers (agents) are assumed to put their self-interest first rather than shareholders' and may at times make sub-optimal decisions which increase their utility at the expense of shareholders. Shareholders recognise this possible outcome ex-ante and are only willing to buy the shares at a discount that they think is appropriate.

It is widely accepted that managers in general will know more about the company that they are running than outside investors. This situation is known as information asymmetry and affects more small companies than large ones. In this respect, I think that Waterlife suffers from a relatively serious asymmetric information problem, which will become more evident when Waterlife goes to the capital markets. Investors could be unable to evaluate the fair value of the securities issue. Thus, the decision to issue debt or equity will be interpreted as a sign of what managers know/think about the future prospects of Waterlife. Investors know that if Waterlife cannot meet its debt obligations, it will land in serious trouble and managers will lose their jobs. Thus, if Waterlife decides to issue debt, then the market will interpret this as a sign of managerial optimism about the future. If, however, Waterlife decides to issue equity, then the market will interpret this as a sign of pessimism. Management do not want to issue debt because they think that the earnings generated by the new project might not be enough to honour debt-financing commitments with something left over for shareholders. Further, investors might also interpret this as a sign that management think the stock is overvalued and might try to 'cash in' on this situation. Hence, the announcement to issue equity will be accompanied by a share price decrease.

On balance, I think a debt issue is a dangerous financing strategy and unless Waterlife decides to enter the national market, it will most likely lead to financial distress. On the other hand, a share issue will induce a share price decrease. It will, however, give Waterlife the safety it needs during this time of weak economic performance as well as preserve its financial flexibility. Therefore, I suggest that Waterlife issues 616,280 shares at €8.6 to raise €5.3 million required to finance the new project.

A few points that a manager should bear in mind when faced with a capital structure decision are:

- the tax rate – what is the marginal (not average) tax rate that the company pays? Will it have enough earnings in the future to shield it from tax by borrowing? Are there any less risky alternative ways, such as depreciation, to shield the income?

- Business and financial risk – what is the business risk of the company? How sensitive is the firm's income to variations in GDP? Are its sales more like those of a supermarket (stable throughout the business cycle) or like those of luxurious goods (very high during expansion periods and very low during recession periods)? How likely is financial distress and bankruptcy given the actual and future economic conditions?
- Asset structure – what type of assets does the company employ? Are they tangible, fixed assets such as land, buildings, machineries and equipment which maintain most of their value should the company sell them in the second-hand market or are they intangible assets such as patents, brand names, research and development which have value only in the firm as a going concern?
- Debt capacity – what is the actual level of debt and the maximum the firm can employ without leading to financial distress and a significant increase in probability or bankruptcy? How valuable is financial slack? Is it likely that the company will need external finance at short notice or financial slack will lead to a 'sleepy' management?

Appendix 1: Cost of Capital

(a)

Market Risk Premium $MRP = r_m - r_f = 12 - 4 = 8\%$

Equity Beta $\beta = \dfrac{Cov(r_m, r_w)}{Var(r_m)} = \dfrac{150}{10^2} = 1.5$

Cost of Equity $r_E = r_f + \beta(r_m - r_f) = r_f + \beta(MRP) = 4 + 1.5 \times 8 = 16\%$

(b)

$rE1 = 4 + 1.5 \times 10 = 19\%$

$\Delta rE = rE1 - rE = 19 - 16 = 3\%$

$rE2 = 4 + 1.5 \times 6 = 13\%$

$\Delta rE = rE2 - rE = 13 - 16 = -3\%$

(c)

The formula for the Weighted Average Cost of Capital is:

$$WACC = r_D * \dfrac{D}{D+E} * (1 - Tax\ Rate) + r_E * \dfrac{E}{D+E}$$

Therefore, we need the proportions of debt and equity Waterlife employs in its capital structure as well as the tax rate.

There are several ways to compute the implied tax rate that Waterlife pays. The first one is to employ the following formula:

Tax Rate $TR = \dfrac{Tax\ Paid}{EBIT - Interest\ Paid} = \dfrac{2{,}700}{608{,}000 - 599{,}000} \times 100 = 30\%$

Where the numerator and denominator come from the Income Statement (Appendix 2).

Another way to calculate the implied tax rate paid by Waterlife is the following:

We know that *Value of Tax Shield = Tax Rate × value of Debt*.

Therefore, Tax Rate $TR = \dfrac{Value\ of\ Tax\ Shield}{Value\ of\ Debt} = \dfrac{1{,}590{,}000}{5{,}300{,}000} = 30\%$

Now we can compute Waterlife's cost of capital:

$WACC = 8 * \dfrac{2{,}000{,}000}{12{,}700{,}000} * (1 - 0.3) + 16 * \dfrac{10{,}700{,}000}{12{,}700{,}000} = 14.36\%$

Appendix 2: Leverage and WACC

The current leverage ratio is around 15.8%. Now, suppose this ratio increases to 25% without increasing Waterlife's financial distress/bankruptcy risk. Then we have:

$WACC1 = 8 \times 0.25 \times 0.7 + 16 \times 0.75 = 13.4\%$

Therefore, a 58% increase in the leverage ratio leads to a 6.7% decrease in WACC.
Now, suppose that the leverage ratio increases from 15.8% to 30%, assuming again that this does not lead to an increase in financial distress/bankruptcy risk. Then we have:

$WACC2 = 8 \times 0.3 \times 0.7 + 16 \times 0.7 = 12.9\%$

Therefore, a 90% increase in the leverage ratio leads to a 10.3% decrease in WACC. Thus, we may conclude that although Waterlife's WACC is not extremely sensitive to changes in the leverage ratio, it still decreases with increases in debt levels.

Appendix 3: Interest Coverage and Tangibility of Assets

(a)

A useful indicator of financial safety or distress is the Interest Coverage ratio given by the following formula:

$$Interest\ Coverage = \frac{EBIT}{Interest\ Paid}$$

This ratio measures the 'financial safety' of the firm, i.e. to what extent can it cover the interest payments to its debt-holders? A rule of thumb for this ratio is that firms should be concerned if this ratio falls below about 5.
For Waterlife, depending on the probability scenario we have the following estimates:

Scenario 1 (35% probability): $\frac{320{,}000}{599{,}000} = 0.54$

Scenario 2 (35% probability): $\frac{606{,}000}{599{,}000} = 1.02$

Scenario 3 (30% probability): $\frac{880{,}000}{599{,}000} = 1.47$

Therefore, Waterlife should be very worried as it is close to financial distress.

(b)

A useful indicator of tangibility of assets is the Tangibility of Assets ratio given by the following formula:

$$Tangibility\ of\ Assets = \frac{Fixed\ Assets}{Total\ Assets} = \frac{7{,}000{,}000}{11{,}000{,}000} = 63.6\%$$

We can also compute the Intangibility of Assets ratio as follows:

$$\frac{\text{Total Assets} - \text{Fixed Assets}}{\text{Total Assets}} = \frac{11{,}000{,}000 - 7{,}000{,}000}{11{,}000{,}000} = 36.6\%$$

By construction these two ratios have to add up to 1 (or 100%):

63.6 + 36.4 = 100%

Appendix 4: Capital Structure and WACC

(a)

We can compute the Value of the Tax Shield to Waterlife employing the following formula:

*Value of Tax Shield = Tax Rate*Value of Debt.*

We computed the tax rate in Appendix 1 in the following way:

$$TR = \frac{\text{Value of Tax Shield}}{\text{Value of Debt}} = \frac{1{,}590{,}000}{5{,}300{,}000} = 30\%$$

Therefore, if the current level of debt is rolled over permanently, the financial benefit to Waterlife will be:

*Value of Tax Shield = 0.3*2,000,000 = €600,000*

If, however, the debt level is increased to €7,300,000, then the value of the tax shields to Waterlife will be:

*Value of Tax Shield = 0.3*7,300,000 = €2,190,000*

(b)

The Trade-off theory of Capital Structure can be represented graphically in the following way:

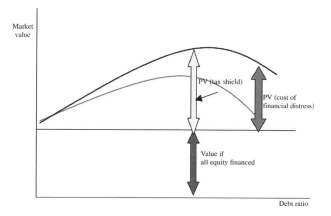

Case 29
Solution to Good Eating Company plc
John Cotter, University College Dublin

REPORT ON ISSUES FACED BY GOOD EATING COMPANY (PLC) AND ITS EMPLOYEE PENSIONS

Prepared by: J Milkins
Consultant

For: Finance Director of Good Eating Company (plc)

1. Terms of Reference

Further to our discussions of xx/xx/xx, I present the report requested. With respect to the pension situation, we examine three different scenarios in valuing the pension fund of Good Eating Company and discuss the associated analysis. We first look at the most common valuation by calculating the present value of the assets and liabilities and the implications of the related analysis. We then measure the future value of the pension fund and comment on the various estimation issues involved and the related implications. For scenario 3, we illustrate findings for the case where we look at various different values for the inputs in scenario 1 and the resulting implications of changes in the inputs. We then turn our attention to the composition of Good Eating Company pension assets and comment on their risk and return attributes. Using the analysis of the company's pension assets and liabilities we discuss alternative pension schemes for the company in the future. In particular, we outline the attributes of a defined benefit scheme supported by the Pension Protection Fund (PPF) as an alternative to its current defined contribution scheme. The numerical analysis in the report relates to a set of figures provided by the finance director of Good Eating Company, are taken in good faith and have not been independently verified for the purposes of this report.

2. Recommendations

(a) There is a (very) large pension deficit using today's prices and the company should be concerned about the contribution requirements for current employees.
(b) This pension deficit would be difficult to eliminate and would require a very different set of assumptions than those used to do the calculations. Changing these assumptions to such an extent may not be plausible.
(c) The company should examine and explore alternative pension schemes and compare these to the current defined contribution scheme in operation.
(d) A defined benefit scheme, available in the UK under the auspices of the PPF, could offer a viable alternative to the defined contribution scheme.
(e) Membership of the defined benefit scheme would allow the company to change its investment strategy and invest in riskier assets so as to reduce its level of pension insolvency.
(f) The costs of joining the PPF are reasonably small and would be attractive to current employees, who would receive their full pension entitlements.

3. Issues Relating to Good Eating Company (plc) and its Employee Pensions

Much of the analysis of this report is based on the time value of money and converting assets and liabilities into either future values or present values. In Appendix 1, assets are presented in their present value form, as they are given in current market prices, but, in contrast, liabilities are given as future values based on future contributions that must be made to current employees when they take retirement. In order to assess the attributes of the pension fund of Good Eating Company we will examine three different scenarios and comment on the respective findings. (Throughout the following scenarios, it is assumed that the employees' expected pension payments represent a future liability, when, of course, given that the scheme is a defined contribution scheme, Good Eating Company is not actually obliged to make these payments if the value of the pension fund's assets is insufficient.)

Scenario 1: Current Value of Pension

The current value of the assets can be obtained directly from Appendix 1 and is €10 million. However, liabilities of the pension are given in the context of their future contribution values and must be discounted by the time value of money. In this case we assumed that the discount factor is the same as the Fixed Income 'returns' in Appendix 1 of 3%. The timeframe that we apply to our calculations is based on the number of years of the scheme and we are going to simplify the calculations by dealing with one single time period of 10 years. (We could also deal with other timeframes and deal with, for example, an assumption that the payments made yearly over the length of the scheme would be discounted on an annual basis.) We also assume that converting the assets and liabilities into cash values is equivalent and is costless, although, obviously, there are different transactions costs and liquidity issues in trading equities compared to properties, etc. Given these assumptions and the timeframe involved we suggest that a reasonable estimate of the liability contributions is:

$25m/(1.03)^{10} = 25m/1.34 = €18.65$ million.

As the net value of the fund is obtained using the value of the assets less the liabilities, we find that there is a negative value of €8.65 million (18.65 − 10). This represents a deficit and if Good Eating Company was audited at the moment, it would represent an insolvent pension fund (as the value of the pension contributions in today's terms is exceeded by the liabilities). The problems facing Good Eating Company plc are even clearer when you consider a ratio of fund assets over liabilities of 0.536:

Assets/liabilities = $10/18.65 = 0.536$.

This ratio clearly suggests that Good Eating has difficulties at present with its pension fund. Essentially, employees would only receive approximately 50% of their pension contributions or approximately €12,500 from €25,000. As Good Eating Company is currently using a defined contribution pension scheme, this must be a worry for all stakeholders of the company. These figures and analysis are based on the assumption that current market conditions prevail, but even if there were changes, they would have to be very large so as to change the overall assessment that Good Eating Company has a serious pension deficiency.

Scenario 2: Future Value of Pension

The second scenario that we will explore is the future value of the pension fund. We will take one date, like the first scenario; we assume this is 10 years in the future. We are also consistent with scenario 1 in terms of the discount factor and eliminate any trading costs that may exist. In this scenario, the future value of the liabilities is available, but we need to calculate the corresponding future value of the assets of the fund. We also make the assumption that the respective growth rate of the assets corresponds to the respective expected returns of the assets in Appendix 1. Thus, given the current market prices of assets in Appendix 1, the expected future value of each of the pension's assets is:

Equity – $€5m(1.20)^{10} = €30.96m$
Fixed income – $€3m(1.03)^{10} = €4.03m$
Property – $€2m(1.20)^{10} = €12.38m$

Combining these future values, the expected future value of the portfolio of pension assets is €47.37 million. This represents an average expected value of the portfolio of pension assets.

Now if we want to work out the value of the Good Eating Company plc pension fund, we have to make an assumption on whether the expected returns will actually happen or not. Let's first assume that these outcomes will occur. Using the same analysis as earlier on we find a positive fund value with assets exceeding liabilities by €22.37m (47.37 − 25). There is a certain amount of good news for Good Eating Company plc in these figures, especially as they will not have a pension deficit based on the assumptions underlying the calculations. Also our ratio of assets to liabilities is 1.895 (47.37/25), suggesting that there is a big cushion between pension assets and pension contributions. On this basis, the employees of Good Eating Company should receive their full pension contributions. However, they must recognise that having a surplus in the pension fund implies that they are underutilising resources to grow the firm by using this excess for some other revenue generating scheme.

Our analysis thus far is based on the assumption that the expected returns are realised. However as we can see in Appendix 1 each of the assets has an associated risk with equities being most risky with a standard deviation of 30%, followed by property with 12% and even the Fixed Income securities have some variability with a risk measure of 0.5%. We should incorporate these levels of uncertainty of the pension assets into our analysis and there are a number of ways of doing this. One such way is to create a portfolio and estimate the portfolio returns and the portfolio risk. On this basis the portfolio returns are the weighted average of the individual assets expected returns given the amount respectively invested. On this basis, the portfolio return is:

$0.5(0.2) + 0.3(0.03)$ and $0.2(0.20) = 0.149$ or 14.9%.

Using this we can work out the future value using the same mechanism as before $10(1+0.149)^{10} = $ €40.10 million.

However, there is uncertainty associated by these investments and in a portfolio context, (assuming the asset returns are uncorrelated with one another) we can use the previous expression to get a weighted average of each asset's individual risk:

$0.5(0.3) + 0.3(0.005)$ and $0.2(0.12) = 0.1755$ or 17.55%.

Allowing for this uncertainty to grow during the lifespan analysed (assuming volatility grows in proportion with time) gives a potential level of uncertainty of:

$10(1+0.1755)^{10} = $ €50.37 million.

Thus, in this case the future expected value of €40.10 has a level of uncertainty of €50.37 around it, using the same assumptions that the growth effects of returns and risk are the same. Obviously our analysis in estimating the future value of Good Eating Company plc pension fund would have to incorporate both the future value of the effect of the expected returns and risk. One such way to do this is to treat the risk as the deviation from the expected value and say that our expected returns are €40.10 million, with deviation plus and minus this estimate of the portfolio's standard deviation of €50.37 million. This creates two outcomes: the positive deviation case and the negative deviation case; and if the former is analysed, then Good Eating Company plc has excess assets over liabilities by a large amount, but in the negative case the value of the assets would be zero, implying an extreme deficit.

Scenario 1 is a more reasonable situation and is one that analysis would commonly follow, but scenario 2 shows the potential impact of risk on the pension's assets and there can be two effects arising from this: either a negative or positive effect.

Scenario 3: Changing Assumptions of Scenario 1

There are two assumptions relating to scenario 1 and they affect the measurement of liabilities of the Good Eating Company (plc) pension fund. We assumed that the lifespan of the pension contributions would be 10 years. This would represent an average estimate of the lifespan of an employee after they retire and would be less/more for any one employee. The discount factor utilised was the same as the yield or return on the fixed income securities and is related to prevailing current market conditions. (We also assumed 100 employees that were entitled to a defined contribution scheme in Appendix 1 and this was based on the current numbers of 102 and the view of the finance director that this represented a 'steady state' going forward, so we will not comment on this further.)

First, looking at the timeframe of the pension fund, we need to comment on mortality rates. We know that lifespans are increasing and the average lifespan of males and females can be obtained. We also know that these average lifespans vary for males and females, so we need additional information on the numbers of male and female employees that the company usually has in employment. However, if the average lifespan of Good Eating Company employees increases (decreases), then the period over which payments will be made will increase (decrease), thereby increasing (decreasing) the future value of the pension liabilities. So, assuming an increase in life expectancies, we find that, in this case, the present value of liabilities would be even greater than that calculated in scenario 1, implying a greater pension deficit and a lower ratio of assets to liabilities. This would make the restructuring of the pension fund an even more pressing problem for Good Eating Company. In contrast, if the average lifespan of employees is reduced, the reverse will happen, and the deficit will get smaller.

Secondly, if we examine the discount factor, we find that if we increase its value, then the present value of the liabilities will decrease, thereby reducing the pension deficit. In contrast, if the discount rate falls, then the present value of the fund liabilities will increase, implying an even larger deficit. One final note is that predicting future interest rates is a difficult issue and a detailed discussion of this is beyond the realms of this report.

Valuation of Pension Assets

We now turn our attention to the types of asset chosen by Good Eating Company. First, we note that there are two types of asset chosen by the company. The choice of fixed income securities suggests that 30% of the pension fund is put into safe assets. In the context of the CAPM, these assets would be relatively risk-free assets: this is supported by having such a low level of risk associated with this asset class. The other assets – equities and property – can be considered as risky assets, implying that they offer relatively high expected returns but are also associated with relatively high levels of risk.

To utilise the CAPM, we would create a portfolio of these risky assets based on the proportions invested in them to get the estimate of the expected returns and the expected levels of risk. So for every dollar invested, the weight for equities is 5/7 and the weight for property is 2/7, and these would affect the expected returns and risk in a similar manner as when we calculated portfolio risk and return earlier. In order to calculate the expected return according to the CAPM we are, however, missing one estimate and this is beta. Beta will tell us the sensitivity between movements in our portfolio of equities and property relative to some market benchmark. We can, however, comment on what the size of the beta may entail and how this may impact upon the asset portfolio of Good Eating Company. For example, if we find a beta of 1, then we say that the portfolio of risky assets for Good Eating Company moves by the same amount as the general market. If the beta is greater than 1, we have chosen relatively risky assets compared to some market benchmark. In this case our risky portfolio should have higher return and risk levels than the market benchmark. For a beta less than 1 we find that the market is more risky, with higher returns than the chosen portfolio. Good Eating Company should be aware of the composition of its pension assets and the likely outcomes in terms of risk and returns of its chosen assets.

Analysis of Alternative Pension Schemes

The final issue that we want to raise in our report concerns the alternative pension schemes available to Good Eating Company. This is the key issue in our report and our analysis earlier will help us advise the company on the relative merits of the alternative schemes.

First, if the company does not change from the defined contribution scheme, it will only have to pay on the basis of the market value of the assets. In this case, if we follow the most commonly applied analysis, we will examine scenario 1. As we saw in scenario 1, Good Eating Company has a very large pension deficit, with liabilities far exceeding the value of the pension fund assets. In fact, employees would only be looking to receive pension entitlements of approximately half of the €25,000 that they could receive if the deficit did not exist. Good Eating Company, whilst legally obliged to pay only the amount of the value of the assets, must also take into consideration other factors. Paramount to these is the reputation that Good Eating Company has developed. It is seen as a stable and successful company and problems relating to pension payments would have adverse effects on the image of the company. Given that its success is supported by having an image of being quality producers of food products, pension problems may tarnish its image.

The main alternative for Good Eating Company (plc) is to change the type of pension being offered to a defined benefit scheme. If it does this, it also has the choice of becoming a member of the Pension Protection Fund (PPF). Let's first comment on the defined benefit scheme. For the defined benefit scheme it would have to pay €25,000 per employee over his/her retirement period. In terms of public relations, employees would be much more supportive of the defined benefit scheme as they will not be affected by the uncertainties of the market place. This payment would have to take place regardless of the level of deficit on their pension fund. Thus Good Eating Company Ltd would then face the dilemma of how to deal with this situation. Again let's concentrate on the findings of scenario 1. Three options spring to mind. First, they can move funds from other parts of the company's balance sheet to eliminate the deficit. This would solve the problem but mean that Good Eating Company would be removing capital from other areas of the business and this may affect the growth possibilities of the firm going forward. Second, they could allow the deficit to continue and hope that it is reversed as time passes. Essentially this would be following a 'do nothing' strategy but given the large negative working capital for the assets and liabilities of the pension fund, it would be a very optimistic outcome that is being hoped for. Essentially we would not recommend that the company would get involved in negative net present value projects. Also, given the potential changes in the determinants of the liabilities, such as length of pension and discount factor, we could actually envisage the situation getting worse rather than better.

The third strategy would be to join the PPF. This would also allow for an insolvency of the fund, but in this case the government-backed PPF would ensure that payments would be made to employees up to the value of €25,000. This figure is exactly in line with the payment contributions of the current pension scheme run by Good Eating Company. Thus the potential negative publicity of having an insolvent pension scheme would be reversed once it is realised that employees' pension rights are protected. Good Eating Company could also change its investment stance and invest in more aggressive and risky assets with the hope that it will experience more positive returns so that the pension deficit is reduced. If that happens, the insolvency issue is reduced, but again if the assets perform poorly, Good Eating Company is secure in the knowledge that its employee benefits will be covered. There is a cost to membership, but the maximum levy would be €125,000 (€25 million liabilities × 0.5% levy). Whilst this is not negligible, it does represent a relatively small price to pay given the other alternatives that are available and the extent to which the liabilities of Good Eating Company pension exceed its assets.

Case 30
Solution to Personal Financial Planning: Tom Smith

Anne Marie Ward, University of Ulster

PERSONAL FINANCIAL PLAN
FOR TOM SMITH AND FAMILY AS AT 2XX9

Prepared by: A. N. Advisor

For: Tom

Date: 30 September 2XX9

	Table of contents	Page
1.	Terms of Reference	181
2.	Introduction	181
3.	Recommendations (immediate action)	182
4.	Expected Net Worth and Financial Position (After Immediate Action has been Implemented)	185
5.	Other Recommendations	186
6.	Education Issues	187
7.	Investment, Risk and Return and Portfolio Theory	188
8.	Conclusion	189

Appendices

Appendix 1	Schedules Detailing Relevant Background Information	191
Appendix 2	Schedule Detailing Primary and Secondary Objectives	193
Appendix 3	Statement of Net Worth (Before Recommendations are Considered)	194
Appendix 4	Debt Schedule (Before Recommendations are Implemented)	195
Appendix 5	Statement of Annual Net Cash-Flows in 2XX9	196
Appendix 6	Statement of Expected Net Worth (Amended to Reflect Recommendations for Immediate Action)	197
Appendix 7	Statement of Expected Net Income (Amended to Reflect the Recommendations for Immediate Action)	198

1. Terms of Reference

This draft financial plan has been prepared in response to a request from you (Tom Smith) for financial advice. In particular, you have requested information on your current net income and financial position and how this can be improved in light of your financial aims. Schedules detailing the current and the proposed scenario are to be prepared and evaluated.

In addition, the financial plan provides advice in respect of the decisions your children are facing and outlines the principles underlying portfolio theory and how this theory can be applied to you.

2. Introduction

2.1 Background Information

This draft financial plan has been prepared from the information supplied by you (Tom Smith). You are 54 years old, are in full-time employment as a civil engineer and are in good health. You are married to Angela. She is 45 years old, is a nurse and does not adopt a healthy lifestyle. You have three children: Dan (aged 22), Sheila (aged 16) and Ted (aged 10). Dan has just left university and is looking for your advice on whether to take up a trainee accountant post or to become a labourer (higher immediate earnings). Sheila has just completed her examinations and has two years left at school if she chooses to continue in her education. Sheila has been offered a job in the bank and you have also requested my advice on this matter. Ted is still at primary school. See Appendix 1 for full background details. In section 6, I have highlighted some issues and opinions that you might consider before you provide advice to your children in respect of their education and future careers. In addition, in Appendix 1 I have included estimates of the annual cost to expect if you decide to finance your children's education.

2.2 Personal Aims

Your aims are summarised in Appendix 2. I have assumed that your primary aim in the short-term is to improve your liquidity position by reducing your debt burden, and in the long-term your primary aim is to be debt free and to have surplus funds when you retire. Other aims include funding your children's education, building up savings and investments and leaving funds for your children when you die. These aims influence the recommendations made in sections 3, 4 and 5.

2.3 Current Net Worth and Financial Position

At present you and Angela have net assets of €342,690 (see Appendix 3 for full details). This is made up of assets of €475,000 and debt of €132,310. Your assets range from your private home to motor vehicles. Your investment strategy to date seems to be limited to savings accounts, which are earning low returns. The land is not earning anything.

Your debt is analysed more fully in a debt schedule (see Appendix 4). This schedule provides information on how much each debt source is increasing per month, the annual rates of interest being charged, the credit limits, the amounts outstanding, the monthly repayment amounts and the payment terms. You (and Angela) have eight different sources of debt with annual costs that range from 6% (the mortgage) to 28.3% (the joint credit card). With the exception of the mortgage, all the other debt sources are very expensive and clearing these is a priority.

From the information you have supplied a statement of your annual net cash-flows for 2XX9 has been prepared (see Appendix 5). From this it can be seen that your yearly cash outflows exceed your cash inflows by €7,683.60. This situation cannot continue. You will run down your savings and find yourself in financial difficulty in the near future if you do not take steps to redress this problem.

3. Recommendations (Immediate Action)

At present you are utilising more cash than you are generating. This has been possible over the past number of years because you have been subsidising the family's joint incomes from the funds received as a legacy from your father. In addition, cash spent on credit cards has been increasing and an overdraft is being used. If steps are not taken, you will find yourself in financial difficulty in the next couple of years. A number of steps can be taken now to strengthen your financial position and to ensure that the family has surplus cash each month after all cash commitments have been satisfied. These suggestions are as follows:

3.1 Immediate Action – Debt Management

(a) Pay off all expensive debt using your savings as these are earning such a low return. This will improve your cash-flow position immediately. Ted and Sheila's education funds should be used (just because of the sheer cost of the debt) and steps to deal with financing their education should be postponed for one or two years. I recommend you make the following transactions (see Appendix 6).

　A. Use the €10,000 from the deposit account, which is only earning 3% per annum, to reduce the balance on the joint credit card, which costs 28.3% per annum. The balance on this credit card will fall to €2,000.

　B. Use the €1,000 from the deposit account you have earmarked for Ted's education, which earns 2%, to reduce the balance on the joint credit card account. The balance outstanding will now be €1,000.

　C. Use the €6,000 from the deposit account you have earmarked for Sheila's education, which earns 3%, to clear the final €1,000 balance on the joint credit card. The remaining €5,000 should be used to clear the Succeeding credit card balance of €4,200 as this credit card charges 25.34%, and the remaining €800 should be used to reduce the balance on the Dot Hawkins credit card. At this point the Succeeding credit card is fully paid off and should be destroyed.

D. Remove €8,150 from the legacy deposit account, which is earning 4% per annum. Use €1,000 of this to clear the Dot Hawkins credit card, €3,200 to clear the Debenporks credit card, which costs 19.56% per annum, and the remaining €3,950 to clear the overdraft, which costs 18% per annum. At this point both the Dot Hawkins and the Debenports credit cards are fully paid off and should be destroyed.

E. Finally, transfer the €15,000 from the term deposit account against the mortgage account, reducing the balance from €75,000 to €60,000. The term deposit account earns interest at 5%, but this will be subject to taxation, hence the net return will be about 3% (assuming a tax rate of 40%). The mortgage costs 6% (it is assumed that there are no tax deductions in relation to mortgage interest). Therefore, reducing the mortgage is indirectly a good investment option at this stage.

F. These transfers will not impact on your net worth, as highlighted in Appendix 6. It will remain the same at €342,690; however, you will now have much lower debt and only three sources. This will be easier to manage. In addition, the expensive debt has been paid off. This means that there will be yearly interest savings and cash-flow savings from not having to repay the capital.

(b) The car finance needs to be investigated further. Before providing advice in this area I would need to know if there would be penalties for breaking either credit agreement. Penalties can be expensive, if they are, keep the cars until the end of the credit agreement term (at least). If the penalties are negligible, then it will be worthwhile paying off the car debt in advance of the mortgage. Typically, many car deals can be broken when 50% of the car is repaid. However, this option is normally allowable when the 50% is paid very quickly, i.e. not after four or five years. When repayments are quick, the value of the asset is always greater than the value of the debt and the agreement is less likely to be broken. If the value of the vehicle is below the outstanding balance on the finance, the debt-holder would just cancel after the 50% threshold has been reached and let the lender reclaim the lower value vehicle. Therefore, it is assumed that the penalties for cancelling the agreement are high.

In future, the couple should be encouraged to buy their cars in cash and to go for more modest vehicles until they are financially secure.

(c) The family will need about €30,000 – €35,000 to fund Sheila – starting with about €15,000 in the first year (if a second-hand vehicle is purchased). These estimates assume that Sheila spends three years at university (see Appendix 1) and lives at home. Note – these figures assume the worst-case cash requirement.

(d) Dan is now working. He should be able to afford his own car in one to two years' time and his current car could go to Sheila. This would reduce the amount required to finance her through university by €5,000 – €7,000 in the first year. However, this depends on the condition of the vehicle.

3.2 Immediate Action – Cost Management

(a) It would seem that your family have allowed spending to spiral out of control, particularly on credit cards (see Appendix 4 and 5). I would recommend that you analyse all costs thoroughly with your family and agree to become more frugal for the next few years. From the information you have supplied it would seem that possible savings can be made on the following non-essential items.

(b) You could cancel Sky (€30) and limit the mobile-phone spend. This can be achieved by changing to pay-as-you-go deals for your children. Their allowance could be capped to €10 per month, with yourself and Angela agreeing to limit calls to less than €20 per month. This will provide an overall saving of €90 per month. Indeed, Dan should now be taking responsibility for his own phone bill. You could consider getting a bundle deal whereby one provider supplies phone, Sky and broadband. This can be obtained for approximately €30 – €40 per month.

(c) Reduce spend on consumables, such as amount spent on coffee, cigarettes, alcohol. Or eliminate consumable expenditure for a period until finances are stronger.

(d) Sheila is 16. She will have been issued with a national insurance number and she should be encouraged to get a part-time job – this would save an additional €520 per year as you could stop providing pocket money to her. It may also give Sheila an appreciation of the value of money. Sheila could be encouraged to start to take responsibility for the cost of her own telephone calls, providing further cash savings.

(e) Another possible area where cash can be saved is in respect of childcare costs. At present, childcare costs for Ted amount to €2,340 per year. Would it be possible for Sheila to look after Ted now that she is 16? You could treat the arrangement as a part-time job – wherein she is paid per hour for undertaking this role. Is this a viable option? If Sheila is considered mature enough to work in a bank, she is mature enough to look after her brother for the three evenings that Angela is at work. She could be paid a lower rate than is currently being paid to the child-minder and this could become her pocket money. Savings of €2,000 overall might be possible (reduction in childcare costs, phone bill costs and Sheila's pocket money). Another option may be that Angela change shifts to work one weekend day, saving one-third of the cost. Other factors to consider include: is the neighbour registered? Can she be paid with childcare tax-deductible vouchers? If she can, this will result in a tax saving that will have an immediate impact on the amount of cash taken home by either Tom or Angela, depending on who elects to administer the vouchers. This will save €936 in cash each year (€2,340 × 40%).

(f) Angela should be encouraged to stop using her credit cards for a period of 12 months at the outset and then to limit her spend. Angela seems to enjoy shopping and credit cards provide easy access to funds – in this instance the access is too easy. I would recommend that Angela should not use credit cards at all as she is not good at managing her funds. At the minute she seems to be spending €428 per month on clothes, which is too high given the family's current financial situation. See footnotes 4, 5 and 6 in Appendix 4 for this calculation.

3.3 Immediate Action – the Land

I would recommend fencing the land and renting it out immediately. The neighbour may be able to claim squatter's rights if you do not start to use the land. A costly legal battle may be the result as you try to reclaim the land and you may even lose it.

4. Expected Net Worth and Financial Position (After Immediate Action Has Been Implemented)

As mentioned previously, your net worth will not change immediately, though it will start to improve yearly from now on (assuming the recommendations are followed). Your cash-flow position will improve (see Appendix 7) and I predict a cash surplus at the end of the next year of €8,416.40, increasing to about €10,000 in the succeeding year as the expenditure to fence the land is a one-off. The improvement from a net cash deficit of €7,683.60 to a surplus of €8,416.40 has come about because of the following incremental cash-flows.

4.1 Incremental Sources of Cash

(a) The land will be rented, earning approximately €1,200 per year.
(b) Expenditure on consumables by you and Angela should fall to €20 each per week, saving €3,120 (€5,200 - €2,080) each year.
(c) Household bills may fall from €7,800 to €2,600, providing a cash saving of €5,200 (cutting out Sky, reducing mobile phone expenditure, etc.).
(d) Sheila's pocket money will fall if she gets a part-time job, or takes responsibility for Ted's childcare (saving about €780) – only €260 is reflected in the projections as this would have to be agreed with Sheila. She may not want to take a part-time job if it results in her losing her free pocket money.
(e) All the credit card repayments will end, saving approximately €13,200 in cash (assuming all clothes shopping ceases for the next year).
(f) The transfers to Sheila and Ted's education deposit accounts have been cancelled. The most pressing issue after the restructuring of your finances will be to build up a suitable emergency fund and then to focus on funding Sheila's education. If Sheila continues in her education, funding will be required in only two years' time. Funding Sheila will take precedence over funding Ted in these first few years.

4.2 Incremental Applications of Cash

(a) Interest income will fall from €988.40 to €44.40.
(b) Payment protection insurance and life assurance will cost about €1,000 per year.
(c) Net payments to the pension fund will result in a net cash reduction in take-home wages of €1,180 (see Appendix 7 for the calculation).

4.3 Other points

(a) In line with your objectives, I have not reduced your mortgage repayment amounts, even though the capital balance on your mortgage will have been reduced by €15,000. This will speed up the repayment of your mortgage.

(b) No savings or incremental cash-flows have been included in respect of childcare costs as there are a variety of options available. Savings are possible, which will increase your yearly cash surplus even more.

(c) I have assumed that it would not be cost-efficient to refinance the vehicles. More detail on the finance agreements will enable us to determine if savings are possible.

5. Other Recommendations

5.1 Given the expected yearly cash savings, you now are in a position to decide what to do with the annual cash surplus. The following points might be considered.

(a) It is always advisable to maintain a certain amount of cash for emergencies, such as losing your job. The annual surplus funds (predicted to amount to €8,416.40 in the first year) could be used to build up an emergency cash balance in the current account/instant access deposit account. As mentioned, fencing the land is a one-off expense, so the annual surplus is more likely to be €10,000 per year in future years. This will increase by even more in the year after as childcare costs fall – Ted will now be going to secondary school. The family is then more likely to be in a position to fund Sheila's education out of the cash funds built up and the annual yearly surplus expected in three to five years time. Sheila could subsidise her education costs with a student loan as this is a very cheap form of finance. This would enable you to retain funds to achieve your other aims.

(b) Under the current mortgage repayment schedule the balance will be repaid within the next seven to eight years. This will achieve one of your key aims (to be mortgage free on retirement) and allow time to build up the €25,000 fund that you would like. The €25,000 aim is seriously underestimated! Where did you get this figure from? You could live for 30 years or more after retirement – a nest egg of €25,000 seems very low. I would recommend that you aim to put aside much more than this.

(c) Ted's education: at present I would recommend that you focus on repaying the expensive debts that you have accumulated and on funding Sheila through university. In about five years time both cars will be fully paid for and the family should be in a better position to start thinking about their retirement years and the funding of Ted's education. It is recommended that the family do not change the cars for as long as possible (assuming repair bills do not become too high).

(d) Though the current economic climate is not favourable towards pensions, they are one of the best ways to invest in the stock market. I would not recommend a pension as the sole investment for retirement; however, in this instance I would recommend that you take out the company pension. A total of 9% (5% + 4%)

of your wages will be contributed to the pension fund. This will cost you 2.36% (4% × 59%) of your wages. This is the cost net of taxation (assumed at 41%). The company will bear most of the cost (5%) and the government contributes the other 1.64%. The stock market has not been performing well over the last two years. However, it is likely that the markets will regain strength when the economy picks up. This will allow you to reap the rewards that should fall to pension companies when the value of stocks and shares rises.

(e) An option that you might consider is to sell your house and build a new house on the site. This will leave you in a very strong financial position when you retire and may even release as much as €200,000 towards your retirement fund. However, this option may take several years to complete and will not solve the immediate cash problem. Your current home will be hard to sell in the current economic climate. If you are considering building, it might be worthwhile looking into the possibility of including a granny flat for your mum.

(f) As soon as you have built up sufficient levels of emergency funds, you and Angela should consider building up savings. In Northern Ireland €5,100 per year can be put into a tax-free cash ISA. I recommend that the family remain frugal for the next couple of years until a sufficient emergency fund and savings have been established.

(g) It is assumed that the value of Tom's mum's house and wealth will cover her care in her old age (more detail is required). Tom's mum may be willing and able to provide an interest-free loan to help with Sheila's education, if need be – though this should not be necessary if the family initiate the steps recommended in this draft financial plan.

(h) Reducing risk exposure: I would recommend that you obtain income protection insurance. This insurance would guarantee a minimum income level for a period of 12 months in the event of either you or Angela losing your job. *This is particularly important when you do not have a sufficient emergency fund in reserve.* The family clearly requires both incomes to run the house and service the debts at this stage and the loss of one income would cause financial distress for the family. In addition, I would recommend that you consider life assurance for the mortgage debt. This will repay the mortgage in full, in the event of either you or Angela dying.

6. Education Issues

6.1 Your children have performed very well in their studies to date and in my opinion this will provide them with a platform to launch their future careers in top-earning jobs. Though it is too early yet to comment on Ted's future, it is clear that Dan and Sheila are top performers. Both are facing a dilemma as they have to decide whether to continue with their education or to accept employment which has been offered to them. I will provide my opinion on the advice that you should give to them.

6.2 Dan is deciding on whether to accept a job that has been offered by a local contractor on a nearby building site. Dan has a first-class honours degree in Accountancy and has obtained an accountancy trainee post with a top accountancy firm, which provides a starting salary of €12,000 per year (see Appendix 1). This is less than the salary on offer by the contractor. However, it should be noted that the accountancy firm allows study leave, pays for Dan's ICAI membership fees, study and examination fees. The gross salary is more like €20,000 and is likely to increase each year by large amounts (depending on Dan's performance). Indeed, an article in the *Financial Times* in September 2007 reported that the holders of accountancy degrees are the highest earners. I recommend that you inform Dan of the additional perks being provided in the trainee contract and also highlight the long-term benefits associated with becoming a qualified accountant and not to focus on short-term perceived financial gains.

6.3 I must also point out that the contractor is breaking the law by offering to pay Dan in cash. If Dan agrees to accept cash, he will also be breaking the law as this is a form of tax evasion. In addition, Dan will not be earning enough to qualify for the payment of his 'stamp' – the minimum national insurance contributions which are required to be paid to enable Dan to get state benefits and a state pension when he retires. Also, he would have little rights as an employee and would not be entitled to, for example, sick pay. Working for a contractor may not be stable work and Dan is likely to be made redundant if the contractor experiences any financial difficulties. Finally, working as a labourer on a building site may be hard work, particularly in winter when the weather is wet and cold. This may be acceptable when Dan is young, but may be a concern when he is older.

6.4 Sheila has also shown great potential and though the bank's offer is good, it will restrict Sheila's future career to working within the bank. Sheila should be advised to continue in education and obtain a degree, after which several opportunities may become available, particularly if she performs as well as Dan has.

6.5 The decision on whether to put aside funds for Ted's education will be based on his performance in his examinations and his interest in studying. Research has shown that certain degrees do not add value and Ted needs to be directed towards those degree areas that lead to the best careers.

7. Investment, Risk and Return and Portfolio Theory

7.1 At present you do not have a notable investment policy. You had put cash into a number of savings accounts with returns ranging from 2% to 5% before taxation. Before providing advice on the correct investment strategy for you and your family I would require more detail on your attitude towards risk and return as both are related. In general, low-risk investments will offer low returns, as in the case of deposit accounts. Indeed, the real rate of return may be negative as the rate of inflation may exceed the net return received on the investment. In low-risk investments the capital invested is usually not exposed to the possibility of loss, whereas high-risk investments, such as holding shares in one company, stand the chance of making a very high return if the company performs well, or may suffer a loss in the capital invested if the company does not perform well. Therefore, any advice given will be influenced by your view on risk and return.

7.2 There are some steps that can be taken to improve your overall return whilst managing your exposure to risk. *Portfolio theory* suggests that an investor can diversify away the risk associated with holding one type of share or investment by holding a *well-diversified portfolio of shares/investments*. The larger the number of differing types of share or investment held, the more likely that the risk associated with one type will be reduced. In the context of investing in equity shares, it is thought that holding eight to 10 carefully chosen shares is sufficient to diversify away the risks that are specific to each one. It is important to select shares that are not correlated with each other, or that are negatively correlated with each other. This means that when economic conditions change, one will react in the opposite manner to the other. So when one share goes down in price, another rises in price so as to even out the overall performance of the portfolio.

7.3 In terms of your investment strategy and depending on your attitude to risk, I would recommend that you try to create a portfolio of different types of investment for your retirement. This may include as a minimum: term deposit accounts (high interest), gilts, investment in the stock market (through your pension) and property (the land and building site). If you are a risk taker who believes that there are high returns to be made by investing in the stock market, then you could consider investing directly in shares.

8. Conclusion

8.1 You need to undertake immediate steps to strengthen your finances. At the present time you and Angela have assets of €475,000, debt outstanding of €132,310 and are paying out more cash per year than you are generating (€7,683.60 more). This will have been running down your savings and you will find yourself in financial difficulty in the near future if this is allowed to continue.

8.2 Your debt situation is particularly worrying as you are paying very high interest charges on seven of the eight different types of debt that you have amassed. The first key recommendation is that you should use the funds from your deposit accounts, which are earning low rates of interest, to repay all the credit cards and overdraft immediately. This alone will reverse your cash crises and leave you in a net cash-generating position. However, on its own this is not enough. Sheila may well go to college in two years time and you have stipulated that you would like to finance her education. Therefore lifestyle changes are required – a more frugal lifestyle should be pursued. Savings can be made if non-necessary expenditure is eliminated. The following cash outflows should be considered – consumables, clothing, mobiles, Sky, etc. All cash outflows require scrutiny and serious cuts to spending are required for the next couple of years to ensure that your financial aims are met.

8.3 I am also recommending some expenditure. You have not considered risk, or current investment opportunities. From the financial plan it is clear that both salaries are required to service the family, therefore I recommend that you take out income protection insurance. This is particularly important in the first year as your emergency fund will not be sufficient to cover the family's cash outflows for a six-month period. This will be replenished as a priority from the surpluses made in the next year. In addition, it is recommended that you take out life assurance on the mortgage (if this is not included as part of the occupational pension scheme). These two insurances should not cost more than €1,000 per year.

8.4 I also recommend that you join the occupational pension scheme. Though 9% of your salary will be paid into this scheme, this will only cost you 2.36% and allows access to an already created portfolio of diversified shares (as selected by the pension company). Pension companies also invest in commercial property, gold, etc. and you may reap rewards in the future when the recession ends and the economy recovers.

8.5 Finally, I would recommend that you encourage both Dan and Sheila to continue with their education as this is an investment in their human capital value, which will reap rewards in the long-term.

Appendix 1: Schedules detailing relevant background information

1. General Information – Profile

	Self	**Partner**
Surname:	Smith	Smith
Christian name:	Tom	Angela
Age:	54	45
Occupation:	Civil engineer	State-employed nurse
Telephone number (home):	079 456456	079 456456
Telephone number (work):	0780 123122	0750 253621
Mobile number:	0779 458982	0779 526852
Fax:	–	–
E-mail:	T.Smith@coolmail.com	A.Smith@coolmail.com
Home address:	15 Country lane Jenkinstown Dundalk Co. Louth	15 Country lane Jenkinstown Dundalk Co. Louth
Correspondence address (if different from home address):	–	–
Married	Yes	Yes

2. General Information on Health and Risk

	Individual	**Partner**
Health:		
Current health *(answer as good/ok/poor)*	Good	Ok to poor
Risk factors: *(Answer as yes or no)*		
Smoker	No	Yes
Drink alcohol beyond recommended levels	No	Yes
Other high-risk factors *(provide detail)*	3 children No pension No insurances Elderly mother	3 children No exercise No insurances

Appendix 1 (continued)

3. General Information on Children

Education: *(Answer as yes or no)*

	Individual	Partner
Do you have any children?	Yes	Yes

If you have children who are dependent on you, please provide the following details:

	Name	Age	Years of education to finance	Expected yearly cost
Child 1	Dan	22	(N) 0	0
			(P) 0	0
			(S) 0	0
			(U) 0	0
Child 2	Sheila	16	(N) 0	0
			(P) 0	0
			(S) 2 years	€1,500[1]
			(U) 3 – 4 years	€10,000+[2]
Child 3	Ted	10	(N) 0	0
			(P) 1 year	€800
			(S) 7 years	€1,500
			(U) 3 – 4 years	€10,000

Where (N) is Nursery school, (S) is Secondary school, (P) is Primary school, (U) is University.

Other information:

Dan has a first class honours degree in Accountancy and has been offered a trainee accountancy post with a starting salary of €12,000. He has also been offered a job as a labourer on a nearby building site. The construction manager has offered to pay him €4,000 through the books plus €1,000 cash each month.

Sheila has 8 A's and 2 B's in her GCSE's/intercerts. She has also received an offer of a job in the bank with a starting salary of €800 per month (€9,600 per annum). Tom already has €6,000 invested in a deposit account for Sheila's education. He has suggested that he will give this to her – and that she is likely to purchase a car with the funds.

Sheila gets €15 per week pocket money and clothes.

Tom has €1,000 invested towards Ted's future education.

1. Pocket money of €15 per week amounts to €780 per year. In addition, it is estimated that about €60 per month is spent on clothes and shoes for Sheila, making a total yearly cost of €1,500.
2. Funds spent on Dan's education (per the information provided in the question).

Appendix 1 (continued)

One-off	
Car	€6,000
Yearly (for three years)	
University fees	€3,200
Insurance	€1,200
Car tax	€165
Car repairs	€350
Petrol (€20 × 52)	€1,040
Weekly allowance (€40 × 52)	€2,080
Textbooks (€200 × 3)	€600
Total annual	€8,635

The expenditure for Sheila is therefore prudently estimated at about €10,000 per year, assuming that she also remains at home and travels to university and you purchase a vehicle for her.

Appendix 2: Schedule Detailing Primary and Secondary Objectives

Schedule to identify primary and secondary objectives (rank in order of importance)

Objectives	Example responses	More information
Primary		
Short-term	Debt control	You would like to be mortgage-free when you retire in 11 years time.
Long-term	Would like to have surplus funds on retirement	You would like to have at least €25,000 surplus cash after all debt has been repaid when you retire.
Secondary		
Short-term	Finance children's education	You have set funds aside for Sheila's education. If it is in Sheila's best interests to continue in education, you would like to be able to pay for this.
	Be debt-efficient/ intelligent	Reduce expensive bad debt. Reduce the financial pressure experienced each month.
	Start saving/investing regularly	Analyse current income and expenditure and highlight potential savings to be made and investment opportunities.
Long-term	Finance children's education	You are currently setting funds aside for Ted's education. If it is in Ted's interests to continue in education, you would like to be able to pay for this.
	Consider inheritance	Make a will/start a trust. You would ideally like to leave some wealth to your children when you die.

Appendix 3: Statement of Net Worth (Before Recommendations are Considered)

Statement of Net Worth

	Return	Tom €	Angela €	Total €
Assets				
Legacy account	4%	10,000		10,000
Sheila's education account	3%	6,000		6,000
Ted's education account	2%	1,000		1,000
Term Deposit account	5%	15,000		15,000
Deposit account	3%	10,000		10,000
House				350,000
Contents (estimate)				20,000
Land			50,000	50,000
Cars		6,000	7,000	13,000
Total assets				475,000
Liabilities	Cost			
Overdraft	18%			(3,950)
Mortgage	6%			(75,000)
Car finance – Tom[1]		(12,960)		(12,960)
Car finance – Angela[2]			(19,200)	(19,200)
Credit card (joint)[3]	28.3%			(12,000)
Debenporks card[4]	19.56%		(3,200)	(3,200)
Dot Hawkins card[5]	22.42%		(1,800)	(1,800)
Succeeding card[6]	25.34%		(4,200)	(4,200)
Total liabilities				(132,310)
Net assets				342,690

1. €360 x 36 = €12,960.
2. €400 x 48 = €19,200.
3. $(1 + 0.021)^{12} - 1 = 28.3\%$.
4. $(1 + 0.015)^{12} - 1 = 19.56\%$.
5. $(1 + 0.017)^{12} - 1 = 22.42\%$.
6. $(1 + 0.019)^{12} - 1 = 25.34\%$.

NOTE: In addition to the above assets you are likely to inherit the family home and any other assets belonging to your mum. These assets are not anticipated as they may be used to cover future care costs for your mum.

Appendix 4: Debt Schedule (Before Recommendations are Implemented)

Debt type	Monthly increase in balance	Annual Rate	Credit limit	Outstanding balance	Repayment amount	Payable
	€		€	€	€	
Overdraft		18%		(3,950)		
Mortgage		6%		(75,000)	1,100	Monthly
Car finance – Tom[1]		15.38%		(12,960)	360	Monthly
Car finance – Angela[2]		19.56%		(19,200)	400	Monthly
Credit card (joint)[3]		28.3%		(12,000)	800	Monthly
Debenporks – 1.5%[4]	100	19.56%	4,000	(3,200)	100	Monthly
Dot Hawkins – 1.7%[5]	80	22.42%	3,000	(1,800)	80	Monthly
Succeeding – 1.9%[6]	80	25.34%	4,500	(4,200)	120	Monthly
Total				**(132,310)**	**2,960**	

1. Tom's Passat
   Amount borrowed is €18,500 + €500 (set-up fee) for a seven-year period.
   The terms are 84 monthly repayments @ €360.
   The Present Value = X x 84 periods at x%
   €19,000 = €360 x 84 period annuity at x%
   52.77 = 84 period annuity at x%

Use interpolation (try 1%)

$$\frac{1-(1.01)^{-84}}{0.01} = 56.65$$

Try 1.2%

$$\frac{1-(1.012)^{-84}}{0.012} = 52.73$$

The interest rate is 1.2% per month, which equates to an annual rate of: $(1.012)^{12} - 1 = 15.38\%$ (rounded).

2. Angela's Eos
   The amount borrowed is €19,500 + €500 (set-up fee) for an eight-year period.
   The terms are 96 monthly repayments @ €400
   The Present Value = X x 84 period at x%
   €20,000 = €400 x 96 period annuity at x%
   50 = 96 period annuity at x%
   Use interpolation (try 1%)

$$\frac{1-(1.01)^{-96}}{0.01} = 61.53$$

Try 1.5%

$$\frac{1-(1.015)^{-96}}{0.015} = 50.7$$

The interest rate is 1.5% per month which equates to $(1.015)^{12} - 1 = 19.56\%$ (rounded)

3. Spend on credit card (Joint) €12,000 × 2.1% = €252 – Interest. The credit card is at the maximum limit so the monthly spend must be €800 - €252 = €548.
4. Spend on Debenporks credit card per month (€100 + €100 - €39 (balance half way through year €2,600 × 1.5%) = €161.
5. Spend on Dot Hawkins credit card per month (€80 + €80 - €22 (balance half way through year (€1,800 – (6 × €80)) × 1.7% = €138.
6. Spend on Succeeding credit card per month (€80 + €120 - €71 (balance half way through year (€4,200 – (6 × €80)) × 1.9%) = €129.

Appendix 5: Statement of Annual Net Cash-flows in 2XX9

Income	Tom €	Angela €	Total €
Wages (€2,900 × 12)	34,800		34,800
Wages (€1,400 × 12)		16,800	16,800
Consultancy (€300 × 12)	3,600		3,600
Child benefit (€18.8 + €12.2) × 52			1,612
Legacy a/c 4% (1 – 0.40) × €10,000	240		240
Sheila a/c 3% (€6,000 + €3,600)/2 × 1.8%	86.4		86.4
Deposit a/c 2% (€1,000 × (2% (1 – 0.4)	12		12
Term Deposit a/c 5% (€15,000 × (5% (1 – 0.4)	450		450
Deposit a/c 3% (€10,000 × 3% (1 – 0.40)	180		180
Total income			57,780.4
Cash outflows			
Tax on consultancy (40% × €3,600)	1,440		1,440
Childcare costs (€15 × 3 × 52)		2,340	2,340
Groceries (€600 × 12)			7,200
Diesel (€50 × 52)	2,600	2,600	5,200
Car Insurance (€60 × 12)	720	720	1,440
Car Tax	110	110	220
Car repairs	300	300	600
Consumables (€30 × 52)	1,560		1,560
Consumables (€70 × 52)		3,640	3,640
Household bills (€150 × 52)			7,800
Sheila – pocket money (€15 × 52)	780		780

Appendix 5 (continued)

Debt

Overdraft (interest estimated at €700 per annum)		700
Mortgage (€1,100 × 12)	13,200	13,200
Car finance – Tom (€360 × 12)	4,320	4,320
Car finance – Angela (€400 × 12)	4,800	4,800
Credit card (joint) (€800 × 12)		9,600
(expenditure on credit card accounted for above) €548 × 12[1]		(6,576)
Debenporks (€100 × 12)	1,200	1,200
Dot Hawkins (€80 × 12)	960	960
Succeeding (€120 × 12)	1,440	1,440

Savings

Transfers to Ted's account (€100 × 12)	1,200	1,200
Transfers to Sheila's account (€200 × 12)	2,400	2,400
Total expenditure		65,464
Net yearly outflow		(7,683.60)

1. The spend on the joint credit card of €548 per month (on average) is assumed to be on a variety of costs, including household bills and food. The yearly cash outflow would have been much worse in the previous three years because of financing Dan through university.

Appendix 6: Statement of Net Worth (Amended to Reflect the Suggested Immediate Steps)

	Rate	Total	Change	New position
Assets		€	€	€
Legacy a/c	4%	10,000	D (8,150)	1,850
Sheila a/c	3%	6,000	C (6,000)	-
Deposit a/c	2%	1,000	B (1,000)	-
Term Deposit a/c	5%	15,000	E (15,000)	-
Deposit a/c	3%	10,000	A (10,000)	-
House		350,000		350,000
Contents		20,000		20,000
Vehicles		13,000		13,000
Land		50,000		50,000
Total assets		475,000		434,850
Liabilities				
Overdraft	18%	(3,950)	D 3,950	-
Mortgage	5%	(75,000)	E 15,000	60,000
Car – Tom		(12,960)		12,960
Car – Angela		(19,200)		19,200

Appendix 6 (continued)

Credit card (joint)	28.3%	(12,000)	A 10,000 B 1,000 C 1,000	–
Debenporks credit card	19.56%	(3,200)	D 3,200	–
Dot Hawkins credit card	22.42%	(1,800)	C 800 D 1,000	–
Succeeding credit card	25.34%	(4,200)	C 4,200	
Total liabilities		(132,310)		92,160
Net assets		(342,690)		(342,690)

Also it would be wise to transfer the €1,850 from the legacy account to the current account, for day-to-day emergency transactions, the balance on this account to be built up over the coming year.

Appendix 7: Statement of Net Income (Amended to Reflect the Suggested Immediate Reductions in Non-necessary Expenditure)

	Tom €	Angela €	Total €
Income			
Wages (€2,900 × 12)	34,800		34,800
Wages (€1,400 × 12)		16,800	16,800
Consultancy (€300 × 12)	3,600		3,600
Rent of conacre (€80 × 15)[1]			1,200
Legacy account 4% (1 − 0.40) × €1,850	44.4		44.4
Child benefit (Government subsidy)			1,612
Total income			58,056.4
Cash outflows			
Tax on consultancy (40% × €3,600)	1,440		1,440
Insurances (payment protection, life assurance)			1,000
Pension (€50,000 × 4% × 59%)			1,180
Childcare costs (€15 × 3 × 52) – likely to be lower and will only last for two more years		2,340	2,340
Groceries (€600 × 12)			7,200
Diesel (€50 × 52)	2,600	2,600	5,200
Car Insurance (€60 × 12)	720	720	1,440
Car Tax	110	110	220
Car repairs	300	300	600
Consumables (€20 × 52)	1,040		1,040
Consumables (€20 × 52)		1,040	1,040

Appendix 7 (continued)

Household bills (€50 × 52) – possibly too low		2,600
Sheila – pocket money (€10 × 52)	520	520
Debt		
Overdraft	–	–
Mortgage (€1,100 × 12)	13,200	13,200
Car finance –Tom (€360 × 12)	4,320	4,320
Car finance – Angela (€400 × 12)	4,800	4,800
Fencing land (one-off expenditure)		1,500
Total cash outflows		49,640
Cash surplus expected		8,416.40

1. There will be no corresponding tax cash outflow in this year as the fencing expenditure is tax deductible.

Section C

Solutions to integrated Cases in Management Accounting/ business finance

Case 32
Solution to Toffer Group plc
Ciaran Connolly and Martin Kelly,
Queen's University Belfast

MEMORANDUM

To: Board of Directors of Toffer Group
From: Independent Consultant
Date: XXXX
Subject: Management Accounting and Business Finance Issues

Question 1

For decision-making, only future costs and revenues are relevant. Past costs are gone (sunk) and should be ignored, although there may be psychological influences to the contrary. Marginal costing, because it concentrates on variable costs, is more in line with decision-making theory. This is not to say that fixed costs are not relevant; they can be manageably variable, i.e. to the individual company a general manager's salary is a fixed cost, but to James Grant in the future such a cost is manageably variable.

Question 2

Marginal costing allows a greater degree of flexibility to a decision maker, particularly for short-term strategies. It may be that James Grant is looking for short-term improvement to justify investment, or the concentration on volume output, or the switching of production between plants, all of which are more easily accomplished on a marginal approach. In the longer term, however, all costs must be accounted for and contributions must be sufficient to cover every fixed cost.

Question 3

There are a number of possible alternatives:

(a) The hi-low approach (or variations upon it) which, by comparing the highest and lowest levels of activity isolates the variable element. For example:

Hours of activity	Overhead
	€
Lowest 3,000	6,000
Highest 9,000	13,200

A step of 6,000 hours gives an increase in overhead of €7,200, therefore €7,200/6,000 = €1.20 per hour, i.e. the variable element.

At the 3,000 level of activity, variable cost is €3,600 (€1.20 × 3,000) so fixed cost must be €2,400 (€6,000 − €3,600). At 9,000 hours, VC = €10,800 and FC = €2,400.

(b) Scatter graph techniques (lines of the best fit).
(c) Method of the least squares.

Question 4

Contribution per hour, Department Y the constraining factor:

Product	Alpha	Beta	Gamma
Contribution	€30	€55	€64
Hours in Department Y	6 hours	8 hours	10 hours
Contribution per hour	€5.00	€.875	€6.40

Question 5

This may be achieved by maximising profit in the short term, and subject to employment and redundancy legislation. The maximum profit could be achieved by producing products in the order of their highest contribution factor per unit of limiting factor (Alpha, Beta and Gamma).

Hours available in Department Y:

6 hours × 5,000	=	30,000
8 hours × 2,000	=	16,000
10 hours × 3,000	=	30,000
		76,000

The available hours are allocated to the products in the order of their contribution per hour. The maximum demand for Beta and Gamma is 4,000 units of each. The remaining hours are allocated to Alpha. Maximum profit is therefore:

		Hours		€
Beta	4,000 × 8	32,000 × €6.875	=	220,000
Gamma	4,000 × 10	40,000 × €6.40	=	256,000
				476,000
Alpha	Balance	4,000 × €5.00	=	20,000
		76,000		496,000
Fixed overhead				(152,000)
Profit				344,000
Extra profit over original budget				44,000

Question 6

Redundancy in Departments X and Z:

Produce	Units
Alpha (See note)	666
Beta	4,000
Gamma	4,000

Note: 666 units of Alpha are to be manufactured, i.e. 4,000 hours in Department Y at 6 hours per unit.

Product	Original hrs		Max. profit hrs		Reduction in hrs
Department X:					
Alpha	5,000 × 30	150,000	666 × 30	19,980	
Beta	2,000 × 15	30,000	4,000 × 15	60,000	
Gamma	3,000 × 32	96,000	4,000 × 32	128,000	
		276,000		207,980	68,020
Department Z:					
Alpha	5,000 × 15	75,000	666 × 15	9,990	
Beta	2,000 × 8	16,000	4,000 × 8	32,000	
Gamma	3,000 × 32	96,000	4,000 × 32	128,000	
		187,000		169,990	17,010

Then redundancy:
Department X	68,020 / 1,920	=	35 employees
Department Z	17,010 / 1,920	=	9 employees

Question 7

Bebe:

Financial statement for last year in marginal form:

	No. of units	Per unit (€)	€'000
Sales	8,000	1,000	8,000
MC of sales:			
Variable cost of product	12,000	500	6,000
Less stock	(4,000)	500	(2,000)
			4,000
Contribution			4,000
Fixed costs:			
Production		2,880	
Selling		1,200	(4,080)
Loss			(80)

Note:
Per Appendix 3, profit under an absorption approach is €880,000. Under marginal costing, there is a loss of €80,000, resulting in a total difference of €960,000. This is explained as follows:
Stock values per machine, €740 (absorption) and €500 (marginal).
Therefore, €240 × 4,000 units stock = €960,000.

Question 8

(a) Absorption costing principles

	No. of units	Per unit (€)	€'000
Sales	12,000	1,000	12,000
Production cost:			
Variable cost	12,000	500	6,000
Fixed cost	12,000	240	2,880
		740	8,880
Stocks:			
Opening	4,000	2,960	
Closing	4,000	2,960	–
			8,880
Factory profit			3,120
Selling etc.			(1,200)
Net profit			1,920

(b) Marginal costing principles

	No. of units	Per unit (€)	€'000
Sales	12,000	1,000	12,000
Cost of sales:			
Variable cost	12,000	500	6,000
O/stock & C/stock	4,000		-
Contribution			6,000
Fixed costs (€2,880 + €1,200)			(4,080)
Net profit			1,920

See how, when production and sales are the same, profit is €1,920,000 under either system of accounting. Profit differences arise where there are changes in the level of stocks.

Question 9

(a) Absorption costing principles

	No. of units	Per unit (€)	€'000
Sales	16,000	1,000	16,000
Production cost:			
Opening stock	4,000	740	2,960
Variable cost	12,000	500	6,000
Fixed cost	12,000	240	2,880
			11,840
Factory profit			4,160
Selling etc.			1,200
Net profit			2,960

(b) Marginal costing principles

	No. of units	Per unit (€)	€'000
Sales	16,000	1,000	16,000
Cost of sales:			
Opening stock	4,000	500	2,000
Variable cost	12,000	500	6,000
Contribution			8,000
Fixed costs (€2,880 + €1,200)			4,080
Net profit			3,920

When sales exceed production, the marginal system reports higher profits (profit difference is stock movement 4,000 × €240 = €960,000).

Question 10

Could use the following approaches:

- dividend with and without growth;
- net assets;
- historic earnings x P/E; and
- current (potential earnings) x P/E.

Dividends – No Growth

Value per share = €350,000/0.06 = **€1.16**
5,000,000

Dividends with Growth

Value per share = €0.07 x (1.03) = **€2.40**
0.06 – 0.03

Note: Bebe is unlisted and a higher dividend yield could be used

Net assets

€14,910 – €18,000 + €8,500 + €2,000 + €1,500 (excluding goodwill)
Value per share = €8,910,000/5,000,000 = **€1.78**

P/E – Average Historic Earnings

$$\frac{€955 + €525 + €695 + €555 + €607}{5} = €667,400$$

Use average PE (discounted as Bebe unlisted) = 15 × (2/3) = 10
Value per share = 10 × €667,400/5,000,000 = **€1.35**

P/E – Current Potential Earnings for this Year

This year's earnings potentially (see solution 8) = €1,920,000

After tax = €1,344,000
Value per share = 10 × €1,344,000/5,000,000 = **€2.68**

Note: Also, future earnings from solution 9 (above) if assumptions re. sales and closing inventory of Nets are correct then earnings basis would indicate an even higher valuation.

Question 11

Net Assets

A company such as Bebe Limited is usually bought as a source of future cash streams, rather than to access and sell the assets, so the net asset value, which looks at the book values only, is not particularly relevant, unless it is the intention to liquidate the company. The non-current assets have been adjusted for recent fall in property prices, etc. (as per valuations of independent valuer in question). Asset valuation can often act as a 'floor value' for negotiation between seller and purchaser. Intangible assets are hard to identify and value, especially in an unquoted business such as Bebe. Students could also refer to comments in e-mail to James Grant from Q. Director. Goodwill is included on balance sheet of Bebe and it is unlikely that a perspective purchaser would be prepared to pay for this.

Earnings

Earnings basis assumes that previous earnings are typical and that the market will view Bebe in a similar light to the three competitors shown in Appendix 4. Not told in question what Toffer's P/E is. As Bebe is unlisted there is an argument to discount the P/E due to lack of liquidity and perception of higher risk. Earnings figure should really be maintainable earnings for the future. Conversely, another company may be prepared to pay more if it can see synergistic benefits on acquisition. Clearly, from information in case, there is potential for future benefits from sales of Nets or diversification into other related markets. More information would be needed, but there may be a case for arguing that there is significantly more potential (especially intellectual capital/other markets) that would point to higher PE than average of 10 used above. Clearly, there are very talented people working at Bebe who could contribute significantly to goals of Toffer Group. Should be mentioned that gearing levels will affect P/E ratios.

Dividends

Dividend-valuation model assumes constant growth in dividends (3%) in perpetuity. It is more appropriate for minority shareholdings who would be unable to alter dividend policy. What happens if a company pays no dividends? However, it is useful to look at this method in comparison to earnings and net assets valuations.

The preferred approach to valuation would be to estimate future cash-flows and discount them at an appropriate cost of capital. This method is also called shareholder value analysis. Share valuations are essentially a process of negotiation but a price of around €2.50–€3.00 per share, based on earnings approach, would not appear to be unreasonable.

Other Points

- Level of secured debt in Bebe needs investigating (secured on what).
- Need for cash of around €15 million to finance acquisition.
- Overall reliability of figures presented/other risks.
- Effect on EPS/share price of Toffer Group.
- HR issues that occurred in integrating KTE into Toffer have to be avoided and hopefully on hindsight the experience will be helpful in integrating Bebe into the group.

Question 12

Strategies for Enhancing Value after Acquisition Include:

- review Bebe (and individual parts) or costs that could be cut or assets that are surplus to requirements;
- consider what economies of scale could be enjoyed across the Toffer Group to reduce costs/improve efficiency and improve revenues;
- ensure that the acquisition does not demotivate staff, particularly in Bebe, by improving and maintaining good communication with the workforce. Ian would have an important role to play here given his experience with KTE acquisition;
- review contracts and budgetary planning and control systems as a matter of urgency;
- look at possibility of entering other markets or enhancing the Net product;
- re-evaluate the group cost of capital, which may have changed to reflect investors' new perception of risk in the shares.

Question 13

Equity

- Public issue of equity would not be common for a listed company such as Toffer. Need to raise around €15 million to fund acquisition. Difficulty setting an issue price.
- Problem regarding loss of control for shareholders and cost would be significant.
- Rights issue would make sense as it is cheaper and issue price is relatively unimportant (assuming market efficiency). Control stays with existing shareholders.
- However, as Director P points out, there may be issues regarding timing and students should refer to 'bear market'/EMH in their answers. Director P favours a 'Chartists' approach to forecasting share prices.
- Underwriting of rights issue.
- Reduce gearing (not told in question what percentage of debt is). Effect on EPS, share price and dividends.

Debt-Convertible Loan Stock

Preferred by James Grant, but there is a need for caution, as highlighted in e-mail from Q. Director.

- Self liquidating (cash-flow advantages) providing holders of convertibles convert.
- Cheaper source of finance for Toffer Group as interest would be less than straight debt and hopefully by time conversion occurs Bebe will be well integrated in to the group.
- Tax-deductibility advantage and issue costs of debt are lower than equity.
- Problem if other lenders want to impose restrictive covenants.
- Currently interest rates are low so it would make sense to increase level of gearing but to take account of increase in financial risk.

- Effect on cost of capital of Toffer Group.
- Debt does impose sense of discipline (Agency theory).

Students may mention other debt instruments – flexibility/risk/cost/control, etc. Effect of gearing on share prices as mentioned by Q. Director – Modigliani and Miller/Traditional theories of gearing.

Retained Profits

- Often these are already committed for working capital and commercially may not be a realistic option.

Question 14

Wide range of points could be made, but would expect reference back to issues raised by Directors P and Q.

- What do we mean by a dividend policy? Historical dividend pattern of Toffer group.
- Dividends as a residual (Investment decision first (NPV'S) and what is left can be paid out to shareholders.
- Clientele effect – different types of shareholders will have preference for income now.
- Is paying more dividends or stable dividends a signal to market of confidence about the future on the business. Share price implications.
- Liquidity – effect on cash reserves. Director Q appears to ignore what other investment calls there are on the funds.
- Relationship of share price and dividends. Director Q's comment that remuneration packages are tied into share value and anything that reduces value would be resisted at the board.
- Reduced dividends may be cheap way to finance expansion and avoids need to raise additional equity.
- May be best for Board of Toffer Group to have a consistent pattern of dividends and avoid major changes.
- Share buy back option is possible alternative if have cash but no further attractive investment proposals.
- What are competitors doing?
- Relationship between Investment, Financing and Dividend decisions.

Question 15

Executive share option plans (ESOPs) have become popular in recent years, partly in an attempt to aid goal congruence within companies. Goal congruence arises when goals of different groups coincide. The two main groups are shareholders (principals) and managers/directors (agents). Other parties include employees, creditors, government and the local community. ESOPs enable managers to buy a company's shares at a fixed price over a specified future period. The aim is to give managers a stake in the firm so that they will make decisions consistent with shareholders' interests. However, share options typically form only a limited part of the remuneration package. If share prices fall, managers may decide not to take up the option. Once they have taken up options, managers may feel that share price movements have little to do with their efforts, but reflect external market movements. ESOPs are viewed as a useful instrument for encouraging congruence between shareholder and manager, but one that is by no means perfect. Recently, there has been a backlash from the public over what has been seen as rewards given to managers for presiding over corporate failures. Good corporate governance now demands that directors look at the 'sustainability' of current business practices and evaluate the impacts they are having on the environment and society. It is likely that in the future these impacts will also be tied into executive remuneration packages.

Case 33
Solution to Glenview House Hotel
Margaret Healy and John Doran, University College Cork

REPORT ON PROPOSALS FOR EXPANSION AT GLENVIEW HOUSE HOTEL

Prepared by: Andrew Healy
Healy Dolan Consulting

For: Paul and Collette O'Connor
Glenview House Hotel
x/x/xxxx

I. Terms of Reference

This report evaluates each of the alternatives presented by Paul and Collette O'Connor as being under consideration with regard to the future development and operation of Glenview House Hotel. Critical aspects of expansion via renovation of the existing stable area are highlighted, as is the need for additional market research into the probable revenues, cost structures and general market conditions underpinning each of the proposed options. Business and financial issues relevant to the consideration of the leasing alternative are also identified and discussed. The report also addresses the use of relevant costing principles in decision making generally, as well as outlining the principle methods of determining the transfer price of inter-business transactions, should the riding holidays option be pursued.

All calculations are based on information provided by Glenview House Hotel, which has not been independently verified in the production of this report. It should also be noted that taxation aspects relevant to each of the options are outside the terms of reference of this specific report, but would merit serious consideration prior to any final decision being made.

2. Recommendations

(a) The expansion proposals under consideration need to be balanced with empirical market research to firm up on the revenue and cost estimates (including occupancy rates) used before such a major investment is entered into. We have significant concerns about the reliability of the figures provided (and which we have used in our calculations) as they are mainly subjective estimates.

(b) The proposal to renovate the stables for self-catering accommodation offers only a marginally profitable return on investment, except in a best-case scenario, which is believed to have a likelihood of 25% (i.e. a 1-in-4 chance).

(c) The proposal for Glenview Riding School should only proceed under terms agreed upon as a written partnership agreement between the parties.

(d) Research should also more broadly examine trends in the tourism industry generally. Specifically, any additional options that are available to the business should be identified and evaluated, as those analysed here have been arrived at to some extent as a reaction to external events or suggestions.

(e) The leasing alternative provides the most predictable stream of income over the medium term. However entry into this arrangement should be considered in light of the financial and strategic business risks it would encompass.

3. Evaluating the Proposals for Expansion

There are two proposals available to Glenview House Hotel for expanding the business in the medium term, each presenting varying levels of personal commitment and involvement on the part of the O'Connor family. The proposals are mutually exclusive, offering summary financial outcomes as presented and discussed in (a) below. A number of mechanisms for setting the daily rate chargeable for hotel guests using the Glenview Riding School are presented in (b). The main principles involved in making relevant costing-type decisions are outlined in (c).

(a) Proposals for the Re-development of the Existing Stables Area

Self-Catering Accommodation Proposal Based on the available estimates, the proposal to convert the stables to self-catering accommodation is estimated to require an investment of €976,910 (see Appendix 1) and to generate annual contribution (Appendix 2) dependent on market conditions as follows:

	Probability	Contribution	Gross Yield	Payback (in years)
Best-case scenario	25%	€86,735	8.9%	11.3
Middle-case scenario	50%	€45,513	4.7%	21.5
Worst-case scenario	25%	€25,163	2.6%	38.8
Expected (weighted average) outcome		€50,731	5.2%	19.3

It should be noted, however, that the probabilities used in the calculations of the likely contributions for the self-catering units are subjective and also based on historical experience. We are concerned by the evidence from both tourist trade and financial sources that the future for the tourist trade may differ significantly from historical experience. In this case past probabilities are not a good guide to future performance. Based on the information provided, the self-catering accommodation proposal would only be worthwhile in a best-case scenario. It should also be noted that the figures do not take into account the costs of wear and tear and the probable need for further investment to renew the facilities even before the end of the payback period. The building cost estimates also need to be finalised, with firm quotations being received in writing.

Riding Holidays Proposal Based on the information available, this proposal requires an investment of €252,000 (see Appendix 1). However, whilst some effort has been made to identify the annual cash outflows of the business, less clarity exists regarding the annual income streams. Based on having eight horses available for use, the average number of working days per horse required to breakeven is 180 days (see Appendix 3). The nature of that activity must also be considered. If users are predominantly hotel guests, the pattern of use will show demand peaking and waning depending on the days of the week and time of the year. Local trade, however, may lead to a more even spread of demand. Greater consideration as to the anticipated sales mix is needed, towards refining the breakeven calculation and determining the extent to which the margin of safety currently envisaged is reflective of the potential trading environment.

A number of other issues are also relevant to the consideration of this proposal.

- The previous track record of Sean's business is of concern, particularly given the lack of evidence indicating the O'Connors have any knowledge or experience of running a riding school. Combined with the circumstances of 'friends going into business', the potential for future fractious relations needs to be addressed. A partnership agreement should be drafted and should include operating procedures for the future management and decision-making needs of the business. This agreement should include provision for (i) profit sharing; (ii) terms if either party wishes to withdraw; and (iii) distribution of assets/surplus on winding up or termination of the venture.
- The estimated revenues from the proposal do not specify the proportions originating from hotel-based clients versus others. Greater investigation of the market potential of the venture is needed.

- The capital costs of the initial investment are largely covered by Sean's proposed cash inflow of €200,000, thus reducing the financial commitment required of the O'Connors. The potential to lease the hotel premises to a management company (considered later in this report) and proceed with the riding school initiative should also be investigated. Future investments required for the business (e.g. replacement of horses) need to be incorporated into the negotiations.
- The impact of the riding school on the 'image' of the Glenview House Hotel (under its current business model and/or following acceptance of the leasing arrangement discussed later) needs to be considered.
- Issues concerning the valuation of the business and the finalising of its ownership structure also need to be urgently addressed.

(b) Determining the Transfer Price for Guests Availing of the Riding Holiday Facilities

A number of mechanisms exist through which a transfer price for use of the riding facilities can be set between Glenview House Hotel and the proposed Glenview Riding School. The ideal is that the chosen method and its resultant price should lead to goal congruence as between the activities of Glenview House Hotel and Glenview Riding School, in relation to the operation of the riding holidays proposal. Three alternatives are discussed in the following paragraphs.

Market-based transfer pricing Market-based transfer pricing uses the publicly available price of a similar service to determine the transfer price. This can lead to optimal decision-making when markets are perfectly competitive, inter-dependencies between the sub-units are minimal, and there are no additional costs or benefits to using the market place instead of contracting internally. Given the involvement of Paul O'Connor in both businesses, and the suggested extent of excess capacity currently available to Sean, these conditions do not apply. However, use of market price may constitute an initial starting point, and ceiling level, from which all parties can initiate the negotiation process. Identification of the availability of riding facilities from other sources in the immediate vicinity and the associated price levels for these services would quickly identify the extent to which the Glenview House Hotel can seek to influence the outcome of the negotiations.

Cost-based transfer pricing Cost-based transfer pricing determines the price based on the costs (either budgeted or actual) of producing the riding service. Whilst this approach can be helpful when market prices are unavailable, it can also lead to sub-optimal decision making where the fixed costs and proposed mark-up of the selling entity become regarded as variable costs to the transaction. A more detailed analysis of the cost structure of the Glenview Riding School would be needed to inform the use of this method and the determination of an appropriate profit margin for the Riding School.

Negotiated transfer pricing Negotiated transfer prices arise as the outcome of a bargaining process between the buyer and seller of a service. Where there is excess capacity (as in this instance), the transfer price range generally lies between the minimum price at which the selling entity is willing to sell (its variable costs) and the maximum price the buying entity would be willing to pay (the price at which the service is available from outside suppliers). Additional information and market research is needed to determine and verify each of these before the current negotiations can produce a mutually acceptable charge.

In addition to the specific matters mentioned above, there are a number of other matters bearing on the transfer price negotiations:

- Paul O'Connor is a member of both parties negotiating. His ability to maintain clear, impartial business judgment, supported by relevant financial data, in the particular circumstances and extant relationships between the parties will be crucial to the outcome and to the successful operation of the venture, should the proposal proceed.
- Sean Farrell's willingness to invest in the venture substantially reduces the investment cost for the Glenview House Hotel. However, the trade-off for that investment needs to be 'ring-fenced' in terms of the associated percentage of the ownership of the Glenview Riding School, rather than be allowed to become a bargaining tool for use in the setting of the transfer price.

(c) General Principles of Relevant Costing

Relevant costs are expected future costs that differ between alternatives. Relevant costing focuses on the costs that will change in a given decision scenario. There are two types of relevant cost: avoidable outlay cost and opportunity cost. Avoidable costs are costs that only happen if a particular course of action is followed; if it is not, then the costs do not occur. Opportunity costs relate to the net cash benefits given up for the next most desirable alternative. There are other costs that are not relevant: sunk costs (costs incurred prior to a decision being made); committed costs (costs that have to be paid, regardless of the outcome of the decision); and allocated costs in the future based on expenditure (e.g. depreciation). Limitations of decision-making using relevant costing concern how to identify all relevant opportunities and how to foresee all of the relevant costs and revenues.

4. The Management Company Leasing Option

The following financial and strategic business issues need to be considered in evaluating the leasing option alternative.

- Due diligence: the current owners should investigate the track record of the management company and their prior experience in any similar operation.
- Relationship Management: as the financial future of the owners will, to a large extent, be in the hands of the new management team, it is vital that they spend considerable time getting to know their potential future business partners and assessing both their reliability and the likely quality of the ongoing relationship.

- Adequate capitalisation of the management company: it is vital to ensure that the management company would have sufficient capital in place to fulfill its business plan, but also to sustain operations through a period where the 'worst case' scenario applies.
- Management commitment required: the leasing option will not require day-to-day management time and this would allow the current owners of Glenview House Hotel to pursue other interests.
- Release of capital investment: the continued operation of the hotel will inevitably involve upgrading and reinvestment in some form. This would tie up the capital of the owners and their ability to make alternative investments.
- Risk related to occupancy rates: leasing contracts need to be constructed carefully to ensure that the property owners will not carry a residual risk should the expected occupancy rates fluctuate. Clauses need to be included in the contract to make clear who bears this residual risk.
- Core competency: the current proprietors must consider carefully what represents the unique selling point (USP) of the existing hotel business. A significant but not quantified portion of the current revenue comes from customers who have built a close relationship with the owners. Is this merely a perception or is this custom dependent on the current style of ownership?
- The move to a new ownership structure would need to be carefully managed, with perhaps a transitional involvement in customer relations of the original proprietors. The lease payments for the first year or two may be conditional on reaching certain sales targets. While this might initially seem undesirable to the original proprietors, it might allow for a better price to be achieved overall as it would give the leasing company some assurance in projections of future turnover.
- Strategic Implications: the real interest of Trixie O'Connor in the property would need to be clarified. If her interest is real, what timescale does she place on her wish to become involved? Would a 10-year lease without a guarantee that the lessee could renew be more suitable? In that case there would need to be clarity as to if, and if so how, the lessor would be compensated for vacating the lease and for any improvement works that might have been performed to the premises in the interim.
- Labour relations: the transfer arrangement would need to clarify the position of existing staff. Would these be retained such that the new owners would merely take over the running of the business? Or would they be made redundant? And if made redundant, would there be a guarantee of re-employment by the new operator? The redundancy process of staff will also need to be handled carefully to minimise damage to the brand image and goodwill of the business, as well as to the personal reputation in the community of the original employers. Financial provision might also be made for severance payments. The amount involved would vary depending on whether re-employment was guaranteed.
- Employment Law implications: legal advice should be taken as to the position of existing staff and the responsibilities of their employer in the event of a new operator leasing the premises. The status of the employees would be affected by issues related to the transfer, including whether the premises would operate continuously during the transfer or would close for refitting prior to reopening under new management.

Appendix 1: Glenview House Hotel – Review of Expansion options

Cash-flow Details Under Each Option
(Assuming all 10 self-catering units are constructed)

	Self-catering Accommodation	Riding School
Initial Investment:		
- Site works	100,000	150,000
- Construction	350,000	50,000
- Internal fit-out of units (40,000 × 10)	400,000	-
- Installation of services	50,000	-
- Planning fees	2,000	2,000
- Playground	10,000	-
- Refurbishment of existing stables	-	40,000
- Purchase of riding equipment	-	10,000
- Laundry facilities (100 × 10)	1,000	-
Project cost	913,000	
- Architect design fees (7% of total project)	63,910	-
TOTAL INVESTMENT	**€976,910**	**€252,000**

Appendix 2: Glenview House Hotel – Self-catering Accommodation

Contribution Statement Under Each Scenario

High Season	**Best Case**	**Middle Case**	**Worst Case**
Contribution per unit – high season (revenue – variable costs)	€330	€330	€330
Number of units available	10	10	10
Contribution per week – full occupancy	€3,300	€3,300	€3,300
Expected occupancy	90%	50%	25%
Expected weekly contribution	€2,970	€1,650	€825
Length of season – weeks	13	13	13
Contribution – high season	€38,610	€21,450	€10,725
Low Season	**Best Case**	**Middle Case**	**Worst Case**
Contribution per unit – low season (revenue – variable costs)	€275	€275	€275
Number of units available	10	10	10
Contribution per week – full occupancy	€2,750	€2,750	€2,750
Expected occupancy	50%	25%	15%
Expected weekly contribution	€1,375	€687	€412

Appendix 2 (continued)

Length of season – weeks	35	35	35
Contribution – low season	€48,125	€24,062	€14,437
Total annual contribution	**€86,735**	**€45,513**	**€25,163**
Likelihood of Occurrence	**25%**	**50%**	**25%**

NOTE: it is possible to calculate an expected value of €50,731 by weighting the contributions by their probabilities. However, there are only three discrete possibilities and only one will occur. Expected values are more appropriate where there will be a large number of repetitions of the event.

Appendix 3: Glenview Riding School

Calculation of Breakeven Level of Users

Annual Costs

Insurance	5,000
Staff wages	90,000
Animal Feedstuff	48,000
Veterinary fees	10,000
Advertising	5,000
TOTAL	**€158,000**
Net Income per day's riding	€110
Breakeven level of users	1,437
Breakeven no. of days riding per horse (based on current level of eight horses)	180 days

Case 34
Solution to Delaney's Bakehouse Breads
John Doran and Margaret Healy,
University College Cork

**REPORT ON SUPERMARKET CONTRACT
NEGOTIATIONS FOR DELANEY'S
BAKEHOUSE BREADS**

Prepared by: James O'Connell
O'Connell Consulting

For: Noleen Delaney
Delaney's Bakehouse Breads
Date: x/x/xxxx

1. Terms of Reference

This report considers the issues raised from our discussion on xx/xx/xxxx. The report analyses the cost structure of the speciality breads proposal using absorption costing and activity-based costing (ABC). The impact that the choice of accounting method may have on this decision is considered. Issues arising from the ongoing contract negotiations process are also considered. All calculations are based on information provided by Delaney's Bakehouse Breads and have not been verified in the production of this report.

2. Recommendations

(a) Reconsideration of the current terms of the speciality breads proposal is advised. The proposal generates favourable returns for only two of the three products

included in the bundle if activity-based costing methods are used.
(b) Cross-subsidisation of the projected losses on the Sultana Loaf should only be considered if the production and sale of all three products is maintained at contract levels.
(c) If production is to be maintained at the Macroom Bakehouse, greater consideration of production process efficiencies is needed and can be informed by the contents of the ABC analysis.
(d) Greater consideration of the longer-term working capital implications of the supermarket contract is needed. In particular, issues concerning inventory management and debtor payment terms need to be urgently addressed.

3. Proposed Speciality Breads Initiative

(a) Costing Calculations

Costs have been produced for the speciality breads proposal under both the existing costing practices of the bakery and under ABC. Results are presented in Appendices 2 and 3. In summary the calculations show:

All Amounts in Cents	Harvest Pan	Sultana Loaf	Bagel Loaf
Production Cost (per loaf)	cents	cents	cents
-under existing costing practices	16.18	23.91	17.18
-under ABC	14.37	44.85	17.66
Target Selling Price	20.00	30.00	25.00
Budgeted Net Margin (per loaf)			
-under existing costing practices	3.82	6.09	7.82
-under ABC	5.63	(14.85)	7.34

The implications of the results above are twofold. The commercial implications of these cost estimates are discussed under (b) below. The critical impact that the choice of cost-accounting regime may have on estimates of profitability and commercial viability generally is discussed in (c).

(b) Commercial Implications of the Cost Estimates

On the basis of the ABC calculations it would appear that the Harvest Pan and the Bagel Loaf offer a return on sales of 28.1% and 29.4%, respectively. However, the Sultana Loaf produces a loss on sales of 49.5%. On this basis Delaney's Bakehouse Breads has a number of options if the contract is to be pursued:

- proceed with the production of the Harvest Pan and Bagel Loaf, but drop the proposed Sultana Loaf offering;
- re-price the Sultana Loaf as a premium product. However, this would have to be explored both with the retailer customers and tested with end consumers to assess its viability;

- customer pressure may require that all three products are supplied as a 'package' at close to the original prices. If so, then the projected losses on the Sultana Loaf should not necessarily be seen as a 'deal breaker'. Although the projected loss on this product is almost 50% of revenue, the low volumes projected would limit the damage to budgeted margin to around €89,000. This would leave a combined annual margin on the complete contract of €655,000. In effect, the projected losses on the Sultana Loaf could be cross-subsidised by the other two products;
- this cross-subsidy can only operate if production of all three products is maintained at or close to the budgeted levels. To rely on this Delaney's Bakehouse Breads must ensure that contract negotiations focus on capping the volume of the loss-making product supplied and also guarantee minimum orders of the two more profitable products;
- the bakery should examine the possibility of reconfiguration of the business processes which drive the Sultana Loaf cost up to 44.85 cent per unit. The ABC cost per unit (working in Appendix 2) indicates that the relative cost of this loaf is primarily increased at two stages of the production process; mixing and baking. The combination of a longer baking time (50 minutes) and a smaller production run (15 units) account for the higher cost of this loaf. If the production lot size is driven by management policy, then this should be reviewed. If it is driven by technical constraints, then technological innovations should be explored to see if changes are possible, e.g. through larger ovens, revised material mix or temperature changes.

(c) Cost-effectiveness of the Product-costing Mechanism

The cost analysis above shows very different results depending on which costing mechanism is adopted. The main options open are those used in section (a) above;

- continue using the existing system of absorbing overhead costs into product costs on the basis of the products direct labour cost component;
- adopt a system of ABC. This would group indirect (overhead) costs into groups around activities. The costs of each of the activities would then be shared amongst the products on the basis of each product's usage of a cost driver. The costs in each pool are assumed to be variable in proportion to the level of the driver activity rather than the quantity of output;
- a compromise between the two systems would be to continue to use absorption costing for financial accounting purposes but conduct occasional ABC exercises to monitor product costs for cost management purposes and whenever new product launches are being considered. The five cost pools used in this ABC exercise might also be reduced to four. The two smallest cost pools – 'Shaping/Proofing' and 'Mixing' – could be integrated as the cost drivers for each (the weight of materials and the number of loaves) are likely to be highly correlated.

The choice of product-costing mechanism is dependent on the trade-off between the benefits to be gained by the extra information and the costs of maintaining the system as the ABC system requires a greater analysis of costs into pools. This introduces increased record-keeping. The existing absorption costing basis may have been appropriate up to now because of the homogeneous nature of the products in their impact on overhead costs. However, the information in Appendix 1 shows that this will not be the case for newer speciality breads.

In general, an ABC system is justified in cases where:

- indirect costs are a higher proportion of total costs;
- there is increased competition, particularly if competitors are segmenting the market and concentrating on some product offerings (you can survive with poor costing information and weak cost management if it is no worse than your competitors);
- a diverse range of products consumes resources in differing proportions. It is clear that some costs in the bakery are driven at batch level via the number of production runs or sales orders while others are volume related;
- there are clearly identifiable links between cost drivers and ABC cost pools.

4. Contract Risks and Benefits

As well as commercial implications discussed in the earlier sections, there are a number of other risks and benefits to the proposed contract terms that Delaney's Bakehouse Breads needs to consider, specifically in relation to working capital. These are discussed below.

- Based on Appendix 4, there is a higher net present value to be derived from ownership of the ovens by Noleen than by passing ownership to the supermarket chain. This derives from the high level of rebates that the supermarket chain would demand for taking on ownership of the ovens.
- In addition, vesting the ovens in the supermarket chain is also linked to ceding property rights over the brand. This both limits future opportunities beyond this one customer site and also risks Noleen losing control of her intellectual property rights. At a minimum it creates a risk of a fraught and inequitable future relationship.
- The cost related to loss of brand control is real, although hard to quantify.
- Ownership by Noleen/Delaney's Bakehouse Breads of the in-store ovens may also make it more difficult for the supermarket chain to shift supplier or take the venture in-house should it be successful.
- Reliability of volume estimates will need to be determined. Market research will need to be performed to confirm that the volume estimates used are attainable. If Noleen owns the ovens, then she will carry a higher fixed cost and consequent operational leverage and residual risk related to in-store fixed assets.
- Price support in the longer term should not be ignored. Reliance on one large customer will make the bakery very vulnerable to imposed contract variations

when the term of the first supermarket contract expires. It may be that this contract should be seen as the first of several to diversify the customer base. If possible, Noleen should avoid any commitment to exclusivity in this supermarket contract in relation to the brand. If exclusivity were demanded, then it should, at a minimum, be tied to a longer-term commitment from the supermarket chain.
- The data supplied is silent about the staffing of the project. Calculations here are based on the assumption that all in-store labour costs under either option are borne by the individual supermarkets / the supermarket chain.
- Costs of promotional activities need to be quantified.
- Maintenance and repair costs of the ovens have not been quantified or included, nor has responsibility for matters such as insurance.

Appendix 1: Delaney's Bakehouse Breads – Cost Driver Information

	Harvest Pan	Sultana Loaf	Bagel Loaf	Total
Budgeted sales price	€0.20	€0.30	€0.25	
Direct-material cost (per loaf)	€0.05	€0.09	€0.06	
Direct-labour cost (per loaf)	€0.03	€0.04	€0.03	
Projected units of output (loaves)	8,000,000	600,000	4,000,000	12,600,000
Production batch size (average)	100	15	50	
Sales order batch size (average)	50	15	50	
Weight of materials (grams per loaf)	400	450	300	
Baking time required (minutes per batch)	40	50	25	
From these above, can be further estimated:				
Number of production run	80,000	40,000	80,000	200,000
Number of sales orders	160,000	40,000	80,000	280,000
Total weight of materials used (kgs)	3,200,000	270,000	1,200,000	4,670,000
Total time required – mins (baking time × no. of production batches)	3,200,000	2,000,000	2,000,000	7,200,000

Appendix 2: Delaney's Bakehouse Breads – Speciality Breads Costing – ABC Method

Cost pool – charged to product by driver	Harvest Pan	Sultana Loaf	Bagel Loaf	O/head Total
Direct-material cost	€400,000	€54,000	€240,000	€694,000
Direct-labour cost	240,000	24,000	120,000	384,000
Set-up	176,000	88,000	176,000	440,000
Mixing	83,597	7,054	31,349	122,000
Shaping and Proofing	50,794	3,810	25,397	80,000
Baking	113,333	70,833	70,833	255,000
Packing and Delivery	85,714	21,429	42,857	150,000
Total Budgeted Cost	**€1,149,439**	**€269,125**	**€706,436**	**€2,125,000**
Number of units	8,000,000	600,000	4,000,000	
Unit Cost	**€0.1437**	**€0.4485**	**€0.1766**	

Each bread type is charged with the (Product's share of absorption basis / Absorption basis) × Total O/h in this cost pool. Allocation bases are as follows:

Set-up	*number of production runs*
Mixing	*weight of materials*
Shaping and proofing	*number of loaves*
Baking	*time required*
Packing and delivery	*number of sales orders*

Cost per Unit (in cents)	Harvest Pan	Sultana Loaf	Bagel Loaf
Direct-material cost	5.00	9.00	6.00
Direct-labour cost	3.00	4.00	3.00
Set-up	2.20	14.67	4.40
Mixing	1.04	1.18	0.78
Shaping and Proofing	0.63	0.63	0.63
Baking	1.42	11.81	1.77
Packing and Delivery	1.07	3.57	1.07
Total production cost per unit (cents)	**14.37**	**44.85**	**17.66**

	Harvest Pan	Sultana Loaf	Bagel Loaf	Total
Total budgeted revenue	€1,600,000	€180,000	€1,000,000	€2,780,000
Total budgeted cost	€1,149,439	€269,125	€706,436	€2,125,000
Budgeted Margin	450,561	(89,125)	293,564	655,000

Appendix 3: Delaney's Bakehouse Breads – Speciality Breads Costing – Conventional Costing Method

Overhead cost-pools combined

Set-up	440,000
Mixing	122,000
Shaping and proofing	80,000
Baking	255,000
Packing and delivery	150,000
Total Overhead	**1,047,000**

Total Cost (except direct materials and labour) per euro spent on direct-labour:
Total O/H / Direct labour cost = €1,047,000 / €384,000
 = 272.7% of direct-labour cost

	Harvest Pan	Sultana Loaf	Bagel Loaf	Total
Direct-material cost per unit	5.00	9.00	6.00	
Direct-labour cost per unit	3.00	4.00	3.00	
Other production costs per unit (O/H)	8.18	10.91	8.18	
Total production cost per unit (cents)	16.18	23.91	17.18	
Number of units	8,000,000	600,000	4,000,000	
Total budgeted cost	**€1,294,375**	**€143,438**	**€687,188**	**€2,125,000**

Appendix 4: Delaney's Bakehouse Breads – Review of Oven-ownership Options

Assuming worst-case scenario of ovens being valueless after two years, the Bakery-owned ovens option still gives a higher NPV.

Cash-flow Details Under Each Option

	Supermarket Owned	Owned by Bakery	
Investment in ovens (20 × €10500)	€0	€210,000	
Investment in inventory (20 × €1500)	€0	€30,000	
Investment in debtors (by baker)	€417,000	€225,875	
Credit term (months)	2 months	1 month	
Net investment in working capital	€417,000	€255,875	
Net investment by Baker	€417,000	€465,875	
Incremental Investment			€48,875
Gross Revenue (Appendix 2)	€2,780,000	€2,780,000	
Price rebate	10%	2.5%	
Rebate Cost	€278,000	€69,500	
Incremental Saving			–€208,500

Supermarket-owned Ovens

NPV – Year:	0	1	2	NPV
Budgeted Margin (Appendix 2)		655,000	655,000	
Rebate Cost		–278,000	–278,000	
Net Contribution		377,001	377,002	
Investment in Equipment	0	0	0	
Investment in Working Capital	–417,000	0	417,000	
Net Cash-flow	–417,000	377,001	794,002	
Discount Factor	1.000	0.926	0.857	
	–417,000	349,075	680,729	612,804

Bakery-owned Ovens

NPV – Year:	0	1	2	NPV
Budgeted Margin (Appendix 2)		655,000	655,000	
Rebate Cost		–69,500	–69,500	
Net Contribution		585,501	585,502	
Investment in Equipment	–210,000	0	0	
Investment in Working Capital	–255,875	0	255,875	
Net Cash-flow	–465,875	585,501	841,377	
Discount Factor	1.000	0.926	0.857	
	–465,875	**542,131**	**721,345**	**797,601**

(Assuming 100% depreciation of the ovens in the lifetime of the contract.)

Case 36
Solution to Malvern Limited
Ciaran Connolly and Martin Kelly, Queen's University Belfast

MEMORANDUM

From: A. Adviser
To: Kate Black
Re: Malvern Limited

Question 1

(a) Raw Materials Budget (kgs)

	June	July	August	September
	(kgs)	(kgs)	(kgs)	(kgs)
Opening inventory	100	85	50	26
Purchases	150	160	150	140
	250	245	200	166
Production (1.5 kgs per unit)	(165)	(195)	(174)	(135)
Closing inventory	85	50	26	31*

Finished Goods Budget (Towing mechanisms)

	June	July	August	September
Opening inventory	110	100	105	106
Production	110	130	116	90
	220	230	221	196
Sales	(120)	(125)	(115)	(100)
Closing inventory	100	105	106	96**

(b) Sales Budget

	June	July	August	September	Total
	€	€	€	€	€
Sales (€300 each)	36,000	37,500	34,500	30,000	138,000

Production Cost Budget

	June	July	August	September	Total
	(110)	(130)	(116)	(90)	
	€	€	€	€	€
Material (€40 × 1.5 kgs)	6,600	7,800	6,960	5,400	26,760
Wages & var. o/hs (€70)	7,700	9,100	8,120	6,300	31,220
	14,300	16,900	15,080	11,700	57,980

Closing Inventory at 30 September 2XX6

Raw materials	*31 kgs @ €40	= €1,240
Towing mechanisms	**96 towing mechanisms @ €110	= €10,560

Receivables at 30 September 2XX6

	€
August sales	34,500
September sales	30,000
	64,500

Payables at 30 September 2XX6

September purchases (140 × €40)	€5,600

(c) Cash Budget

	June	July	August	September
	€	€	€	€
Receipts:				
Debentures		150,000		
Sales (W1)	5,900	13,100	36,000	37,500
Total receipts	5,900	163,100	36,000	37,500
Payments:				
Machinery		130,000		
Raw materials (W2)	3,400	6,000	6,400	6,000
Wages & var. overheads (W3)	7,700	9,100	8,120	6,300
Fixed overheads	3,500	3,500	3,500	3,500
Total payments	14,600	148,600	18,020	15,800
Net cash-flow	(8,700)	14,500	17,980	21,700
Balance b/f	(17,250)	(25,950)	(11,450)	6,530
Balance c/f	(25,950)	(11,450)	6,530	28,230

Workings:

1. **Sales**
   - April – receivables of €5,900 (Appendix 1 of case study) received two months later, in June.
   - May – receivables of €13,100 (Appendix 1 of case study) received two months later, in July.
   - June – credit sales of €36,000 (see sales budget) received in August.
   - July – credit sales of €37,500 (see sales budget) received in September.

2. **Raw material purchases**
   - May – credit purchases of €3,400 (Appendix 1 of case study) paid for one month later, in June.
   - June – credit purchases of €6,000 (€40 × 150 kgs) paid for one month later, in July.
   - July – credit purchases of €6,400 (€40 × 160 kgs) paid in August.
   - August – credit purchases of €6,000 (€40 × 150 kgs) actually paid in September.

3. **Wages and variable overheads**
   - These vary with production and there is no delay involved in payment (see production cost budget).

(d)
How Cash-flow Problems can Arise

- Continually making losses – eventually business will have cash-flow problems;
- inflation – business will need ever-increasing amounts of cash to replace worn-out assets;
- where business is expanding (as is the case for Malvern Limited), it needs more non-current assets (e.g. machines, etc.) and will have to support higher amount of receivables and inventory;
- where there is a seasonal nature to the business cash-flow problems can arise at certain times of the year;
- one-off payments – repayment of loan capital and purchase of machine; and
- poor working capital management.

Methods of easing cash shortages
If problem relates to operational aspects of business, external finance may be difficult to obtain in which case the following could be considered:

- postpone capital expenditure – upgrade of machine, but this could affect growth plans;
- accelerate cash inflows, e.g. improved inventory management and ensuring receivables pay quicker (via discounts/factoring, etc.);

- sale and lease back; and
- negotiate reduction in cash-flows – taking longer to pay suppliers; rescheduling any finance payments.

Question 2

(a) and (b)

The budgeting information that you have prepared has proved most useful in the recent past as an aid to planning and for negotiations with our lenders. However, we can make further use of this information by using it as a means of controlling actual activities. We can record the actual activities and compare this with the planned activities. If we discover any differences between the two, we can undertake an investigation to discover why actual activities are not as planned and take remedial action where necessary.

In order to identify those responsible for the variances, the information must be reported in responsibility-centre format. Therefore, I suggest you analyse the monthly budget figures into the following responsibility centres: stores, production, selling and distribution and administration. Each report should only include those revenues and costs for which the manager is responsible. A possible layout for the monthly departmental reports might be:

	Monthly Values			Cumulative Values		
	Actual	Budget	Variance	Actual	Budget	Variance
Department	€	€	€	€	€	€
Cost line						

Where appropriate, each report should include non-financial information, such as number of units produced, to support the financial data.

Within 10 days of each period end, forward the reports on stores and production to Fred and the other two directly to me. This timing is very important as it ensures that corrective action may be taken, where necessary, as soon as possible. Fred may be reluctant to use the information at first. He may feel that you are 'spying' on him and, because he has coped up to now without this information, he may question why it has suddenly become necessary. You should explain to him that the reports are designed to help him control his areas of responsibility and that they show him the financial consequences of his operational decisions, and emphasise that he has nothing to fear from the reports and that they will form the basis of discussions between us on a regular basis in the future.

In instigating the new system, you must be prepared to change and adapt the reports as our knowledge of the business improves. Be prepared to amend the reports on the basis of the users' comments and in the light of their changing needs.

Question 3

(a)

Year	0	2XX7	2XX8	2XX9	2X10	2X11	2X12
	€	€	€	€	€	€	€
Sales		208,000	237,952	326,211	339,259	255,497	
Labour		(51,000)	(58,262)	(63,672)	(64,945)	(55,204)	
Materials		(40,000)	(44,000)	(60,000)	(60,000)	(40,000)	
Overheads		(1,000)	(1,000)	(1,000)	(1,000)	(1,000)	
Operating cash-flows		116,000	134,690	201,539	213,314	159,293	
Working capital	(20,800)	(2,995)	(8,826)	(1,305)	8,376	25,550	
Capital cost	(450,000)					50,000	
Tax on profits			(34,800)	(40,407)	(60,462)	(63,994)	(47,788)
Tax on CAs*		33,750	25,313	18,984	14,238	10,679	17,036
Final CF	(470,800)	146,755	116,377	178,811	175,466	181,528	(30,752)
Discount Factor	1	0.909	0.826	0.751	0.683	0.621	0.564
Present Values	(470,800)	133,400	96,127	134,287	119,843	112,728	(17,344)

NPV = €108,241 positive, therefore <u>accept</u> the project. Need to do sensitivity analysis and determine accuracy/reasonableness of using 10% cost of capital. Students should discuss assumptions made.

*Capital Allowances:

Year		€	30%	Year for tax relief
	Cost	450,000		
0	WDA (25%)	(112,500)		2XX7
		337,500	33,750	
2XX7	WDA	(84,375)	25,313	2XX8
		253,125		
2XX8	WDA	(63,281)	18,984	2XX9
		189,844		
2XX9	WDA	(47,461)	14,238	2X10
		142,383		
2X10	WDA	(35,596)	10,679	2X11
		106,787		
2X11	Proceeds	(50,000)		
	Balancing allowance	56,787	17,036	2X12

(b)

- ARR flawed principally because it ignores the wealth maximisation of shareholder wealth objective;
- ignores the time value of money;
- definitional problems regarding which 'capital employed' figure to use;

- accrual-based profits/income may well be useful for assessing businesses over short segments of their life, but it is flawed for investment appraisal purposes; and
- managers may generally feel they understand an accounting-based approach rather than a discounted cash-flow approach.

(c)

The after-tax cash-flows associated with financing should be discounted at the after-tax cost of borrowing, which is 6% x (1 – 0.30) = 4.2% (say 4%).

Year	Lease Payment	Tax Shield 30%	Cash-Flow	Discount Factor	Present Value
	€	€	€		€
2XX7	(94,500)		(94,500)	0.962	(90,909)
2XX8	(94,500)	28,350	(66,150)	0.925	(61,189)
2XX9	(94,500)	28,350	(66,150)	0.889	(58,807)
2X10	(94,500)	28,350	(66,150)	0.855	(56,558)
2X11	(94,500)	28,350	(66,150)	0.822	(54,375)
2X12		28,350	28,350	0.790	22,396
				NPV	(299,442)

Year	Capital	Tax Shield 30%	Cash-Flow	Discount Factor	Present Value
	€	€	€		€
0	(450,000)		(450,000)	1.000	(450,000)
2XX7		33,750	33,750	0.962	32,468
2XX8		25,313	25,313	0.925	23,415
2XX9		18,984	18,984	0.889	16,877
2X10		14,238	14,238	0.855	12,173
2X11	50,000	10,679	60,679	0.822	49,878
2X12			17,036	0.790	13,458
				NPV	(301,731)

Leasing has the lower cost, therefore it is preferable to lease the machine; although in this instance the decision is very marginal.

(d)
Qualitative Factors

- Risk – sensitivity analysis (entering new markets can be risk);
- accuracy of cash-flow projections for the Airtow machine;
- inflation; and
- discount rate – no indication of why it is 10%.

Non-Quantifiable Factors

- Working capital assumptions re. cash-flow being realised at end of project;
- use of casual labour and effect this will have on current employees;
- alternative projects – alternative might be to source other contractors to see if they have excess demand with view to looking at sub-contracting out;
- changes in technology may render machine obsolete before five years;
- competition;
- payback would be important; and
- resistance to change from staff.

Question 4

Budgeted Income Statement for the Four Months to 30 September 2XX6

	€	€
Sales (per sales budget)		138,000
Cost of sales:		
Opening inventory of finished goods	12,100	
Production costs (per production budget)	57,980	
	70,080	
Closing inventory of finished goods	(10,560)	(59,520)
Gross profit		78,480
Expenses:		
Fixed costs (€3,500 × 4)	14,000	
Depreciation (€500 + €16,000 + €5,500)	22,000	(36,000)
Operating profit		42,480
Accrued debenture interest (€150,000 × 10% × 3/12 months)		(3,750)
Retained profit for the year		38,730
Retained profit brought forward (per 31 May 2XX6 balance sheet)		56,450
Retained profit carried forward		95,180

Budgeted Balance Sheet as at 30 September 2XX6

	€	€	€
	Cost	Accumulated Depreciation	NBV
Non-current Assets			
Land and buildings	120,000	(20,500)	99,500
Machinery (incl. additions €130,000)	180,000	(60,000)	120,000
Vehicles	52,000	(21,500)	30,500
	352,000	(102,000)	250,000
Current Assets			
Raw materials (see closing inventory calculation)		1,240	
Finished goods (see closing inventory calculation)		10,560	
Trade receivables (see receivables calculation)		64,500	

Bank (see cash budget closing balance)	28,230	
	104,530	
Current Liabilities		
Trade payables (see payables calculation)	(5,600)	
Accrued debenture interest (see income statement)	(3,750)	95,180
		345,180
Non-current Liabilities		
10% debentures		(150,000)
		195,180
Equity		
Ordinary share capital		100,000
Retained earnings		95,180
		195,180

Question 5

(a)
Operating Cash Cycle:

= Receivables (days) + Inventory (days) − Payables (days)
= 57 days + 24 days − 28 days = 53 days (on average).

Receivables four months to 30 September 2XX6
Sales = €138,000 (4 months)
€64,500/€138,000 × 365/3 = 57 days

Payables four months to 30 September 2XX6
Purchases €600 × €40 = €24,000 (4 months)
€5,600/€24,000 × 365/3 = 28 days

Inventory four months to 30 September 2XX6
Inventory (€1,240 + €10,560) = €11,800
€11,800/€59,520 × 365/3 = 24 days.

The cash-operating cycle is also known as the 'working capital cycle'. It is calculated as the average number of days between outlay of cash on raw materials and inflow of cash from sale of company's products.

Significance in Relation to Working Capital Management

- The length of the cycle represents the time for which Malvern Limited requires funding for working capital. The longer the cycle, the more need for working capital investment;

- if Malvern Limited can reduce the length of the cycle, it can reduce its need for working capital and allow it to improve its profitability as expressed in terms of capital employed;
- calculation of the operating cycle focuses attention on areas where the company could improve its working capital control; and
- investigation of the operating cycle over several years may enable Malvern Limited to identify what proportion of its working capital is effectively 'permanent', requiring long-term financing, and what proportion is 'temporary' and therefore appropriate for short-term financing.

(b)
Evaluation of Factor's Offer Using Overdraft Interest of 4%:

	€
Current level of receivables	64,500
New level of receivables = 30 days	34,027
Estimated reduction in receivables	30,473
Savings in finance costs €30,473 × 4%	1,219
Savings in administration costs	2,000
Increased finance cost = €34,027 × 1% × 80%	(272)
Factors fee 1% × (€414,000*)	(4,140)
Net cost of factoring	(1,193)

* Based on current sales for four months to 30 September 2XX6 annualised.

Students may decide to take the average for four months' sales: €138,000 + (115 towing mechanisms × 8 × €300 each).

On this basis, Malvern Limited should not accept the Factor's offer. Note we have not been told if there are any bad debts: if they were > € 1,193 this would make the offer attractive.

(c)
Benefits Include

- Business can pay suppliers promptly and so be able to take advantage of any early payment discounts available;
- optimum inventories can be maintained because company will have enough cash;
- growth can be financed via sales/revenue growth;
- finance linked to volume of sales;
- managers do not have to spend their time in chasing up slow-paying trade receivables;
- cost of running own sales ledger department minimised and can use expertise of factor in receivables management; and
- factor can manage receivables more efficiently due to economies of scale.

(d)
The Factors to be Taken into Account Include

- Matching – non-current assets should be financed by long-term sources of finance and current assets by a mixture of long-term and short-term sources. If Malvern Limited finances illiquid assets from short-term debt (e.g. overdrafts), it faces the risk of insolvency;
- cost – Malvern Limited will seek to minimise its cost of capital. Transaction costs vary depending on the type of finance being used. Relative interest rates carried by short-term and long-term debt will vary over time. Rates are generally higher on long-term loans than on short-term due to risk;
- security – Malvern Limited may find it easier to raise short-term debt with low security than long-term debt. Type of security – secured and unsecured;
- risk – in opting for short-term debt the business may face the risk that it may not be able to renegotiate the loan on such good terms, or even at all, when the repayment date is reached;
- flexibility – long-term debt may carry early repayment penalties. Short-term debt is more flexible since it allows the firm to react to interest rate changes and to avoid being locked into an expensive long-term fixed rate commitment at a time when rates are falling; and
- effect on gearing and financial risk of the business.

Case 38
Solution to Drumview Limited
Ciaran Connolly and Martin Kelly, Queen's University Belfast

REPORT

To: Board of Directors, Drumview Limited
From: ACA
Date: 2XXX
Subject: Management Accounting and Business Finance Issues

Question 1
(a)

	Fixed Budget	Flexed Budget	Actual	Variance
Sales units:				
Standard	1,300	1,000	1,000	
Deluxe	1,500	1,700	1,700	
Sales revenue:	€	€	€	€
Standard	(1,300 × 150) 195,000	(1,000 × 150) 150,000	(1,000 × 140) 140,000	10,000A
Deluxe	(1,500 × 400) 600,000	(1,700 × 400) 680,000	(1,700 × 420) 714,000	34,000F
Total revenue	795,000	830,000	854,000	24,000F
Materials:				
Hardwood	(1,300 × 30) 39,000	(1,000 × 30) 30,000	(1,400 × 28) 39,200	9,200A
Pine	(13,500 × 10) 135,000	(15,300 × 10) 153,000	(15,500 × 13) 201,500	48,500A
Fabric	(2,800 × 10) 28,000	(2,700 × 10) 27,000	(2,700 × 6) 16,200	10,800F
Labour	(11,400 × 8) 91,200	(11,500 × 8) 92,000	(12,000 × 10) 120,000	28,000A
Packaging	(2,800 × 15) 42,000	(2,700 × 15) 40,500	(2,800 × 15.20) 42,560	2,060A
Variable overheads	(11,400 × 6) 68,400	(11,500 × 6) 69,000	72,000	3,000A
Total VC	403,600	411,500	491,460	79,960A
Contribution	391,400	418,500	362,540	55,960A
Fixed costs	70,000	70,000	80,000	10,000A
Profit	321,400	348,500	282,540	65,960A

Reconciliation of Budgeted and Actual Profits:

	€	€
Budgeted profit		321,400
Sales margin volume variance – standard (W1)	15,900A	
Sales margin volume variance – deluxe (W1)	43,000F	
Sales margin Price variance – standard (W1)	10,000A	
Sales margin Price variance – deluxe (W1)	34,000F	51,100F
Manufacturing variances (W2)		79,960A
Fixed cost variance (W3F)		10,000A
Actual profit		282,540

Workings:

1. Sales Variances

	Standard		Deluxe	
		€		€
Margin volume:				
AQ × SM	1,000 × (150 – 97)	53,000	1,700 × (400 – 185)	365,500
SQ × SM	1,300 × (150 – 97)	68,900	1,500 × (400 – 185)	322,500
		15,900A		43,000F
Margin price:				
AQ × AM	1,000 × (140 – 97)	43,000	1,700 × (420 – 185)	399,500
AQ × SM	1,000 × (150 – 97)	53,000	1,700 × (400 – 185)	365,500
		10,000A		34,000F

2. Summary of Manufacturing Variances

		€	€
Hardwood (W3Ai)	Usage	12,000A	
	Price	2,800F	9,200A
Pine (W3Aii)	Usage	2,000A	
	Price	46,500A	48,500A
Fabric (W3B)	Usage	0	
	Price	10,800F	10,800F
Labour (W3C)	Efficiency	4,000A	
	Rate	24,000A	28,000A
Packaging (W3D)	Usage	1,500A	
	Price	560A	2,060A
Variable overhead (W3E)	Efficiency	3,000A	
	Rate	0	3,000A
Total manufacturing variances			79,960A

3. Manufacturing Variances Workings:

A. Materials

i) Hardwood

SQ @ SP		AQ @ SP		AQ @ AP
1,000 × €30		1,400 × €30		1,400 × €28
= €30,000		= €42,000		= €39,200
	DM Usage		DM Price	
	€12,000 (A)		€2,800 (F)	
		€9,200 (A)		

ii) Pine

1,700 × 9		15,500		15,500
× €10		× €10		× €13
= €153,000		= €155,000		= €201,500
	DM Usage		DM Price	
	€2,000 (A)		€46,500 (A)	
		€48,500 (A)		

B. Fabric

2,700		2,700		2,700
× €10		× €10		× €6
= €27,000		= €27,000		= €16,200
	DM Usage		DM Price	
	€0		€10,800 (F)	
		€10,800 (F)		

C. Labour

SQ @ SP		AQ @ SP		AQ @ AP
11,500		12,000		12,000
× €8		× €8		× €10
= €92,000		= €96,000		= €120,000
	DL Efficiency		DL Rate	
	€4,000 (A)		€24,000 (A)	
		€28,000 (A)		

D. Packaging

2,700		2,800		2,800
× €15		× €15		× €15.20
= €40,500		= €42,000		= €42,560
	DM Usage		DM Price	
	€1,500 (A)		€560 (A)	
		€2,060 (A)		

E. Variable overheads

11,500		12,000		12,000
× €6		× €6		× €6
= €69,000		= €72,000		= €72,000
	Efficiency		Rate	
	€3,000 (A)		€0	
		€3,000 (A)		

F. Fixed overheads

Actual €80,000 − Budget €70,000 = €10,000
(Standard marginal costing system, fixed overhead volume variance not required.)

(b) Possible Causes for the Variances Calculated Might Include:

Hardwood

Adverse-usage variance: €12,000

- Purchase of cheaper quality wood making it more difficult to use and leading to more waste;
- inefficient cutting leading to higher wastage and/or scrap;
- incorrect standard.

Favourable price variance: €2,800

- Purchase of lower-grade material than planned for (see adverse-usage variance);
- suppliers have not imposed a planned price increase;
- negotiation of better purchase discounts;
- competitive action by rival suppliers causing price reduction;
- incorrect standard.

Pine

Adverse-usage variance: €2,000

- Purchase of cheaper quality wood making it more difficult to use and leading to more waste;
- inefficient cutting leading to higher wastage and/or scrap;
- incorrect standard.

Adverse price variance: €46,500

- Unforeseen supplier price increase;
- failure to take advantage of purchase discounts;
- incorrect standard.

Fabric

Nil usage variance

- Usage in line with standard (but does not necessarily mean standard is appropriate).

Favourable price variance: €10,800

- Purchase of lower-grade material than planned for (but not necessarily supported by usage variance);
- suppliers have not imposed a planned price increase;
- negotiation of better purchase discounts;
- competitive action by rival suppliers causing price reduction;
- incorrect standard.

Labour

Adverse efficiency variance: €4,000

- Workers less efficient than planned due to being less motivated, using poorer quality equipment or materials;
- workers working more slowly due to problems with hardwood and pine (see variances above);
- discontent over having to package goods;
- lack of training;
- incorrect standard.

Adverse rate variance: €24,000

- Use of higher-skilled workers on higher rates of pay;
- Wage increase implemented not planned for;
- Recruitment of new staff on higher rates of pay;
- Incorrect standard.

Packaging

Adverse-usage variance: €1,500

- Labour discontent at having to pack goods (see labour efficiency variance);
- purchase of cheaper quality packing (i.e. arising from bulk purchase) making it more difficult to use and leading to more waste;
- inefficient cutting leading to higher wastage and/or scrap;
- incorrect standard.

Adverse price variance: €560

- Unforeseen supplier price increase;
- failure to take advantage of purchase discounts;
- incorrect standard.

Variable Overheads

Adverse efficiency variance: €3,000

- Driven by adverse labour variances.

Nil rate variance

- Rate in line with standard (but does not necessarily mean standard is appropriate).

Question 2

(a)

Students should be familiar with some strategic analysis tools. They may attempt a PEST Analysis, a SWOT analysis or use McKinsey's 7-S framework (staff, strategy, shared values, systems, style, skills and structures). Students may also use other appropriate models of which they may be aware.

Some students, however, may not use any of these, but may instead discuss the pertinent issues. Generally, students should identify that Drumview Limited operates in a competitive, and possibly global, environment and therefore not only needs to take account of, and deal with, issues specific to the country in which it operates, but also be aware of the threat posed from foreign competitors.

Given that Drumview Limited operates in a very competitive market, price is likely to be largely outside its control. Consequently, in order to maintain or increase profitability, the company must control costs. It is not important that students get the issues under the right headings, but rather that they identify them as important. For example:

External:

Political Influences

- Possible threat of industrial action by 'unhappy' skilled workers;
- general demand for minimum wage.

Economic Influences

- Growing economy and threat of cheaper foreign competition.

Technological Influences

- Operations appear to be largely labour-intensive and therefore there could be a threat from cheaper, mass-produced goods;
- however, perhaps this is an opportunity for the company to target customers who place greater emphasis on traditionally made, high-quality goods.

Sociological Influences

- Moves towards higher minimum wage.

Internal

Staff

- Company has three departmental mangers, a management accountant and a chairman. Operatives are possibly dissatisfied and underpaid, though, and are expressing this through dysfunctional behaviour (e.g. with respect to packaging).

Systems

- Production and information systems seem to be professional, although budgetary control systems are only now being developed and possibly more work needs to be done in order to gain the support of all the departmental managers. The recent buying problems suggest there are communication problems.

Skills

- It is difficult to assess if the operatives are skilled;
- accounting skills are evident.

Strategy

- Different pricing strategies for the two models.

Style

- Attempting to introduce a more participative style of management, but suffering a number of teething problems. Departmental managers appear to need more experience with this new approach. Control is apparently exercised via accounting information.

Structure

- Hierarchical, but still relatively flat, structure appears evident, and seems appropriate for the size of the organisation.

Shared Values

- Christopher appears to be trying to encourage shared values, but obviously needs more time;
- some evidence of dysfunctional behaviour, or at best poor communication. For example, recent bulk-buying decisions.

(b)

The Management Accountant would need to consider:

- likely minimum wage levels;
- rates which would currently satisfy the operatives;
- future raw material costs in the light of minimum wage and growing economy;
- short-term impact of not meeting production and/or sales targets;
- potential for a sales price increase;
- potential for reducing fixed costs;
- potential for greater efficiency in production via technology and motivation.

(Students may offer a variety of other examples.)

Possible sources (internal and external) of information include:

- market research;
- opinion-gathering;
- accounting system;
- formal channels (e.g. official documents, newspapers, various media sources);
- informal channels (e.g. networks of acquaintances, gossip).

(Students may offer a variety of other sources.)

Question 3

(a)

Forward contract

Cost = $500,000

Therefore, in Euro, the spot cost is €(500,000/1.32) = €378,788.

The forward rate is calculated by adding the appropriate discount to the relevant spot rate as follows:

Forward rate is 1.32 + 0.02 = 1.34.

The contract is a binding contract to buy or sell a specified quantity of a particular currency at a pre-determined rate of exchange on fixed future date, therefore the forward rate fixes the cost at:

€(500,000/1.34) = €373,134, compared to the predicted spot rate of 1.22, which would leave Drumview facing a payment of €(500,000/1.22) = €409,836.

(b)

Money market hedge

If a company has an asset denominated in a foreign currency, it can mitigate the effect of the exchange rate movements on the value of the asset by borrowing in that currency, thus creating an equal and opposite liability. Since interest rates can be fixed in advance and all currency translation is done at spot rates, the uncertainty is removed:

Spot rates:
SFr/€ 1.52 – 1.56   Interest rates: Eurozone – 6 months   2.5%
                                      Switzerland – 6 months   2%

200,000SFr to be received in six months. Therefore borrow an amount equal to x SFr now, such that with interest 200,000 SFr will be owing in six months time:

x SFr x 1.020 = 200,000
x SFr = 196.078

Convert to Euro immediately to remove exchange risk:
SFr196,078/1.56 = €125,691.

In six months time the loan with interest will be 200,000SFr and will be paid off by the receipt.

Note: students may also mention:
- do nothing – but this is not hedging;
- currency options; and/or
- operating bank accounts in foreign currencies/multilateral netting.

(c)

A *futures contract* is similar to a forward exchange rate contract (FEC) as Drumview Limited would be in a no win/loss position. However, the future is for a standardised amount, unlike a FEC, which can be used for any amount. In addition, the company would not be able to buy a future at the bank, as futures are traded on currency exchanges.

Currency options are similar to FEC's, but they would give Drumview Limited the right to buy/sell currency in the future, whereas FEC's are a contractual obligation.

Two types:
- call option – to buy currency; and
- put option – to sell currency.

Options are more flexible as has the right to buy/sell. As a result, options are more expensive and transaction costs are high.

(d)

Budgetary planning and control helps a company to achieve its strategic objectives over a budget period, and calls for:

- preparing plans for future activity;
- implementing those plans;
- monitoring actual performance;
- comparing actual performance with plan;
- taking action to correct any differences.

In formulating the budget for Drumview Limited, the management accountant will need to bear in mind the strategic objectives of the company. In large organisations, a Budget Committee would have responsibility for developing and co-ordinating budgets. However, this would not seem to be appropriate for Drumview Limited. The Management Accountant will need to:

- make forecasts of key factors, such as expected changes in raw material costs, in order to prepare realistic budgets;
- identify the principal budget factor, which is usually sales;
- prepare feasible quantity budgets for sales, finished goods, production, raw materials, and so on. This will require extensive consultation with the other departmental managers if the budget is to be accepted by them. Some of the departmental managers have suggested that the budget needs to be changed;
- prepare financial budgets from the quantity budgets, including a cash budget, and co-ordinate and review these budgets for consistency;
- prepare a master budget, i.e. a budgeted profit and loss account and balance sheet, for the individual budgets, showing overall planned performance for the budget period;
- agree the budgets with Christopher and the departmental managers.

The Management Accountant may considering developing a Budget Manual, which is a collection of instructions governing responsibilities, procedures, forms and records regarding the preparation and use of the required budgetary data, and offers guidance and information about the budgetary process.

Students could also discuss the difference between fixed and flexible budgets:
- a fixed budget is prepared from estimated sales and production volumes and is not adjusted if actual volumes are different in a control period;
- a flexible budget is a fixed budget that has been flexed for a different level of activity than expected, and can be used at the end of a control period to provide control information about performance at the actual activity level in that period.

Question 4

(a) WACC

$$K_e = \frac{D_0(1+g)}{M_v} + g$$

M_v = €1.4 m recent bid as best estimate of market value
D_0 = € 132,000
$(1 + g)^4 = 132/90$
$g = 10\%$

$$= \frac{132{,}000 \times 1.10}{1{,}400{,}000} + 0.10 = 0.20 = 20\%$$

Over draft:
$K_d = 6\% \times (1 - 0.30)$ = 4.2%

Redeemable loan stock:
Calculate the MV using a pre-tax cost of 6%:

Time	flow	6%	PV
1-5	9	4.212	37.91
5	102	0.747	76.19
			114.10

Calculation of kd:

Time	Cash-flow	2%	PV	4%	PV
1-5	6.3	4.713	29.69	4.452	28.05
5	102	0.906	92.41	0.822	83.84
0	(114.10)	1	(114.10)	1	(114.10)
			8		(2.21)

kd = IRR = 2% + $\underline{8}$ × (4-2)% = 3.56%
    (8 + 2.21)

Mv = €800,000 × 114.10/100 = €912,800

Calculation of weighted average cost of capital:

$$\text{WACC} = \frac{(1{,}400{,}000 \times 0.20) + (100{,}000 \times 0.042) + (912{,}800 \times 0.0356)}{1{,}400{,}000 + 100{,}000 + 912{,}800} = 13.1\%$$

(b)

- A company's cost of capital should represent the return required by shareholders. A major problem is that it assumes that all shareholders of Drumview Limited require the same return. Private shareholders and venture capitalist will have different risk exposures.
- Use of DVM assumes that the shareholders will value the shares in terms of future dividends. It is likely that the venture capitalist will want an exit in a couple of years.
- In terms of the €1.4 million as MV of Drumview Limited, the figure is likely to be too low (otherwise Christopher would have sold?) resulting in a cost of equity that is too high. Drumview Limited could have been valued by applying a suitable PE to maintainable profits after tax, but there would be difficulties surrounding the use of a suitable quoted company's PE.
- Growth rate assumes constant growth in perpetuity and thus there are questions over the sustainability of a 10% growth rate.
- An alternative would be to look at cost of equity of quoted companies similar to Drumview, if they exist.
- Unlisted company – what if they stop paying dividends?

(c)

- WACC is only valid as a discount rate if:
  - there is no change in business risk (i.e. project is marginal in nature); and
  - the existing capital structure is optimal (i.e. gearing will stay same).

- The project involves only limited diversification for Drumview Limited, so change in business risk will be limited.
- The acquisition will be financed by debt and as such may involve a significant change in gearing.
- Given issues regarding the use of DVM (in (b) above), it is unlikely that WACC will be an appropriate discount rate.

(d)

Investment Decision

- This category covers both internal and external investment. Working capital, fixed asset expenditure and takeovers/mergers.
- Objective is most commonly assumed to be maximisation of shareholder value (important for venture capitalist!) and such decisions will be taken in reference to rates of return adjusted for risk.
- Effect on cash-flows.
- Non-quantifiable factors of investment decisions, such as environmental, HR and longer-term strategic issues.

Finance Decision

- Need suitable methods of finance.
- Could include shares, debt, retained earnings and sale of assets.
- Costs of the different sources have to be compared. Loan finance has advantage of tax deductibility.
- Debt does increase risk in capital structure (e.g. financing acquisition of supplier).
- Cost of capital and relevance of capital structure on free cash-flow will be important. More problematic to find appropriate discount rates in unlisted companies, such as Drumview Limited.

Dividend Decision

- Do we distribute or do we retain?
- Retained profits cheaper, but consider effect on shareholders of Drumview.
- If Drumview continues to pay dividends, what will be effect on cash-flow? Requirements of stakeholders need to be considered.

Case 42
Solution to Plastic Products
Michelle Carr and Derry Cotter, University College Cork

REPORT TO THE BOARD OF DIRECTORS OF PLASTIC PRODUCTS LIMITED

SUBJECT: ALTERNATIVE GROWTH AND COST-MANAGEMENT STRATEGIES

B. Wyse
Finance Director

Contents

1. Internal Growth

Analysis of the proposed Plastech project:

(a) Payback period.
(b) Accounting rate of return.
(c) Weighted average cost of capital.
(d) Recommendation on 'Plastech' project.
(e) Sensitivity of project to level of fixed overheads.
(f) Financing acquisition of machinery.

2. External Growth

Evaluation of the proposed acquisition of Metal Fasteners Limited:

(a) Valuation of Metal Fasteners Limited.
(b) Recommendation and structuring of consideration package.
(c) Evaluation of alternative methods of financing proposed acquisition.
(d) Assessment of dividend policy of Plastic Products Limited.
(e) Interest rate risk management.

3. Just-in-time Manufacturing System

Evaluation of the proposal to implement a JIT manufacturing system:

(a) Just-in-Time Manufacturing Philosophy.
(b) Recommendation on JIT manufacturing system.
(c) Determination of profit-maximising price and output level.
(d) Conditions necessary for successful implementation of a JIT manufacturing system.

4. Activity-Based Costing System

Evaluation of the proposal to implement an activity-based costing system:

(a) Determination of unit product cost using absorption costing system.
(b) Determination of unit product cost using activity-based costing system.
(c) Comment on pricing and profit implications.
(d) Benefits and limitations of activity-based costing system.

MAIN REPORT

1. Internal Expansion

(a) Payback Period

The payback period can be computed by reference to Appendix 1. The net cash outflow at 31 July 2XX6 is €429,400. Of this amount, €424,960 is expected to be recovered by 31 July 2XX9. Therefore, the payback period is just in excess of three years.

(b) Accounting Rate of Return

One method of calculating the accounting rate of return is to compute the average annual accounting profit before tax as a percentage of average investment over the lifetime of the project. This can be computed by reference to Appendix 1. The average annual profit equals ((total contribution − design costs − overheads − bad debts − discount allowed − depreciation) /4)

Average Annual Profit = $\dfrac{(1{,}200{,}000 - 10{,}000 - 480{,}000 - 24{,}000 - 28{,}800 - 350{,}000)}{4}$

= €76,800

Average investment = (Machinery cost − redundancy costs saved − scrapping costs saved − residual value of machine)/2
= €135,000

Acc. rate of return = $\dfrac{76{,}800 \times 100}{135{,}000}$
= 57%

(c) Weighted Average Cost of Capital of Plastic Products Limited

The weighted average cost of capital (WACC) of Plastic Products Limited is 12% (see Appendix 2). This is computed using the market values of the company's existing sources of long-term capital. The WACC will be used as the discount rate for the 'Plastech' project, for calculating its net present value (NPV).

(d) Recommendation

Neither the payback period nor the accounting rate of return provides a reliable basis for establishing whether the Plastech project should be accepted. Both of these methods of project appraisal fail to take the time value of money into account. It is preferable, therefore, to utilise a discounted cash-flow method, the most reliable of which is net present value.

The net present value of the Plastech project is €67,500, as computed in Appendix 1. Therefore the project should be undertaken, as it should lead to an increase of €67,500 in the value of Plastic Products Limited.

It is assumed that the Plastech project involves the same level of risk as that of the 'average project' undertaken by Plastic Products Limited. If this is not the case, it may not be appropriate to use the company's weighted average cost of capital to discount the project's cash-flows.

(e) Sensitivity Analysis

One method of assessing the risk of a project is sensitivity analysis. In respect of the Plastech project, an important factor is the project's sensitivity to the level of fixed overheads. This can be evaluated by calculating the present value cost of fixed overheads, and expressing this as a percentage of the project's NPV.
The PV cost of fixed overheads can be calculated as follows:

- annual relevant fixed overheads x annuity factor for four years at 12%
  = €120,000 × 3.037
  = €364,440;
- tax effect of annual fixed overheads x annuity factor for years 2–5
  = €120,000 × 40% × 2.712
  = €130,176;
- PV of cost of fixed overheads = €234,264 (i.e. €364,440 - €130,176);
- NPV of project = €67,500;
- sensitivity of project to fixed overheads = (67,500/234,264) × 100
  = 28.8%.

Therefore the level of fixed overheads could increase by 28.8% before the NPV of the Plastech project would be reduced to zero.

(f) Alternative Methods of Financing the Acquisition of the Machinery

The machinery required at 31 July 2XX6 can be acquired either by leasing or by outright purchase. The cost of these alternatives is examined in Appendix 4. As outright purchase has a lower PV cost, it is the preferred financing option.

2. External Expansion

(a) Valuation of Metal Fasteners Limited

A detailed valuation of Metal Fasteners Limited is set out in Appendix 5:

	Earnings basis	Assets basis
	€	€
Value	7.5 million	2.16 million

(b) Recommendation and Consideration Package

There is a large difference in the valuation when using the two alternative bases. There is a strong case for revising the earnings valuation downwards, as the earnings for the year ended 31 December 2XX5 are significantly higher than previous years. Assuming an annual dividend of €100,000, and omitting the start-up year 2XX1, the average after-tax earnings in previous years was €299,000. This could be increased to €389,000[1] if expected synergy benefits are included. A reasonable compromise might be to apply an equal weighting to 2XX5 earnings and to the average earnings of previous years.

A revised earnings valuation would be computed as follows:
[(389,000 × 0.5) + (946,100 × 0.5)] × 8 = €5.34 million.
Average annual retained earnings in previous years = €199,000 (€596,000/3).
Add annual dividend of €100,000 + synergy benefits of €90,000.
Average after-tax profits in previous years = €389,000.

---

[1] Revenue reserves at 1 January 2XX5: €596,000.

Conclusion

It would seem appropriate that Metal Fasteners Limited should be valued on an earnings basis, as future cash-flows relate more to the firm's earnings than to its assets. The analysis above would suggest an approximate valuation of €5.3 million. This is €3.14 million in excess of the value of Metal Fasteners Limited, computed on an assets basis. It should be considered, therefore, that Plastic Products Limited will incur a substantial loss should it be unable to operate Metal Fasteners Limited profitably after its acquisition.

Consideration Package

In structuring the consideration package, Plastic Products Limited should endeavour to establish a link with the future profits of Metal Fasteners Limited. The purchase price should be at least partially dependent on profit targets being achieved. This will reduce the downside risk incurred by Plastic Products Limited, and may encourage George Simpson to retain an interest in the management of Metal Fasteners Limited, thereby ensuring that access to essential management expertise is retained.

(c) Financing the Acquisition of Metal Fasteners Limited

The proposed acquisition can be financed by a long term loan, or by flotation of the shares of Plastic Products Limited on the Irish Enterprise Exchange.

- *Long-term loan*

It seems that, at present, Plastic Products Limited does not have appropriate security to offer in respect of further loan finance. This may result in the Bank applying restrictive covenants. The Bank may establish certain financial parameters which must be achieved, e.g. times interest covered, debt:equity ratio etc. Failure to achieve these required targets could limit Plastic Products Limited's flexibility in relation to its dividend policy or raising additional debt finance, and could place restraints on any further expansion. One significant advantage that would be obtained if loan finance were raised would be the related tax savings.

- *Flotation of shares on the Irish Enterprise Exchange*

The major fear regarding a Stock Exchange flotation seems to be that the company's shares will be under-priced, due to the use of income-decreasing accounting policies by Plastic Products Limited. This would, however, be inconsistent with the concept of market efficiency. The semi-strong form of the efficient markets hypothesis states that share prices should reflect all publicly available information. Therefore, share prices should be determined by investors' expectations of a company's future cash-flows. To the extent that accounting policy choice affects disclosed profit but does not impact on future cash-flows, it should not affect a company's share price.

It should be considered, however, that a Stock Market flotation will result in the existing shareholders suffering some loss of control, and in the board of directors coming under increased pressure to achieve short-term performance targets. A Stock Market flotation is also not without cost, and inevitably results in a loss of privacy, as disclosure requirements of the Stock Exchange must be complied with.

(d) Assessment of the Dividend Policy of Plastic Products Limited

Shareholders in a company with a stock market listing expect a stable dividend, which increases gradually over time. Dividends are often perceived as a signalling mechanism, increasing dividends being a sign that management is optimistic about a firm's future earnings prospects. On the other hand, a decrease in a firm's dividend is often interpreted as 'bad news' and can result in a collapse in the company's share price.

Plastic Products Limited has a policy of paying an annual dividend equal to 30% of after-tax profit. By their nature, earnings are volatile, as is evident from the significant fall in Plastic Products Limited's earnings in 2XX3. A dividend policy which is based on a percentage of earnings will inevitably result in a wildly fluctuating annual dividend. This is not a suitable policy for a company with a Stock Market listing.

Therefore, should Plastic Products Limited intend to float its shares, its current dividend policy will need to be reconsidered.

(e) Interest Rate Risk Management

Should Plastic Products Limited decide to finance the acquisition of Metal Fasteners Limited by means of increased borrowings, it will need to consider its policy in relation to interest rate risk management. Presently, it is uncertain whether borrowed funds will in fact be required, as this is dependent, first, on whether Plastic Products Limited proceeds with the acquisition of Metal Fasteners Limited and, secondly, on the use of debt to finance the purchase. While considering these options Plastic Products Limited may wish to protect itself against possible interest rate increases. This can be done by obtaining an interest rate option, thus giving Plastic Products Limited the right, but not the obligation, to borrow funds at a pre-agreed rate of interest.

If raising debt finance becomes imminent, interest rate increases can be avoided by employing any of the following strategies:

- sell interest rate futures on the London International Financial Futures Exchange (LIFFE);
- arrange a forward rate agreement (FRA) with the company's bank. This will entitle Plastic Products Limited to borrow a specified amount of funds, for a fixed period, at a pre-agreed rate of interest;
- once funds are in place, a fixed rate of interest can be agreed for periods of up to 10 years or more. Unfortunately, however, anticipated future interest rate increases will be reflected in the fixed rate.

Case 42: Solution to Plastic Products

3. Just-in Time Manufacturing System

(a) Just-in-Time Manufacturing Philosophy

Many companies seek to eliminate and/or reduce the costs of non-value-added activities by introducing JIT systems. The aims of a JIT system are to produce the required items, at the required quality and in the required quantities, at the precise time they are required. In particular, JIT aims to eliminate waste by minimising inventories and reducing cycles or throughput times (i.e. the time elapsed from when customers place an order until the time when they receive the desired product or service).

(b) Recommendation on JIT Manufacturing System

Annual Cost Changes are as Follows:		
Direct labour	0.1 × (56+64.60) × 37,500	+452,250
Variable set-ups	0.15 × (3,000) ×500	−225,000
Variable materials handling	0.15 × (500) × 800	−60,000
Variable inspection	0.15 × (4,000) × 500	−300,000
Variable machining	0.075 × (20) × 64,000	−96,000
Variable distribution	700×800	−560,000
Fixed cost	10,450 + 0.15 × (11,330 + 16,445 + 19,940) + 0.075× (67,270)	−22,653
Total saving		**811,403**

The introduction of a JIT manufacturing system would result in Plastic Products Limited incrementally reducing its costs by €811,403. On that basis we recommend that the company implements such a system.

(c) Determination of profit-maximising price and output level

Total Variable Overhead Costs Allocated to each Product are as Follows:	Plasex	Plasent
Set up at €2,550 per production run	637,500	637,500
Materials handling at €425 per order	170,000	170,000
Inspection at €3,400 per production run	850,000	850,000
Machining at €18.5 per machine hour	444,000	740,000
	2,101,500	2,397,500
	37,500	37,500
Variable overhead per unit	56.04	63.9
Direct material	126	146.2
Direct labour	56	64.8
Total variable cost per unit	238.04	274.93

Selling Price	Demand	Unit Contribution	Total Contribution
Plasex			
€200	37,500	−€38	−1,426,500
€287	32,500	€49	1,591,200
€300	25,000	€62	1,549,000
€325	17,500	€87	1,521,800
Plasent			
€220	37,500	−€55	−2,060,000
€280	30,000	€5	152,000
€325	22,500	€50	1,126,500
€375	17,500	€100	1,751,167

The profit-maximising price and output levels are €287 and 32,500 units for Plasex, and €375 and 17,500 units for Plasent.

(d) Conditions Necessary for Successful Implementation of a JIT Manufacturing System

Elimination of Non-Value-Added Activities

JIT manufacturing focuses on the elimination of non-value-added activities. The lead or cycle time involved in manufacturing and selling a product consists of process time, inspection time, move time, queue time and storage time. Of these five steps, only process time actually adds value to the product. All other activities add cost but no value to the product, and are thus deemed non-value-added processes according to JIT manufacturing. Thus Plastic Products Limited should examine its lead time and reduce/eliminate non-value-added activities.

Factory Layout

JIT aims to produce the right parts at the right time, only when they are needed, and only in the quantity required. This philosophy has resulted in a pull manufacturing system, which means that parts move through the production system based on end-unit demand, focusing on maintaining a constant flow of components rather than batches of WIP. With the pull system, work on components does not commence until specifically requested by the next process. JIT techniques aim to keep materials moving in a continuous flow, with no stoppages and no storage. Plastic Product Limited needs to develop a pull manufacturing system.

Kanban Systems

The pull system is implemented by monitoring the consumption of parts at each operation stage, and using various types of visible signalling system (known as Kanbans) to authorise production and movement of the part to the using location. The production cell cannot run the parts until authorised to do so. The signalling mechanism usually involves the use of Kanban containers. These containers hold materials or parts for movement from one work unit to another.

Purchasing Arrangements

JIT purchasing techniques are where the delivery of materials immediately precedes their use. By arranging with suppliers for more frequent deliveries, stocks can be cut to a minimum. Considerable savings in material-handling expenses can be obtained by requiring suppliers to inspect materials before their delivery and guaranteeing their quality. This improved service is obtained by giving more business to fewer suppliers and placing longer-term purchasing orders. Therefore, a critical component of JIT purchasing is that strong relationships are established with suppliers.

Batch Sizes of One

JIT focuses on reducing set-up times to a minimum. Set-up time is the amount of time required to adjust equipment settings and to retool for a different product. Long set-ups and changeover time make the production of batches with a small number of units uneconomic. However, the production of large batches leads to substantial throughput delays and the creation of high inventory levels. JIT manufacturing requires the reduction and elimination of set-up times. For example, by investing in advanced manufacturing technologies some machine settings can be adjusted automatically instead of manually. Alternatively, some set-up times can be eliminated entirely by redesigning products so that machines do not have to be re-set each time a different product has to be made.

4. An Activity-Based Costing System

(a) Determination of Unit Product Cost Using Absorption Costing System

	Plasone	Plastor
Direct materials	1.75	1.90
Direct labour	2.50	1.25
Overhead applied	25.42 × 0.5 = 12.71	25.42 × .25 = 6.35
Unit product cost	16.96	9.50

Pre-determined overhead rate = 1,398,000 / 55,000 = 25.42.

(b) Determination of Unit Product Cost Using ABC System

	Cost Pool	Activity Level	Cost-driver Rate
Machine set-ups	48,000	60	800
Machine depreciation	350,000	37,000	9.46
Purchasing	420,000	280	1,500
Engineering	400,000	2,000	200
Material Handling	180,000	180	1,000

		Plasone
Machine set-ups	800 × 20	16,000
Machine depreciation	9.46 × 25,000	236,500
Purchasing	1,500 × 80	120,000
Engineering	200 × 1,000	200,000
Material Handling	1000 × 100	100,000
		672,500
Overhead allocation	(€672,500/100,000)	6.73

		Plastor
Machine set-ups	800 × 40	32,000
Machine depreciation	9.46 × 12,000	113,520
Purchasing	1,500 × 200	300,000
Engineering	200 × 1,000	200,000
Material Handling	1000 × 80	80,000
		725,520
Overhead allocation	(€725,520/20,000)	36.28

	Plasone	Plastor
Direct materials	1.75	1.90
Direct labour	2.50	1.25
Overhead applied	6.73	36.28
Total unit cost	10.98	39.43

(c) Comment on Pricing and Profit Implications

	Plasone	Plastor
Absorption system	16.96	9.50
ABC system	10.98	39.43

Plasone is over-costed according to the absorption costing system. Plastor is under-costed according to absorption costing. It is claimed that ABC more accurately measures resources demanded by products. Where cost-plus pricing is used, the transfer to an ABC system will result in different product prices. If activity-based costs are used for stock valuations, then stock valuations and reported profits will differ.

(d) Why the Existing Absorption Costing System is a Poor Base for the Allocation of Overheads

When direct labour is used as an allocation base for overhead, it is assumed that overhead cost is directly proportional to direct labour. When cost systems were originally developed in the 1800s, this assumption may have been reasonably accurate. However, direct labour has declined in importance over the last 100 years, while overhead has been increasing. This suggests that there is no longer a direct link between the level of direct labour and overhead. Indeed, when a company automates, direct labour is replaced by machines; a decrease in direct labour is accompanied by an increase in overhead. This violates the assumption that overhead cost is directly proportional to direct labour. Moreover, while the empirical evidence is not entirely clear, it appears that overhead cost may be driven by factors such as product diversity and complexity as well as by volume, for which direct labour has served as a convenient measure.

(e) Importance of Top Management Support for Implementation of an ABC System

Activity-based costing may be resisted by people in an organisation because it changes the 'rules of the game'. It alters some of the key measures used in decision making, such as product costs, and may impact on how individuals are evaluated. Without top management support, there may be little interest in making these changes. In addition, if top managers continue to make decisions based on the numbers generated by the traditional costing system, subordinates will quickly conclude that the activity-based costing system is not viable.

Appendix 1

Time 31.07.	Machinery	Cap. Alls	Design costs	Contribution	Fixed O-Hs	Working Capital	Redundancy	Disc. Allowed	Bad debts	Scrap costs avoided	Taxation (excl. cap. allowances)	Net cash-flow	PV factor @ 12%	DCF
2XX6	−400,000					−109,400	60,000			20,000		−429,400	1	−429,400
2XX7		32,000	−10,000	300,000	−120,000			−7,200	−6,000		−32,000*	156,800	0.893	140,022
2XX8		32,000		300,000	−120,000			−7,200	−6,000		−62,720	136,080	0.797	108,456
2XX9		32,000		300,000	−120,000			−7,200	−6,000		−66,720	132,080	0.712	94,041
2X10	50,000	32,000		300,000	−120,000	109,400		−7,200	−6,000		−66,720	291,480	0.636	185,381
2X11		12,000									−66,720	−54,720	0.567	−31,026
													NPV=	**67,474**

* (60,000 + 20,000) × 0.4

This represents the increased tax charge resulting from a fall in costs at 31/07/2XX6.

Appendix 2: Weighted Average Cost of Capital

Source	Value €'million	% Value	% Cost	Proportionate cost
Equity	42	61.3	15.5 (note 1)	9.5%
Pref. Shares	15.7	23.0	6.7 (note 3)	1.54%
Debentures	10.8	15.7	5.6 (note 4)	0.88%
	68.5	100	WACC =	11.92%

Note 1: Cost of equity capital

Using the dividend growth model;

$$K_e = \frac{DIVI}{MV_o} \times 100 + g$$

$$K_e = \frac{1.85M \times 30\% \times 1.14}{42M^*} \times 100 + 14\% \text{ (note 2)}$$

$$= 15.5\%$$

* Net of discount and issue expenses.

Note 2: Dividend growth rate

As dividends are a constant percentage of earnings, the dividend growth rate can be derived from the rate of earnings growth over the four-year period 2XX1–2XX5.

$$\text{Required PV factor} = \frac{1,100}{1,850}$$

$$= .595$$

This implies an average growth rate (using PV tables) of 14% over four years.

Note 3: Cost of preference shares

$$K_p = \frac{\text{Annual dividend}}{MV_o \text{ (ex-div)}} \times 100$$

$$K_p = \frac{7}{104.5} \times 100$$

$$= 6.7\%$$

Note 4: Cost of Debentures

$$K_d = \frac{\text{Annual interest (net of tax)}}{MV_o \text{ (ex-interest)}} \times 100$$

$$K_d = \frac{6}{108} \times 100$$

$$= 5.6\%$$

Appendix 3: Working Capital

Plastic Products Limited has a choice of allowing three months credit to customers, or introducing a cash discount for payment within one month.

a) Three months credit

	€	
Debtors	145,500	(600,000 − 18,000) / 4
Finance Costs	17,460	(145,500 × 12%)
Bad debts	18,000	
Total costs	**35,460**	

b) Discount for early payment

	€	
Debtors	89,400	[(600,000 / 12 × 60%) + (600,000 − 6,000) / 4 × 40%)]
Finance Costs	10,728	(89,400 × 12%)
Bad debts	6,000	
Discounts allowed	7,200	(600,000 × 60% × 2%)
Total costs	**23,928**	

As total costs of the discount policy option are lower, a cash discount of 2% should be allowed for payment within one month. This will give rise to annual savings of €11,532.

Therefore, the total investment in working capital at 31 July 2XX6 will be:

	€	
Stocks	30,000	(600,000 × 50% × 10%)
Debtors	89,400	
Creditors	(10,000)	[(600,000 × 50% × 40%) /12)]
Total costs	**109,400**	

Appendix 4: Lease versus Outright Purchase

The optimal financing option will be that which has the lower PV cost. This requires a comparison of the PV cost of leasing versus the PV cost of outright purchase, using the after-tax cost of borrowing of 6% (10% × (1 − 0.4)) as the discount rate.

Leasing

PV cost of lease payments	=	€130,000 × 3.673
	=	€477,490
Less PV of tax savings	=	€130,000 × 40% × 3.465
	=	€180,180
PV cost of leasing	=	€297,310

Outright purchase

PV cost of purchase	=	€400,000

Case 42: Solution to Plastic Products 265

Less PV of capital allowances	=	(€32,000 × 3.465) + (€12,000 × 0.747)
	=	€119,844
Less PV of disposal proceeds		€50,000 × .792
	=	€39,600
PV cost of outright purchase	=	€240,556

Conclusion
The machine should be financed by outright purchase.

Appendix 5: Valuation of Metal Fasteners Limited

Two alternative valuation bases are used for the valuation of Metal Fasteners Limited.

(i) Earnings Basis

An earnings valuation is computed as follows:

- calculation of maintainable earnings of Metal Fasteners Limited;
- application of an appropriate P/E ratio to derive an imputed value for Metal Fasteners.

Calculation of Maintainable Earnings

	€
Profit after taxation	880,000
Less additional loan interest*	(27,500)
Add synergy benefit (after tax)	90,000
Add depreciation (€180,000 × 2%)**	3,600
	946,100

*An additional interest charge for 11 months should be levied in respect of the loan raised on 1 December 2XX5, as this will better reflect the finance costs going forward. The increased interest, on an after-tax basis, will be:

- €500,000 × 10% × 11/12 × 60% = €27,500.

** Based on depreciation charge, which will be avoided in 2XX6.

Computation of an appropriate P/E ratio
A listed company in the metal industry has a P/E ratio of 10 (€100m/10m). However, it may be appropriate to make adjustments to this P/E as follows:

- a premium of (say) 10% might be applied, as the valuation of Metal Fasteners Limited is in respect of a controlling interest;
- a discount of (say) 20% might be applied, to reflect the comparative lack of marketability of the shares of Metal Fasteners Limited;
- in view of its high gearing level, an additional discount of (say) 10% might be applied to the P/E ratio used in respect of Metal Fasteners Limited.

Taking the above factors into account, a P/E of about 8 would seem reasonable.

Earnings valuation

The imputed market value of Metal Fasteners Limited could be calculated as follows:

Maintainable earnings after tax × P/E ratio of similar quoted company
= €946,100 × 8
= €7.6 million, less once-off rationalisation costs (after tax) of €120,000
= €7.5 million.

(ii) Assets valuation

An assets valuation of Metal Fasteners Limited can be computed as follows:

	€'000
Balance sheet value of equity shareholders funds	1,476
Disposal value of premises in excess of book value	300
Increase in market value of land and buildings (1.3m – (1.1m – .18m))	380
	2,156

Index

7-S framework 244

absorption costing 6, 21–37, 203–12, 221–8, 259–61
accounting profit 145–55
accounting rate of return 146, 147–9, 153, 154, 233–4, 252–3
accounts receivable management *see* credit control
accuracy 120–22
acquisitions 102, 104–5, 107–8, 131–44, 203–12
activity-based costing 3–10, 45–55, 221–8, 259–61
actual costing 25
administration costs 78–9
agency 3–10
agency relationships 165
ARR *see* accounting rate of return
asset structure 161, 162, 163, 166
assets
    intangible 160
    non-current 208–9
    tangible 160
    valuation 172–6, 208–9
Autoparts SA 77–9
avoidable costs 217

balanced scorecard 15, 23
bank debt 136
bankruptcy 134, 151, 160–61, 162, 163–4, 166
Beara Bay Cheese 3–10
benchmarking 58
Blackwater Hotel Group plc 119–30
bonds 121
bonuses *see* incentive schemes
branding 224
breakeven analysis 3–10, 11–12, 17–18, 42, 59, 119, 215
budgetary control systems 135–7, 210
budgeting 57–75, 93–100, 203–12, 229–38, 239–50
business risk *see* operational risk

Calvin plc 101–8
capacity 26, 29, 30
capital allowances 85
capital asset pricing model 121, 136, 147, 149, 151, 158, 171–7
capital investment 81–9, 121–2
capital structure 101–8, 135–6, 149, 157–69
CAPM *see* capital asset pricing model
cash budgets 93–100, 230–31
cash surplus 101–8, 150–51
cashflow 99–100, 231–2
cashflow projections 110–12, 116
Castlegrove Enterprises 21–37
Chicken Pieces 39–43
company valuation 203–12, 251–66
compensation schemes 77–9
competition 12, 47
competitiveness 39
conflicts of interest 151
contribution margin 4–5, 11–13, 17–18, 58–9, 60, 70–72, 204
The Corner Café 93–100
Corporate Social Responsibility 42
corporation tax 85, 113
cost allocation 5–6, 26, 39–43, 45–6; *see also* costings
cost classifications 25
cost competitiveness 39
cost drivers 46–8, 52, 223, 226
cost leadership 29, 39
cost management 184
cost of capital 110–11, 112, 119–30, 131–44, 145–55, 157–69, 210, 239–50, 251–66
cost of debt 136–7, 158–9
cost of equity 121, 136–7, 158–9, 167
cost of sales 99
cost-volume-profit *see* CVP analysis
costings 24–6
    absorption 6, 21–37, 203–12, 221–8, 259–61
    activity-based 3–10, 45–55, 221–8, 259–61

actual 25
job 24
joint 40
kaizen 15
marginal 203–12
normal 25–6
process 24, 40–41
standard 25
target 97
throughput 25
variable 5, 21–37
costs
administration 78–9
avoidable 217
bankruptcy 134, 151, 163–4
fixed 11, 22, 25, 58, 203–4
labour 25, 45, 58, 260–61
manufacturing 11, 28
marketing 7, 11
materials 25
opportunity 217
quality 11, 13–15
variable 11, 22, 25, 58, 203–4
credit control 86–7
critical success factors 39–40
customer service 39
CVP analysis 3–10, 11–15, 17–19, 39–43

DCF *see* discounted cash flow
debentures 136
debt 135–6, 149, 158–60, 162–4, 166, 210–11, 255
debt management 182–3
decentralisation 61
decision making 3–10, 11–15, 21–37, 39–43, 45–55, 203–12, 213–20, 221–8, 250
finance decisions 131–44, 149, 157–69
investment decisions 81–9, 109–17, 149
under uncertainty 57–75
defined benefit pension schemes 171–7
defined contribution pension schemes 171–7

Delaney's Bakehouse Breads 221–8
depreciation 58, 165
direct labour costs *see* labour costs
direct materials costs *see* materials costs
discounted cash flow 106–8, 122, 145–55
diversification 131–44, 151
dividend policy 101–8, 150, 160, 203–12, 256
dividend valuation model 209
divisional performance 77–9
downward spiral effect 26
Drumview Limited 239–50
due diligence 217
DVM *see* dividend valuation model

earnings before interest and tax 160–61
earnings per share 135, 160
EasyONline 17–19
EBIT *see* earnings before interest and tax
economic value added 146
economies of scale 210
efficiency 47, 161, 210
enterprise resource planning systems 81–3, 85–7
equity 121, 135–6, 149, 158–9, 162–4, 210, 255–6
equity beta 121, 133, 136–7, 146–7, 149, 158–9, 167, 176
ERP systems *see* enterprise resource planning systems
ESOPs *see* share option plans
estimates 120–22
EVA *see* economic value added
exchange rate analysis 110, 113–17
expansion 101–8, 109–17, 119–30, 213–20; *see also* growth
exports 104, 106

factoring 237–8
finance
sources of 93–100, 162–4, 210–11, 255–6

through debt 149, 160, 162–4, 210–11, 255
through equity 149, 162–4, 210, 255–6
financial planning, personal 179–199
financial risk 160–61, 166
financing decisions 131–44, 157–69
firm value 161–2
fixed costs 11, 22, 25, 58, 203–4
footfall 59–60
forecast error 137–8
foreign exchange risk 109–17, 119, 239–50

gearing 102, 149, 162, 210–11; *see also* leverage ratios
Glenview House Hotel 213–20
Good Eating Company plc 171–7
grants 113
gross profit margin *see* profit margins
growth 61, 134–5; *see also* expansion

hedging strategies 246–7
hurdle rates 132, 136–7, 139, 140–43, 147

incentive schemes 61–2, 77–9, 211–12
income statements 21–37, 41
inflation 82, 85–6
information asymmetry 165
infrastructure 112–13
interest coverage ratio 168
interest rate risk 103, 256
internal rate of return 84, 111, 135, 138–9, 143, 146, 150
inventory *see* stock control
investment appraisal 101–8, 109–17, 119–30, 131–44, 145–55, 221–8, 229–38, 251–66
IRR *see* internal rate of return
IXL Limited 81–9

JIT *see* just-in-time manufacturing
job costing 24

joint costing 40
just-in-time manufacturing 81–3, 85–7, 257–61

kaizen costing 15
key performance indicators 40

labour costs 25, 45, 58, 260–61
leasing 213–20
Lennon Department Store Limited 57–75
leverage ratios 159–60, 161, 163–4, 168; *see also* gearing
liabilities 172–6
liquidation 160–61, 162
loan stock 136, 210–11
location 109–17

machine-hours 45–6, 50, 55
macroeconomic forecasts 110, 112–13, 116
Malvern Limited 229–38
management accounting framework 23–4
manufacturing costs 11, 28
marginal costing 203–12
mark-up 46
market risk 133–7
market risk premium 121, 158, 167
marketing 7, 11
materials costs 25
mergers 133, 134
motivation 62

net income 179–199
net present value 81–5, 89, 110–12, 119, 135, 138–9, 145–52, 253–4
net worth 179–199
Newtown Manufacturing Limited 45–55
non-financial performance measures 23, 39–43, 61–2
normal costing 25–6

off-peak rates 19, 120
operational risk 160–61, 166

opportunity costs 217
optimal pricing 17–19, 251–66
outsourcing 3–10, 42–3
overheads 5–6, 25, 58; *see also* costs

payback period evaluation 81–3, 89, 135, 137, 215, 252
payroll costs *see* labour costs
pension deficit 172, 173, 175
Pension Protection Fund 171–2, 177
pensions 171–7, 186–7, 190
performance
   divisional 77–9
   measurement 23, 39–43, 61–2
   non-financial 23, 39–43, 61–2
personal financial planning 179–199
PEST analysis 244
Plastic Products 251–66
portfolio returns 174–5
portfolio risk 174–5
portfolio theory 189
practical capacity denominator level 26
price/earnings ratios 132, 134–5, 208, 209
pricing strategies 17–19, 46–7, 97, 251–66
process costing 24, 40–41
product differentiation 29, 39
product mix 47, 57–62
product quality 39
profit budgets 93–100
profit margins 58
profit opportunity rankings 112
profit statements, projected 57–60, 63–9, 73–5
profitability 18–19, 57–75, 78–9, 147–8, 204–5, 244–6; *see also* CVP analysis
profitability index 111, 146
projections
   cashflow 110–12
   profit statements 57–60, 63–75

quality control 11, 13–15

residual income 146, 147–9, 152–4
retained earnings 158–9, 162–3
return on capital employed 77–8
return on investment 81–9
risk 57–75, 82, 84–5, 121, 122–3, 150
   financial risk 160–61, 166
   foreign exchange risk 109–17, 119
   interest rate risk 103, 256
   market risk 133–7
   operational risk 160–61, 166
   and return 174–6, 179–199
risk exposures 133–7
risk free rate 121, 137
risk management 132–7, 256
ROCE *see* return on capital employed
ROI *see* return on investment
ROR *see* accounting rate of return

Salmon Spray 145–55
scenarios 138
sensitivity analysis 17–19, 85, 105, 119–30, 133, 138, 139, 145–55, 253–4
share issues 165–6
share option plans 211–12
share prices 102, 134–5, 158, 160, 165–6
share repurchase 150
space allocation 57–62
standard costing 25
stock control 28–9
strategic fit 134
strategic planning 61–2
strategy evaluation 57–62
Sun Shine Limited 109–17
SWOT analysis 244
synergies 133

takeover bids 150; *see also* acquisitions
tangibility of assets ratio 168–9
Tannam plc 131–44
target costing 97
tax shield 103, 149, 159, 162, 163–4, 165, 169

taxation 82, 85–6, 103–4, 113, 159, 162, 163–4, 165
Terra Inc. 11–15
term loans 136
throughput costing 25
Toffer Group plc 203–12
trade-off theory 163–4, 169
transfer pricing 216–7

uncertainty 57–75, 119–31, 138, 174–5

valuation methods 25
variable costing 5, 21–37
variable costs 11, 22, 25, 58, 203–4
variance analysis 239–50

WACC *see* weighted average cost of capital
Waterlife plc 157–69
weighted average contribution 4–5
weighted average cost of capital 122, 130, 136–7, 158–60, 162, 167–8, 248–50, 253, 263
working capital management 93–100, 221–8, 229–38